WII
WICK___
WARTIME
Wilmington

Being an account of
murder, malice
and other assorted
mayhem
in N.C.'s largest city during the
Civil War

by
Robert J. Cooke

Dram Tree Books

All photos and illustrations are from the author's collection, or in the public domain, unless otherwise labeled. The abbreviation "NHCPL" refers to images compliments of the New Hanover County Public Library. The abbreviation "LCFHS" refers to images compliments of the Lower Cape Fear Historical Society.

First Edition 2009
Published in the United States of America by Dram Tree Books.

Publisher's Cataloging-in-Publication Data
(Provided by DRT Press)

Cooke, Robert James.
   Wild, wicked, wartime Wilmington : being an account of murder, mayhem and other assorted malice in N.C.'s largest city during the Civil War / by Robert James Cooke.
      p. cm.
   Includes bibliographical references and index.
   ISBN 978-0-9814603-4-5
1. Wilmington Region (N.C.)—History—Civil War, 1861-1865. 2. North Carolina —History —Civil War, 1861-1865. 3. United States —History —Civil War, 1861-1865. I. Wild, wicked, wartime Wilmington : being an account of murder, mayhem and other assorted malice in North Carolina's largest city during the Civil War. II. Title.

F264.W7
975.62722—dc22

10 9 8 7 6 5 4 3 2 1

Volume discounts available.
Call or e-mail for terms.

Dram Tree Books
P.O. Box 7183
Wilmington, N.C. 28406
(910) 538-4076
www.dramtreebooks.com
Potential authors: visit our website or email us for submission guidelines

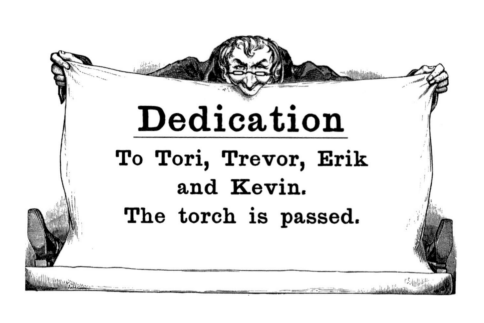

Dedication

To Tori, Trevor, Erik
and Kevin.
The torch is passed.

Contents

Acknowledgements

This book is the culmination of more than ten years of delving into what Wilmington was like during the Civil War years. One eyewitness to those times termed the town turned "topsy-turvy" from its prewar ambiance. Indeed, the collection of these stories and anecdotes indicates that the town hit a new low in that struggle. During the war, the town, which technically would not become a city until after the war, underwent rapid change. Much of the newer population, which grew off the blockade running industry, were resident for the four years of the war only. When the conflict ended, some of those who had come during the war remained, but most seemed to simply vanish like the many blockade runners that had sailed off into the dark of the moon. Wilmington would eventually recover but it would take some time before it reached the heights attained in the Civil War.

I would like to acknowledge the help given me to produce this work. The staff of Randall Library at UNC-Wilmington was most helpful, as was Dr. Chris E. Fonvielle (UNCW), who most graciously allowed me access to his extensive Wilmington files. Beverly Tetterton and Joseph Shepard, "Keepers" of the North Carolina Room at the New Hanover County Public Library, many times went out of their way to secure more information on whatever I happened to be working on. Mr. Ray Flowers, Site Assistant at the Fort Fisher State Historic Site, was not only always supportive of my project, but often gave me valuable information about the lower Cape Fear area and wartime Wilmington. James Burke, of Wilmington, was most helpful in researching the Wilmington and Weldon Railroad. My several visits to the archives at the Lower Cape Fear Historical Society were made more productive by the able assistance of Eli Nieher and the late Ms. Merle Chamberlain.

Trips to the National Archives in Washington, D.C. were always productive, due in large part to the staff that steered me in the right direction, even as the building underwent reconstruction. The N.C. State Archives at Raleigh is yet another treasure trove for researchers and again, I always found helpful staff members there.

Thanks to the editorial efforts of Ms. Blonnie Wyche and editor Jack Fryar many of the grammatical errors have been corrected, and any errors that remain are mine. Finally, thanks to my wife Joan who once remarked that I must have lived another life before this one, one spent in the nineteenth century. She has been my anchor in this life and must be glad to see this book finally in print.

Prologue

Today, Wilmington, North Carolina still retains some of the *savoir faire* of an old Southern town. Many of the homes located downtown were built before or shortly after the Civil War. There are still reminders of that struggle which took place over 140 years ago: artifacts, usually in the form of artillery fragments, are found quite often. Earthworks that once surrounded the city can still be discerned among the golf courses and subdivisions. Confederate trenches below the city can still be viewed if one chances a walk in the woods nearby, and Fort Fisher, located at the mouth of what was once New Inlet, is now a state historic site that offers guided tours of that bastion which for so long protected not only blockade runners entering port, but the city itself.

Before the war, Wilmington was the state's largest town, and also its busiest seaport. Business opportunities abounded with a brisk trade with northern cities (notably New York City). Hence it was no coincidence that a young, recently discharged U.S. Army officer named Sewall L. Fremont made his home there in 1854. Throughout my research his name kept appearing in letters, documents and even the local newspapers. Indeed, a study of Fremont's adult life would acquaint one with the history of the Lower Cape Fear during much of the 19th Century.

Fremont, a graduate of the U.S. Military Academy, was a veteran of the Seminole and Mexican Wars, and was active in setting up the defenses of the Cape Fear. He was involved in blockade running, operated a salt works, and still found time to run a railroad! To begin this story with his pre-war adventures might shed some light on just how this Yankee, born and bred in New England, wound up in Wilmington, and just why he shifted his allegiance and remained here for the duration of the war. The town also changed during the war. Many of Wilmington's earlier residents sent their families to a safer place. Nicknames for various sections of town, such as "Oregon," "California," and "Texas," all suggested a frontier-like existence. Indeed, many of the tales collected in this work show that Wilmington had become much like the vaunted "Wild West" of later years, complete with shootings, robberies, houses of dubious repute, disreputable watering holes, and of course, both heroes and villains.

The wreck of the SS San Francisco (center), with the Three Bells (left) and Antarctic standing by to rescue survivors. The Fremonts, and virtually all other senior officers, had already been rescued by another ship, the Kilby.

A Peacetime Prelude

ajor George Taylor and Captain Sewall L. Fremont had known each other since their days at the U.S. Military Academy. Taylor graduated in 1833, while Fremont finished in 1841. Both men were posted to the 3rd Artillery in Florida, at that time attempting to quell the Seminole Indians, and were later stationed at Fort Johnston in Smithville, (present-day Southport) North Carolina.

The two men also shared another interest. It was almost a custom for the officers to court some of the local girls living in Smithville; Taylor and Fremont soon found themselves married to cousins. Emeline Everitt and Mary Elizabeth Langdon both came from substantial Smithville families: Emeline's father, Sterling B., was a well respected physician while Mary's father was a successful town merchant.

Yet another custom shared by both the soldiers and citizens was the celebration of the nation's Independence Day. The Fourth of July was then, as it is today, a big affair in the small coastal town. In the year 1845, "The Fourth…was ushered in by a salute of 13 guns. At 10:30 there was a procession formed at Fort Johnston, which marched to the Episcopal Church. The Commander, Captain George Taylor, served as Marshall of the Day…and an oration was delivered by Lieutenant Fremont." At the conclusion of the ceremony, the men were marched back to their barracks and dismissed. Later that evening, a ball was held at a local hotel.[1]

National affairs soon eclipsed local doings, and by 1846 the United States was embroiled in a war with Mexico. Both Fremont and Taylor participated in several battles in Mexico, but by 1848 both were back at Fort Johnston. The spoils of that recent conflict gave the United States a large portion of the present-day western states, including California. Soldiers were needed in that turbulent territory, especially after the discovery of gold, so in late 1853 the U.S. War Department ordered the 3rd Artillery Regiment to New York City to embark and head west.

This was the *SS San Francisco's* maiden voyage to California. The ship, built by the well-known shipbuilder William Webb, was well provisioned and "provided with everything that could render [the passengers] comfortable and every luxury that could be procured was placed on board." The vessel, some two hundred eighty-five feet long with a beam of forty-one feet, had cost $300,000 to build and had a newly designed and strengthened bulkhead. The two engines, 1,000 horespower each, were also of a new design. In spite of the purported strength of the vessel, some aboard were uneasy with an ocean voyage, as many steamboat accidents had recently occurred.

Lieutenant Sewell L. Fremont (above), and later in his career, Captain S.L. Fremont (below). (Photos: Robert G. Borrell)

The extreme cold in New York City that December 1853 caused Mrs. Taylor to hurry as fast as she could to board the ship. Shopping in the city, she found she was running late. Major Taylor, her dear husband, had told her that if they missed the steamer to the golden land, they would have to go by the overland route. Not only would it take much longer, but they would have to pay their own way if they missed the embarkation.

On board the *San Francisco*, which lay at anchor in New York harbor, the skipper informed the regiment's commander that the steamer was ready to sail. The Colonel gave the necessary orders, but Taylor's good friend, Captain Fremont, pe0rsuaded the commanding officer to wait a bit longer. Soon after the Taylor's arrival, the ship weighed anchor, slowly making its way past Fort Hamilton, where they were serenaded by an army band.

Taylor had been delayed, but had the foresight to secure a stateroom. When shown to his cabin, he was not happy because it was below decks. Another room, this one in the saloon above decks, was obtained and the couple settled in for the long sea voyage.

On that beautiful wintry 22nd of December, many aboard the *San Francisco* looked upon the journey as a break from the routines of army life. Mrs. Taylor confided to a fellow passenger that she hoped the sea voyage would do her good, as she was not feeling well.[2]

The *San Francisco*, on which the Taylors and Fremont sailed, was to be the pride of the Pacific Mail Company's line. After taking her station, she was scheduled to ply between her namesake city and Panama City, Panama. With the gold rush of 1849-50, regular steamship service was found necessary to convey the many gold-seekers to the promised land. In addition, the U.S. Army's presence in the west, sapped by many desertions to the gold fields, needed to be augmented.

By 1853, crossing the Isthmus of Panama was the most convenient way to go west, but while it took weeks instead of the months to go by sea around Cape Horn, it was also the most expensive. The cheapest way to go was via Cape Horn, however this would take nearly six months to traverse nearly seventeen thousand miles. The War Department naturally selected the most cost-effective way to travel, so the *San Francisco* was prepared for a long trip. Along

The headstone of Major George Taylor in Southport's Old Burial Ground.

with the seven hundred passengers, the ship was well stocked with supplies that included cattle, horses, pigs and chickens. These would be needed not only for the trip itself, but to avoid the higher prices in California.[3]

The weather at the beginning of the trip was beautiful, but only two days out the first signs of a storm were sighted. That evening, a nor'easter hit, pounding the steamer all night long. One passenger reported water streaming in through the portholes, but it was felt the ship could make it. During the night, the engine snapped a piston rod, which completely disabled the ship. Now at the mercy of the seas, the waves crashed against the vessel, smashing furniture and dishes.

Animals broke from their pens. As the frantic animals ran wildly about the deck, orders were given to shoot the hapless creatures, adding gunshots to the overall terror of the night. Water continued to fill the vessel and by morning, many of the passengers were terrified and near panic. One passenger later reported: "[On] the morning of the 24th December, when the wind throughout the night had been blowing a gale...and our foremast was carried away, I could not realize the danger we were in [and] when I was in the cabin, [I heard] a deafening crash...I heard the screams that were stifled by the choking waves....There was indeed horror on board that ship. This is when the upper saloon was swept away by...one tremendous wave."

The upper cabins had been crushed and were in the ocean. Outright panic now spread throughout the ship. Nearly two hundred people had been washed overboard into the frigid waters. Two of those in the tumultuous sea were Emeline and George Taylor. Although they were seen to be wearing life preservers and holding each other's hands, within five minutes they were gone.

Several troopers, taking advantage of the situation, broke into the spirits locker and after consuming the contents, wandered about the ship. One incoherent private, seen carrying a pig, was stopped by an officer. Asked what he was doing, the man answered that he had been told never to go to sea without provisions. Having said this, still clutching the poor porker, he jumped into the water and was never seen again. For those on the doomed ship, the terror would continue until they were finally rescued some days later.

The Fremonts were among the lucky ones. After being rescued, they were taken to New York where they were put up in the Astor House while money and clothing were collected for them. While there, miscreants robbed what little possessions they had left. When found, pieces of jewelry from both Mrs. Fremont and the now-deceased Mrs. Taylor were returned to the families.

The Fremonts returned to Smithville. One of the first things Captain Fremont did, in the spring of 1854, was to resign his commission. Having had a brush with death, the next thing he did was to take out several life insurance policies. For the remainder of that year, he was employed by the government in navigational improvements along the Cape Fear River. In December he was selected to be the Chief Engineer and Superintendent of the Wilmington and Weldon Railroad, a post he would hold until 1871.[4]

Fremont brought order to the Road. Prior to his assuming his post, recordkeeping and the ordering of supplies had been haphazard. Fremont brought military discipline with him, and was soon able to show where attention needed to be directed in order for the road to turn a profit. One who knew him wrote: "...Fremont acquired in his early military education strict discipline and he is sometimes rough, but not unkind in his administration of business and control of subordinates[.]"[5]

The Fremonts relocated to Wilmington, which at that time was North Carolina's largest town and main seaport. The population of New Hanover County was about 22,000. The antebellum town of Wilmington contained nearly ten thousand citizens. As was true of most Southern centers, there were whites, slaves and free blacks. Blacks numbered around 4,350, with nearly 600 of them free.[6]

There were grocers, butchers, barbers, dry good merchants and booksellers who plied their trade. One savings bank and four commercial banks were located in the town. There were doctors, dentists and druggists to provide medical care for the populace. Steam saw mills and turpentine distilleries dotted the area and produced the main products, lumber and naval stores, which were exported from Wilmington. In mid-decade the town was connected to the outside world by telegraph and a Gas Light Company promised to soon finish laying pipe along the main thoroughfare, Market Street.

Although the town was growing, much remained to be done; one newspaper reported that the town commissioners were not paying much attention to the northern section of town. They noted: "There are several streets...which...require improvement...some by grading, others by filling up...A negro in endeavoring to pass over a boggy place in or near the principal street...sank up to his armpits, and remained in the mud all night. He was pulled out this morning much exhausted."

A nineteenth century turpentine distillery.

National "internal improvements" was the topic of conversation in the nation's capital, but for many citizens in Wilmington any improvements should begin at home. They were upset when the town failed to purchase the "Causeway and Ferries" on Eagles Island. They also noted that the approaches to town were either in a dilapidated condition or the tolls so "enormously high" that trade was thought to be affected. The town was "poorly supplied with public promenades" so when a plank road was built from Orange and Front Streets to "the vicinity of the Steam mills in the Southern portion" of town, it was heralded as something to be copied throughout town.

Still, Wilmington was a thriving economic center and the Fremonts settled in to what was a prosperous area. Early in 1853, in addition to the "corn crackers" on the river, over twenty steamboats sailed from the port as others awaited their cargoes at the many wharves along both banks of the river. Commission merchants, whose offices and warehouses were located near the waterfront, sought, for a fee, to send freights northward with tar, pitch and turpentine, the naval stores wooden ships so badly needed. Locally produced items, such as shingles, flour, corn, cotton, peanuts and all other "country goods" grown in the region, could find northern markets as well.[7] What could not be obtained locally could be bought from Charleston, Baltimore, Philadelphia or New York. There was a brisk trade between the latter city and Wilmington, with several partnerships formed between merchants in those cities.

Fayetteville was often the terminus of goods shipped upriver from town, while produce from the interior was carried on the return voyage. The level of the upper Cape Fear varied quite a bit throughout the year; trade declined when the water dropped as much as eighteen feet during the summer and fall months. With "the rising waters of the late winter and early spring" an active trade was resumed between the two towns. November and December were busy months. The beginning of December was when local owners brought their slaves to town to be hired out for the ensuing year. The winter of 1860-61 was different than others. South Carolina had seceded from the Union and a crisis was at hand.

As the new year progressed, many in town – old time Whigs, Unionists and even Democrats – tried to avert a rupture. It was futile. Large secession meetings were held, "a lone star flag was hoisted on Princess St.," guns were fired off at the wharves and a Confederate flag was raised at the corner of Front and Market Streets. To counter this rush towards division, a pro-Union meeting was announced by merchant and former Mayor Oscar G. Parsley: "Notice was given and the American flag hung out. With the hour appointed came only twenty-five people." Parsley attempted to speak on behalf of his beloved Union. The crowd began to hiss and "he broke down in the effort." When his son, William stood to address the gathering, he too was unsuccessful. It was said that Parsley went home and "wept over the ruin of the Union." On the 20th of May 1861, Wilmington celebrated secession by firing ninety cannon shots. Later that evening, skyrockets were fired into the night sky.[8] There was no turning back now.

Endnotes

1. New Hanover County Public Library collection titled, "Fort Johnston." Newspaper article dated July 19, 1970. Bill Reaves, Southport (Smithville), A Chronology, 1520-1887. (Wilmington: Broadfoot Publishing Co., 1978) 31. Smithville was then and continues to be a center for the celebration of the Fourth of July in North Carolina.
2. *The New York Times*, 16 January 1854, "Statement of Mrs. Col. Gates."

3. While the Taylors remained childless, the Fremonts had three young children and all were aboard the steamer. *The New York Times*, 16 January 1854, "Lieut. Winder's Statement", See also 14 January 1854. As coal was cheaper in N.Y. the steamer loaded up with as much as she could carry and may have been seriously overloaded with freight and passengers as well, see *The New York Times*, 8 February 1854, "Lieut. Fremont's testimony."

4. *The New York Times*, 16, 25 January, 8 February 1854. *Harper's New Monthly Magazine*, April 1854; Dorothy Fremont Grant Collection, North Carolina State Archives, Raleigh, North Carolina. One young lieutenant who survived the wreck was Charles Sidney Winder, later to become a Confederate brigadier general who would command the famed "Stonewall" Brigade. Winder would be killed at Cedar Mountain, 9 August 1862.

5. Henry Toole Clark, 9 June 1873, Henry Toole Clark Papers (microfilm), Davis Library, University of North Carolina, Chapel Hill. *"To the Last Man and the Last Dollar: Governor Henry Toole Clark and Civil War North Carolina, July 1861- September 1862"*, thesis presented to North Carolina State University by R. Matthew Poteat, Raleigh, 2005, page 122. Former Governor Clark was writing to his son Haywood, who had been hired by Fremont, likely on the Wilmington, Charlotte and Rutherfordton Railroad.

6. Richard Everett Wood, *Port Town at War: Wilmington, North Carolina 1860-1865*, dissertation presented to Florida State University, 1976, hereinafter cited as *Port Town at War*.

7. *Wilmington Herald*, 9, 19 February 1853; 2, 5 and 5 March 1853; *Daily Journal* 5 January 1860. Martin Schulken purchased the ferry and would operate it during the war, thus gaining an exemption from military service. See the *Herald*, 16 December 1852. Also at the waterfront were the inspectors of wood and naval stores. It was their job to insure the quality and quantity of those items and signed papers to that effect. They charged a small percentage of the value as their fee. "Corn crackers" were the small sailing vessels that traversed the rivers and bays of North Carolina.

8. *Official Records of the Union and Confederate Armies in the War of the Rebellion* (Harrisburg: National Historical Society, 1985) II: 2, 452; Hereinafter referred to as *ORA*.

In addition to protecting the town against traditional crimes, civilian and military authorities were also charged with looking for runaway slaves.

Crime and Punishment

O n the 10th of September [1861], we joined a regiment in Raleigh… Our Company numbered about one hundred men and the regiment about a thousand…In a few days we got on the trains into box cars and left Raleigh on Saturday evening. While we were waiting at the depot, many of the men had their canteens filled with whiskey to comfort them through the night as we were carried slowly to Wilmington…On Sunday morning, about nine o'clock, we were pulled into Wilmington, N.C. and got off under the big car shed at the bank of the Cape Fear River…As I have said, we numbered one thousand men; many at this time were greatly under the influence of whiskey and were where they could get plenty more…We were sleepy, tired and hungry…We wanted to fight and the enemy not being very near, some did fight one another…The patience of good and moral officers was tested at this point. I very well remember hearing a very good and moral officer use oaths on this occasion." Thus was Private John Wesley Bone of the 30th N.C. Regiment introduced to war and its associated debauchery.[1]

Late in 1861, a group of Wilmington citizens met at the town hall to discuss the problem of public drunkenness. The vice of intemperance was to be stamped out. Attending the meeting were most of the town's doctors, as well as Mayor John Dawson and several town commissioners. Resolutions calling for the prohibition of both the manufacture and sale of alcohol were passed and were presented to the civil and military authorities.

Taking their cue, local military leaders soon banned the sale and consumption of intoxicating beverages to soldiers in camp. Anyone found

General Benjamin Huger

General John Bell Hood

supplying the troops would be arrested. Unfortunately, it would take more than ordinances to deter drinking among soldiers.

The town commissioners passed a stricter liquor ban early in 1862, along with an increase in the police force, thought necessary to enforce the ban. Many Wilmingtonians felt their town should follow the example set by General Benjamin Huger, who ordered all the saloons in Norfolk shut down. The railroads and steamboat companies were asked to help by not carrying any "spirituous or malt liquors" into town, but that plea was widely ignored. When it was learned that some "high grade French Brandy" had been destroyed on the docks, it was too much for those whose palate yearned for a drop of whiskey. It was brought out that the sick and wounded soldiers in the hospitals could have used the liquor as a stimulant. Exceptions were allowed for the sick and wounded men; wine, brandy and other spirits were stored in the hospitals or were otherwise regulated by the regimental physician.

For the troops who were well, the question of whiskey rations was a sore one. Northern soldiers, it was claimed, had access to their daily grog, and a "small quantity of whiskey twice a day is almost essential to the health of men who undergo such exposures and hardships." Since coffee was difficult to come by, it was thought "rather hard that our brave fellows should have neither[.]"

Still the town held out against allowing liquor to be sold or produced within its limits. Druggists were excepted from the ban. By producing a note from a doctor, one could purchase liquor for "medicinal purposes." The efforts may have had some success, because one citizen wrote:

In Civil War Wilmington, troops and civilians occasionally found themselves at odds. These encounters sometimes erupted into riots.

"As for what is known as 'running the blockade' that is about played out, and the thirsty traveler, who carrieth not his own private tickler, will search in vain for the fluid wherewithal to 'wet his whistle.'" But even with minor successes, the town was fighting a losing battle.

By the fall of 1863, realizing that it was almost impossible to keep either soldiers or citizens and alcohol apart, the commissioners opted to tax the business. Everyone involved in the buying, selling or manufacturing of spirits was required to purchase a license. Those failing to do so had the law "rigorously enforced against" them. A license could be purchased for one hundred dollars and by the summer of '64, the charge rose to $400. For those who distilled grain to make spirits, the fee was a whopping $1,000. As in pre-war days, there was to be no liquor sold on the Sabbath and those caught doing so would be fined. Bars had to be kept open to public view, so that the police could see into them.[2]

Any soldier found drunk or disorderly was fined twenty dollars and lodged in the Guard House. Police had the right to enter any establishment or home that was suspected of disbursing drinks and if an occupant refused to allow them entry, they could be fined fifty dollars. If there were enough officers, they could legally force their way in and arrest all parties found within the premises. In the fall of 1863, several members of the town guard went to the waterfront to quell a disturbance in an area known as "Paddy's Hollow," where many drinking establishments were located. The guard, three in number, quickly found themselves outnumbered and in trouble; they were up against inebriated members of Hood's brigade of Texans, who were then passing through Wilmington on their way to the bloody battlefield of Chickamauga. A fight ensued and all of the policemen were injured. By the beginning of the new year, the police force was increased by ten more men.

It hadn't always been such a dangerous job. In fact, being in the town guard was a coveted position. New Hanover County had a Police Committee composed of seven magistrates whose job it was to "raise…employ and…equip such additional police force as such committee shall consider…for the protection of the persons and property of the citizens of this County." A policeman's pay had steadily increased from a pre-war rate of $25 until, in 1864, it was $125 per month. The money, however, was not the best part of the job. Members of the guard were exempt from conscription and it was this bonus that made the job an enviable one.

General John Hunt Morgan

Dressed in "common blue pants," blue flannel shirt, adorned with a red cravat, with a "plated star" upon their chest and a black felt hat on their head, the men were quickly recognized. There were originally only twenty men in the force commanded by Captain Nicholas Carr. The guard worked mainly at night, not only arresting drunks, but keeping an eye out for thieves and robbers. They watched the cotton wharves, and were sometimes called upon to guard fire-ravaged buildings to protect against looting.

In March 1864, yet another near riot took place when members of John Hunt Morgan's men passed through town. They raised a ruckus and when Major General W.H.C. Whiting, commander of the Cape Fear area, heard of the trouble and found that one of his men desired a transfer to that unit, Whiting wrote: "The disgraceful and ruffian conduct of a large portion of this com'd. in this city & on the RR during my absence (fortunately for them) is a sufficient reason for me to disapprove the transfer of any good soldier to such a body."[3]

In a letter home, a soldier wrote, "Wilmington is just one of the meanest places in the Confederacy...this town is perfect sink in iniquity (so I am told) of nymphs...I have been told there is 1800 publick [sic] prostitutes here and 9 out of 10 who pass for virtuous women take it on the sly."

Civil War-era prostitute

Before the war patrols of the town by private citizens were the norm. Mainly concerned with keeping the slaves in check, but also to keep the peace throughout the town, these patrols were increased on Saturday night "and at any other time an abnormal degree of lawlessness might be expected." Many citizens tried to avoid such duty, as it was considered "quite onerous."[4]

One of the more successful officers of the law was Paul McGreal. A policeman before the war, and later becoming Chief of Police, McGreal continued throughout the war writing tickets for various violations of the law. There was to be neither "fast riding," defined as no faster than a walk, nor riding of horses on the sidewalks; white persons were fined twenty dollars while slaves or free blacks received 39 lashes for the same offenses. When a citizen wrote a letter to the local newspaper about the impropriety of boys and men bathing in the creek near Oakdale Cemetery, McGreal was quick to publish and enforce the ordnance against nude bathing within the limits of the town. Sailors, however, continued to bathe in the buff in the river off the wharf at Orange Street. Because he was so successful in recovering stolen property, whether it was cotton, gaiters or gold watches, he received the "thanks of the citizens."

Not all in town were enamored of McGreal. In 1864, General Whiting wrote to Mayor John Dawson questioning "the propriety of having such a person in the employ of the city." Just what McGreal had done is not known, but he would remain in office until well after the war ended.

McGreal, like many other citizens and squads of soldiers detailed to look for deserters, was apt to be on hand upon the arrival of the ferry or a train. In the summer of 1862, he was at the depot when a suspicious pair of women got off the train. As he approached them, it became apparent that one of the two was really a man, dressed as a lady. Found out and taken to jail, the man declared that he was from Glasgow, Scotland, and was trying to get to Richmond. The impossibility of obtaining a passport, he said, forced him to dress in petticoats. Further investigation revealed the man was a deserter from one of the Charleston gunboats.

It was difficult to get past the authorities in town; pickets were stationed on all the roads, at the ferry landing and at the railroad depot. Still some tried. There were, in addition to the town guard and army sentries, Robert G. Rankin's Home Guards to patrol the streets. Regardless of the increased police forces, crime steadily rose. The city was divided into two sections and two militia companies were formed from those few men left in town. One writer commented that he "never saw so many police in a small town."[5]

Of course, there had always been crime in Wilmington. Robberies, assaults and burglaries, although not rampant, happened. More common was the jailing of a slave who was found out after curfew, or a free black who had taken a slave wife, or more serious, a slave who had attempted to escape. Captives were lodged in jail, an ad was run in the newspaper announcing their incarceration and, by paying the costs, the owner could reclaim his "property." It was a fact of life in pre-war Wilmington that if a white man murdered another white man, he was charged with murder; if the victim was a slave or free black the charge was usually reduced to "felonious slaying" (manslaughter). If a black killed a white person, he was charged and usually condemned to be hanged. If a black killed another black, he also faced the death penalty.

A most unusual case concerned Peter, a slave belonging to Jesse Craig. A jury found him guilty of rape and sentenced him to be "hung by his neck until dead." County Sheriff W.J.T. Vann "had all the arrangements made for the execution," the militia was called out and Peter was about to be escorted to the gallows when, "to the great relief of Peter, the proceedings were suspended." Governor Henry T. Clark had pardoned Peter and he was remanded back to jail. Being so affected by nearly losing his life, Peter was unable even to speak as he was led away. While some were pleased at the stay, others had come to see a hanging and voiced their disappointment.[6] If a slave or free black was well liked, that went a long way in establishing his guilt or innocence.

Pre-war murders, although much more rare, did occur. In the summer of 1859, two white boys passed several black youths, one of whom was named Fred. The *Journal* continued the story: "Some of the other colored boys said 'there goes the patrol.' Fred replied, 'Hell of a patrol.'" At this time another white boy, H.V. Runciman, came upon the scene and asked what was happening. When he was told that "Fred wanted to raise a muss," Runciman pushed Fred and a fight ensued. The black youngster grabbed a brick and swung at Runciman, who by this time had pulled out a knife. Fred was stabbed and died within a short time. Although only fifteen years old, Runciman was arrested and charged with murder. Released on bail, his trial came up in the fall and he pled not guilty. A jury found him guilty not of murder, but of "felonious slaying," and he was sentenced to two months imprisonment.[7] It would not be the last the law heard of H.V. Runciman.

In March 1863, Runciman and a cohort, William Parker (alias John Finney), were drinking with William Childress. Childress was an Englishman who had come to Wilmington by way of Virginia and who had, just a week earlier, found work in the shops of the Wilmington and Weldon Railroad. Because of his foreign birth and his essential occupation, he was exempt from military service. It was Sunday and the three men wound up at a house "occupied by some women" near Smith's Creek, about a mile out of town. At twilight, Runciman and Parker persuaded Childress to go for a walk. Parker made sure he had his homemade, 18-inch long Bowie knife, "like those used by the Zouaves," with him. As they approached a creek, Parker attacked Childress, and although the Englishman fought back, it was soon over. There were more than twenty wounds inflicted on Childress, at least three of which were fatal. The cuts in Childress's head were so deep that it was thought he had been struck with an axe. After throwing the body in the creek, the two men went back to the house around midnight, asked for water to clean their clohes, went out again and returned at daylight. They brought with them "a number of dead chickens" as a way to explain their bloody clothes. One witness, the man who had brought them water, testified that it was "curious chicken blood– t'wouldn't come out."

The next day the men attempted to sell a gold watch and showed off other newfound wealth, both Confederate and U.S. currency. Parker bragged about his "British protection papers," which he averred would keep him out of the service.

On Tuesday, both men were involved in yet another "affray" and although Runciman was seriously injured, the Provost Marshal arrested them. Childress's British exemption papers were found on Parker and witnesses began to come forward. One described seeing Childress at a bar with the two, and Parker had a watch which several witnesses identified as being in the possession of Childress. When arrested, Parker's knife was examined and found to still have blood on it. In what might be termed an early forensic approach to the evidence, the blade "was applied" by town physician James King, "to one of the mortal wounds upon the body of the deceased [and] fitted in it." Doctor King later swore that any one of three wounds would have caused death.

The evidence pointed to Parker as the murderer, while Runciman swore at his trial that he was not guilty. Runciman's luck held out for a bit longer. A jury found him not guilty of murder, but of felonious slaying. Still suffering from the wounds he had gotten some days before, he was sentenced to two months in jail. Then his luck ran out: Henry Vandross Runciman died of his wounds while still imprisoned. His obituary stated simply that he died "at 9 o'clock...aged about 18 years." His funeral was held at the residence of the town butcher, Thomas E. Lawrence, the same man who had secured his bond in 1859. No other information was given.

As for William Parker, he decided not to wait for a verdict. He, along with four others, broke out of the county jail on the night of 11 August. He remained at large until after the war when he was spotted and recognized in Hillsboro, N.C. He was returned to Wilmington and once again put on trial in October 1867. Although some of the evidence had been lost (mainly the British papers that had belonged to Childress) there were still many witnesses who testified at the delayed trial. Parker was found guilty and, after an appeal, his sentence of death was reaffirmed by the new Supreme Court of North Carolina.[8]

One of the strangest deaths involved a young man who had purchased a knife to "kill a dog." Returning to his boarding house, he saw an acquaintance and began conversing with him. Taking the dagger from his coat, he pressed it against his breast and said, "Lay on, MacDuff!" He then "struck himself in the left breast, the dagger entering about 2 or 3 inches." Uttering "Good Lord!" he fell on the floor, dead. He had actually stabbed himself. When the matter was investigated, it was apparent that the man had done this act before, quoting Shakespeare while using the handle end of a dagger to thrust into his chest. This time he used the wrong end of the knife! A jury termed it an "accidental stabbing."

In the fall of 1863, the jewelry store of Brown and Anderson was robbed. Before long, several men staying at different hotels in town were arrested for the crime. Found in their rooms at the Mechanics and Farmer's hotels were most of the stolen articles. Of the eight men brought before Justice John Conoly, six were committed to jail and two were released, "but were subsequently arrested on the charge of stealing a trunk and valise, taken from the City Hotel." They were quickly placed in prison to await trial.

There were at least three prisons in Wilmington during the war. A city and a county jail kept the common criminals off the streets, while the military lock-up was reserved for soldiers and others arrested by the military. Before the war, that prison, located on the northeast corner of Second and Princess Streets, known to locals as "Exchange Corner," had been the Negro jail. The slave-trading firm of Southerland and Coleman had kept their slaves there before offering their human property for sale at the market. It was a hard old place, a three-story brick building, surrounded by walls eighteen feet high. Containing a kitchen and stable, the premises had been constructed and "fitted up expressly for the safe keeping of slaves." With the war the place quickly filled up. Incarcerated were not only those who might have been drunk or disorderly, but also deserters and soldiers who had committed more serious crimes. When the town jail became overcrowded, civilian prisoners were also sent there.

In the county jail were housed runaway slaves as well as civilian criminals. For their lodging and meals, slaves (or their owners) were charged one dollar per day. If no one came forward to claim the slave, he was "sold for cost." By 1864, with inflation, the county sheriff was allowed eight dollars per day for the prisoners in his care. There were escapes made from the various jails, some successful, most not. Hunted by detachments of soldiers, the miscreants tried to make their way to the Yankee fleet waiting offshore or sought safety in the nearby swamps and thick pine forests.

The citizens of Long Creek district, north of Wilmington, were determined to capture a runaway slave who was hiding out in a nearby swamp. "William's Jim," a slave whose master had died, had hidden away for several months and survived by "killing stock, breaking open smokehouses, stealing, robbing and committing all kinds of depredations." In April 1864, three stalwart denizens started off to find Jim, who had vowed not to be taken alive. They found his camp deep in the swamp and approached cautiously, but were seen by Jim: "When they drew near he sprang up, seized a double barreled gun, and snapped it at them. Mr. Cherry [one of the search party] turning the muzzle aside. Mr. Cherry drew a revolver, but could not use it. In the scuffle, the Negro got Mr. C's left hand forefinger in his mouth, and bit it off...Mr. Cherry hit him several times with a hatchet but failed to make him let go...Finally the Negro got hold of the hatchet and struck both Mr. Montague and Mr. Cherry with it." In the progress of the fight Mr. Montague got possession of the hatchet and used it on the Negro, who was finally subdued, all parties being by this time covered with blood.

Jim was tied up and hauled off to jail. One less desperado lurked in the countryside, but there were many more desperate runaways and deserters still in the district and in the Caintuck and Black River districts, which lie in present-day Pender County.

Deserters, it was well known, could be killed and the killer held "blameless" for the act. "Jim" reported that a deserter named Jeremiah Collins, who was hiding out in the Black River district, was responsible for luring away many slaves and guiding them to the Yankees. Mr. Cherry stated that he was ready to "clear that section of this gang of desperados[.]" The following month, a detail from the 40th N.C. Regiment, an artillery unit stationed in the region, was sent into the Caintuck district to apprehend Collins. After a fruitless search, the men noted a woman walking off into the woods. Trailed by the soldiers, his empty campsite was found; sentries were posted to await his return. That evening Collins came back and was surrounded. He refused to surrender, tried to run off, and was shot and killed.[9]

The local constabulary was also active when danger appeared. Early in the war, County Sheriff Vann was alerted that Yankees were landing east of the city at Masonboro Sound. A vessel had been spotted and in the wee hours of the morning drums sounded the alarm. It was dusk by the time Vann and his men arrived. As they made their way along a path, they were confronted by a group of armed men. Hearing "the ominous click of a gun lock," both parties challenged each other. Facing them was another group of citizens with the same idea of capturing some of the "Lincolnite gentlemen." Fortunately, their challenge was answered "not a second too soon," and all went on their way.[10]

It would appear that Vann was more at home tracking down local criminals. He died in 1863, forty years old and just one month after being married. The office was taken temporarily by County Coroner Richard Jones, later by Robert MacRae, who held the position for about a year. MacRae had lost the use of an arm due to a war wound, but as a returned hero was elected to the job. Unfortunately, he also died soon after taking the job, so in 1864 Edward D. Hall, who had been sheriff before the war, filled the position.

In early 1863 Wilmington suffered through an economic depression. Many of those who had fled the prevailing yellow fever epidemic, which had struck the preceding fall, stayed away because Wilmington was thought to be the next target of a Union attack. Indeed it was to be, except that the new ironclad *USS Monitor* had been lost in a storm off the Carolina coast; yet another had been damaged. When it was realized that the iron vessels would be unable to cross the bar to get into the Cape Fear River, the project was abandoned.

One who left town because of the threat was schoolteacher G.W. Jewitt. His motives, as he later recorded, were several: many of his patrons had already fled town, "and though Wilmington was at no time seriously threatened except by extortioners, panics were of a weekly occurrence." With the fall of New Bern to the Federals in the spring of 1862, any students that were left "scattered to the four winds." Jewitt relocated into the interior at Statesville, where he would remain for most of the war.

In the downturn, many businesses failed, especially hotels. In September 1863, a visitor, lodged in a room with two other men, commented: "One could observe the general demoralization brought about by the turbulent state of affairs. The hotel had neither real service nor furniture."[11]

One of these establishments, the City Hotel, advertised shortly after the end of the yellow fever epidemic that their rooms had been thoroughly fumigated, but still struggled to turn a profit. When an altercation in their barroom turned deadly, it was a portent of things to come.

In 1862, James Thompson, an engineer on the Wilmington and Manchester railroad, invited several others after work to join him for a drink. One man demurred remarking, "No, I have money enough to pay for my own drinks." Three or four others, including Joseph James, another engineer on the line, took Thompson up on the offer. They went to Kelly's Branch Saloon (so-called because it was Kelly's second such establishment) located on the ground floor of the City Hotel. After downing a drink, Thompson jumped up and shouted, "Now I am ready for that man that insulted me down at the station!" With this, he pulled out a knife and swung at those around him. Missing his target by inches, he swore, "Damn you, I can whip the whole crowd," and turned and struck at James. His blade caught the hapless man in the throat. Falling to the floor, James expired in a matter of minutes. Thompson was arrested and charged with murder, but when his case came to trial, in 1864, nearly two years after the deed, the charge was reduced to manslaughter, even though many saw it as a case of willful murder. After paying court costs, his punishment was to be branded on the round of the thumb with the letter "M."

Branding was an archaic punishment which dated back to colonial days, but was still in use during the Civil War. Before the war, legislators in Raleigh had wrestled with what the appropriate punishment should be for horse thievery. It was agreed that for a first offence, a public whipping was suitable; for a second offence it was argued that the thief should be branded on the forehead with a horseshoe! A prewar third offence would result in a hanging. In the spirit of enlightenment, the proposal for branding was soundly defeated, although one lawmaker's reasoning went like this: "Mr. Ramey denounced the practice of branding as…[a relic] of barbarism. He would prefer sending the thief to the grave at once by means of the gallows."

Deserters, when captured, also stood the chance of being branded on the arm, face, hip or back, with a four-inch letter "D." They also faced a very good chance of being forced to perform hard labor by working on the area's fortifications. One of the worst places to be sent was Smith's Island; there a chain gang performed extremely hard labor constructing Fort Holmes.[12] Deserters and murderers were not the only ones who faced the hangman's noose; anyone found spying for the enemy could face summary execution.

Endnotes

1. John Wesley Bone, "Record of a Soldier in the Late War," manuscript provided by Mr. Roger W. Bone.
2. Wood, *Port Town at War.* Wilmington *Daily Journal*, 27 February 1862, 15 January 1863, hereinafter cited as the *Daily Journal.* New Hanover County, City of Wilmington, *Record of Commissioner's Minutes, 1842-1855*, 197, 9 February 1854, hereinafter referred to as *Commissioner's Minutes.*
3. Paddy's Hollow was located "along the river north of Red Cross Street. In its heyday 39 saloons prospered in that small area." Robert Martin Fales, M.D., *Wilmington Yesteryear*, edited by Diane Cashman, privately published, 1984, 84. National Archives, Record Group 109, Military Departments, Letters Sent, District of Cape Fear, North Carolina, Chapter II, Volume 336, letter dated 17 April 1864. These papers, volumes 335-336, 338-339, 344, 346-348 are the official records of Major General W.H.C. Whiting during his time in the region (November 1862-January 1865.) They are hereinafter referred to as the *Whiting*

Papers. Morgan's miscreant's were ordered to Weldon, N.C., "under guard" ibid., 12 March 1864. See also the *Daily Journal*, 20 June 1861, 2 January 1864. After the war Carr would stand trial for the murder of his neighbor. A dispute over their fence line led to the shooting by Carr. Upon rendering the verdict, the judge warned him he "had escaped with his life by the slightest shadow of a distinction." He was instead branded with an "M" on his thumb. See the *Wilmington Herald*, 6 April 1867.

4. Lawrence Lee, *New Hanover County: A Brief History* (Raleigh: State Department of Archives and History, 1971) 56.

5. James V. Albright Diary, Southern Historical Society, Collection No. 1003, Chapel Hill, North Carolina, entry dated 20 January 1864.

6. *New Hanover County Superior Court Minutes, 1856-1871*, (hereinafter referred to as *N.H.C. Superior Court Minutes*), fall term, 1861, labeled number 40. Called as a witness, Craig failed to appear and was fined $80. It is likely he had gone to Raleigh to plead for Peter's life. See also the *Daily Journal*, 11 and 30 November 1860.

7. *N.H.C. Superior Court Minutes*, fall term, 1860. The trial took place in September 1859, see also the *Daily Journal*, 16 July 1859.

8. *N.H.C. Superior Court Minutes*, fall term, 1860; see also spring term, 1864 (25 April 1864); *Daily Journal*, 1 and 2 April 1863, 12 August 1863; *Cases at Law, Supreme Court of North Carolina at Raleigh*, January term, 1868, 473-478, microfilm copy at UNCW, Randall Library; *Daily Journal*, 15 April 1863 (Wilmington) *Evening Star*, 12 October 1867.

9. *Daily Journal*, 13 and 31 October, 16 December 1863; 30 April and 11 May 1864.

10. *Daily Journal*, 11 June 1861.

11. Captain Justus Scheibert, *Seven Months in the Rebel States*, "Confederate Centennial Studies, edited by William Stanley Hoole (Tuscaloosa: Confederate Publishing Co., 1958) 145.

12. *Daily Journal*, 21 November 1862. *N.H.C. Superior Court Minutes*, spring term 1864, dated 27 April 1864. *Whiting Papers*, II:336, letters dated 12 January, 16 January, 5 June and 26 November 1864. *Raleigh Standard*, 12 January 1861. See also Lower Cape Fear Historical Society, "Soldier's Letters," 21 July 1864, hereinafter referred to as LCFHS . Deserters of course also faced the firing squad.

Are There Spies Among Us?

arly in 1861, Joseph Blossom, a commission merchant who also owned one of the largest turpentine distilleries in the lower Cape Fear, saw the writing on the wall. He knew that as a northerner, his business was in danger of being taken by the Confederate authorities. In February of that year, he approached a young man (also from the north, but one who intended to remain in the South) who had gained a reputation as an astute businessman. Cyrus Van Amringe, "a young man without capital, but of much intelligence and experience" was taken in as a partner and given a one-quarter interest in the company for $40,000. With time, his share in the company would increase until he became a full partner.[1]

When the war came, Blossom went north, taking with him a large portion of the firm's assets. To avoid the sequestration laws, he legally transferred control of the company to Van Amringe: "Cyrus was very successful in his operations, and, among other things, made investments in real estate...In 1862 Cyrus died, leaving...[his brother] George Van Amringe...his [executor.]"

The Van Amringes were native New Yorkers who had lived in Wilmington for some time. Brother George, also a businessman, involved himself in blockade running and was captured off Hatteras Inlet in September 1861. The U.S. Naval officer who interviewed him reported that Van Amringe appeared "to be the moneyed man" of the operation. Sent north with the captured prize, the *Sarah Jane*, he was lodged in a prison cell at Fort Hamilton, New York. Moved to Fort Lafayette, he was placed in confinement along with others who had been swept up by the Federal authorities: Robert Tansill,

formerly a Captain in the U.S. Marine Corps (who would rise to the rank of
Colonel in the Confederate army and join General Whiting's staff in
Wilmington). Former U.S. Navy Lieutenant William H. Ward (who would attain
the rank of Commander in the C.S. Navy and would command the *CSS Olustee*).

Captain Michael Berry of Charleston, South Carolina, had been the
skipper of a steamer that plied between Charleston and New York for over forty-
five years. He was arrested in New York harbor for flying the Palmetto flag of
secession and for having "talked secession loudly and publicly[.]" Berry's
residence was listed as "on the high seas!" In November all "Political Prisoners"
were advised: "The Department of State of the United States will not recognize
anyone as an attorney for political prisoners, and will look with distrust upon all
applications for release through such channels, and that such applications will be
regarded as additional reasons for declining to release the prisoners[.]"

In other words, the prisoners were to keep quiet and hope for their
release. That same month, George was sent to Fort Warren in Boston harbor. He
would remain there until being released on 21 February 1862. The Union
Secretary of War, Edwin Stanton, was notified on 17 March that George Van
Amringe had taken his parole. Released less than a week earlier from his N.Y.
cell was Captain Berry; he was in no condition to travel, so he lodged with a
relative in New York and it was there that he died a few months later.

As for George, he returned to Wilmington soon after being released. It
is likely that he took part in his brother's business venture. When yellow fever
killed Cyrus in the fall of that year, George took the helm of the company. At
one point during the war, by order of the military authorities, blockade runners
were not allowed to take turpentine as cargo, likely due to its flammability.
Sales declined to the point that Van Amringe was forced to branch out into
manufacturing camphene (used for lighting), salt, soap, ink, "tanner's oil," axle
grease, varnish and lamp black. After suffering through several fires at his
factory George continued to struggle through the war and at one point reinvested
some $20,000 back into the firm.

Upon the conclusion of hostilities, Joseph Blossom returned to Wilmington
and sued George for having "appropriated very considerable sums to the support
of himself and his father and mother and a younger brother[.]" The younger
brother specified was probably Stacy, who at age twenty-four had enlisted in
1862, but had been discharged the following year because of an "injury of the
intestines and severe contusion of the lower extremities [caused by] a fall."

George's defense, that Blossom had initially deceived the Confederate
government when he turned the firm over to Cyrus, was quickly rejected by the
new North Carolina Supreme Court. As they said, Blossom did but "fight fire
with fire...He is justified...on the ground that artifice, deceit and stratagem may,
during war, be resorted to to deceive the enemy[.]"

A sample of a notice of sequestration. Sequestration was the mechanism employed by the Confederate government to seize the property of those of Northern birth, or those believed to have Northern sympathies. (NHCPL)

Blossom argued that George had changed the name of the company "with a view to complicate and embarrass the accounts" and when all was said and done, Blossom regained control of the company. There was just no way, in 1867, that George Van Amringe was going to win his case. Blossom reestablished himself in Wilmington and went on to a lucrative business career.

The sequestration, or "seizure" laws that so vexed Blossom, were enacted early in the war to prevent monies from flowing into enemy hands; as

DuBrutz Cutlar (NHCPL)

early as August 1861, the Confederate Congress decreed that all males over fourteen years of age, who were not citizens of the Confederate States were "liable to be apprehended, restrained or secured and removed as alien enemies." Such enemies of the State were to be given time "for the disposition of their effects and departure[.]" The time allowed was to be in accordance with the "dictates of humanity and national hospitality" but was to be within forty days of President Davis' proclamation. Once across enemy lines, if an "alien" returned, they were to be arrested and treated as a spy or prisoner of war. There were many businesses throughout the South that were indebted to northern manufacturers, as well as Northerners who owed Southern merchants. Many prominent citizens, including George Davis, who would go on to be Attorney General of the Confederacy, received warning notices from DuBrutz Cutlar, "Alien Custodian and Receiver" of the Confederate States, telling them they owed him money. Banks, as well as steamboat and railroad companies were required to provide Cutlar with lists of their alien enemy stockholders. Other citizens were encouraged to divulge any information they might know about other debtors.[2]

In the first months of war many business partnerships were dissolved and many northerners left Wilmington as well as other cities throughout the South. So many left that the remaining citizens called a meeting to determine what should be done about "persons heretofore citizens of the town of Wilmington, but who, at this hour of peril, have deserted us, or are preparing to [do so.]" As the court house wasn't large enough to hold the numbers of interested people, the meeting was moved to the recently completed Thalian Hall. One of the committee's resolutions declared: "That if any persons now residing here desire to change their residence and remove to the enemy's country, that the Mayor and Commissioners may, in the exercise of their discretion, allow them thirty days to leave."

Yet another resolution called upon the governor to: "require all citizens of this State, now in the enemy's country, to return to the State within a reasonable time, or that they shall be regarded as alien enemies."

Straw and Hat Business.

We would direct attention to the card of Messrs. Orrel & Grady, No. 18 Cortlandt Street, near Broadway, New York, where merchants and others visiting that City may find Hats and Caps, Straw and Millinery goods.

Messrs. Orrell & Grady are both North Carolinians as well by education as by birth, and if we are not greatly mistaken, their's is the *only* strictly Southern House engaged in the same business in the city of New York. Mr. Grady is well known, and favorably known, in this section; Mr. Orrell comes originally from the upper end of the old Cape Fear District. They are good men.

A newspaper advertisement, recommending the wares of Orrell & Grady. (NHCPL)

In what might be termed bad timing, two native North Carolinians had established a business partnership in New York City in April 1860. Selling straw hats and millinery goods, Benjamin F. Grady and Daniel Orrell's store was said to be "the only strictly Southern House engaged in the...business in the city of New York." Grady was the partner who traveled about the South, making contracts and collecting monies owed the company. He returned to North Carolina in April 1861 to collect some of those monies when Fort Sumter was fired upon. He heeded his States' call and offered his services to North Carolina; it was, after all, "where his sympathies and affection lie." He then explained to Collector Cutlar and the Courts that: He [had] communicated...this determination [to return South if war came] to his partner and instructed him to wind up the business in New York as speedily as possible – his object for doing so, being to remove the capital and assets of the firm to the State of North Carolina...and...(from repeated conversations he had with his partner before leaving New York) that [Orrell] concurred."

From time to time, Grady heard from Orrell, who told him he was doing his best to close down the business and in July, Orrell informed Grady that he needed one thousand dollars right away. Grady borrowed the money and sent it to Orrell, along with most of the funds he had already collected from his travels. Grady's attorney, Eli W. Hall, laid his case before the judge: "That since...24th July 1861, the said Daniel Orrell has never written to your petitioner, nor has he

USS Monticello

received any communication direct from him, but he has been informed and believes…that…Orrell received all the remittances…and that he has sold out the entire stock…amounting to…Five thousand dollars."

Orrell had purchased property in Brooklyn, N.Y., as well as in "one of the Western States of the United States." In addition, Grady said that Orrell had been drawing money from the firm and owed nearly four thousand dollars. It was readily apparent that Orrell had no intention of returning to North Carolina and "had fixed his domicile with our enemies." Grady asked the courts to consider the partnership dissolved and also requested to be allowed to keep the money he had yet to collect, some $3,500 from Southern merchants. Poor Grady had returned home with only seventy dollars in his pocket, with no other job prospects than the army.

Another who found himself uprooted was Samuel D. Allen, who before the war ran a dry goods store on Market Street. Leaving his young clerk, George M. Bowen, to sell off or otherwise dispose of his merchandise, Allen sought cooler climes in the North.[3] Bowen, who hailed from Connecticut, got rid of most of the stock and was ready to leave the state as well. As he approached the railroad depot, he was met by the sheriff, who asked him to give up the letters he was known to be carrying northward. Bowen did as he was asked and boarded the train, headed for home.

When the letters were opened and examined, it was apparent that the Reverend Grier, pastor of the newly dedicated First Presbyterian Church, was a Yankee sympathizer. The town's Committee of Safety advised the reverend that he had thirty days to get out of town. Grier did as he was advised, but returned in December 1864 with Union Major General Benjamin Butler's attacking army.

As for Allen, he did not give up without a fight. When the government moved to take his property, his friend and fellow merchant Oran S. Baldwin produced documents indicating that Allen had left Wilmington on his doctor's advice and that he was "in no way hostile to the Confederate States of America and in support of this denial ...alleges that [he left in] extreme ill health." It was no use. His remaining property was seized and Samuel Allen never returned to Wilmington. Of course, anyone who owed Allen money received a summons from Receiver Cutlar. Purchasing most of Allen's stock, Baldwin also wound up with Allen's household furniture.[4]

With the frenzy whipped up by the more rabid secessionists, many of whom were members of the Committee of Safety, it was becoming dangerous for Unionists to remain in town. Joseph Neff, a ship chandler of northern birth, was overheard uttering "disloyal language," and was arrested when he said that " 'Lincoln was in Virginia now and before long he would be in North Carolina and then he [Neff] would fight under the stars and stripes.' They took him to the Court House and tried him, and committed him to gaol...They closed up his store...while they were locking it up – his brother wept like a child." There was not enough evidence to send Neff to jail for good, so he was released. He never left town, but was always suspected of being a traitor.

Not all disloyal persons were Northerners. Francis Savage, a native Tar Heel and former lighthouse keeper, deserted to the Union blockaders with the help of his brother-in-law, John Orrell, and was hired on by the Federals as a pilot. Later, Savage induced Orrell, a

Dr. John Walker
(Tuolumne Genealogical Society)

lieutenant in the Masonboro militia, to desert. Both men provided "good service" to the U.S. Navy. Orrell's knowledge of the coast was put to use to raid the nearby salt works while Savage was employed as a pilot aboard the *USS Monticello.* The Navy paid all pilots $100 per month, but in 1862, offered a special $5,000 bounty to any pilot who could get an ironclad across the bar into the river, up to and back from Wilmington.

When it was learned that Savage had fled the country, Collector Cutlar became involved, because, as he wrote, "the said Savage, [is] being employed and now [is] engaged as pilot on board one of the Blockading Steamers of the

The tug **Uncle Ben,** *seized by Wilmington Confederates.*

enemy off the Cape Fear Bar." Savage lost the forty acres of land he had owned on the Sound, but was able to get his wife and family out of the country.

Others suffered sequestration as well. Dr. John Walker, who had migrated to California during the Gold Rush and had remained there during the war, lost his slave who was sold at auction. He failed to heed his State's call to return "within a reasonable time." Interestingly, Dr. Walker was Major General Whiting's brother-in-law.[5]

In September 1861, Acting Master Edward Cavendy of the *USS Gemsbok* brought his vessel close to New Inlet at the mouth of the Cape Fear. He had disguised his ship by hiding the guns and limiting the number of men on deck. He then hoisted a flag indicating that his steamer required a pilot. He later wrote: "A small boat came off from shore with two men thinking we were a merchant ship wanting a pilot. After getting within hail, I asked them if they were pilots. They answered yes. I told them to be quick, as I wanted to get in as soon as possible. They came alongside and after finding out they were on board a man-of-war, they turned rather pale, but they soon found out they were under the Stars and Stripes and seemed glad."

The two pilots, George Bowen and James Puckett, had been duped, but after taking the Oath of Allegiance, "They proved to be good men." Both men were offered jobs and were assigned as pilots to blockaders. About a month later, Bowen was able to contact his family by means of a "ten-gallon keg" thrown overboard. The keg, washed ashore, was addressed to Mrs. Bowen and assured her that both men were in good health.[6]

The *Journal* and General Whiting suspected there were spies among the population. They were correct. Late in 1864 a man named Schermerhorn, who lived on Myrtle Grove Sound, communicated with the Union Navy and sent a drawing of the roads and defenses around the city. The sketch quickly made its way to the officer commanding the blockaders off the inlets.

An officer aboard one of the blockading vessels reported to his superiors, "I have a weekly communication with the shore and can obtain any information that you require...Do you wish the newspapers we receive from the shore forwarded to you?" Also enclosed in the dispatch was a rude sketch of the area around the sounds.[7]

In August of the first year of war a New York firm, Cromwell's Steamships, wrote to the U.S. Secretary of the Navy that one of their vessels, the steamer *North Carolina*, had been unlawfully detained in that state by their agent in Wilmington. They wrote: "We have received assurances that the motive of her detention was to save the property of her Southern shareholders and for no warlike purposes." Those assurances appeared to be false.

Having made only one or two round trips between New York and Wilmington, the vessel, now under the direct control of agent Edwin A. Keith, was said to be outfitted as a privateer. Cromwell warned the Navy that if the steamer was allowed to go to sea, "she would prove a dreadful scourge to commerce." Although she was not sent out as a privateer, she was loaded with "cotton, rosin and tobacco," and rechristened the *Annie Childs*, she ran the blockade on 5 February 1862. She carried as a passenger Captain James D. Bulloch, the man who would represent the Confederacy abroad.[8]

Yet another vessel had been seized by the citizens at Wilmington. In April 1861, several steamers (actually New York tugboats) were sent to aid Major Robert Anderson, then holding out at Fort Sumter, S.C. At least three tugs made their way southward but hit heavy gales with the storm forcing one of them, the *Uncle Ben*, to seek the shelter of the Cape Fear. When the steamer's mission was learned, even though North Carolina was still technically part of the Union, she was seized and the crew contained aboard the ship. The men were later removed to the Marine Hospital and put under guard.

The Federal naval authorities were approached by concerned Northerners (insurance adjustors) who sent an emissary to Wilmington in an attempt to have the vessel released. There was no way that tugboat was going back North. It was used on the river to haul crib obstructions down to New Inlet in an attempt to close that passage into the river. Others in town wanted the steamer armed and ready to defend the port, but as late as September, that had not been done. It was not until November that she was fitted with at least one gun. In this capacity, she could come down to the river's mouth and assist grounded vessels across the bar. Less than a year later, she lost her engine to a greater cause: the new Confederate ironclad *North Carolina* received it.[9]

Earlier in the war, communication between North and South was carried on via a flag-of-truce boat that brought mail both ways. As the war went on, this formal trade ceased. Surreptitious trade continued throughout the war. It was later stated that there was an "Underground Railroad" that worked in reverse, bringing Southern sympathizers across the lines. A New York City reporter

General W.H.C. Whiting

attempted to prove this trade when, in 1863, he left for the South. After asking local military authorities if he could pass through the lines, he was turned away, and being suspect, was followed.

After losing his shadow, the reporter was eventually directed to go to a certain street near the docks to see a man named Brown. From the mysterious Mr. Brown he received instructions to proceed to a hotel in Maryland. The newsman then met a local man who guided him safely across the Potomac into Confederate lines. A little later he turned up in Wilmington, which, it was recorded, was the Southern terminus of the Road. It was said that the head of the road at Wilmington was none other than Dr. Armand deRosset, Jr., a well-known and respected physician and businessman of the town.

Dr. deRosset had been in partnership with a Mr. Brown before the war and it is likely the Mr. Brown in New York was deRosset's partner. It was also through this channel that Northern newspapers and mail came south. In 1864, Dr. deRosset received a letter from the north. Mailed through official channels, the letter was examined by a military officer before being given to deRosset. The missive was from U.S. General Joseph Gardner Swift.

General Swift, a lifelong army officer, had been in the first graduating class of West Point and had at one time been the Chief Engineer of the U.S. Army. Early in his career, he was sent to the lower Cape Fear area and there became friendly with the deRosset family. He met and married a Wilmington girl, Louisa Walker. The Swift's friendship with the deRosset family extended so far that Armand named a son, Edward Swift deRosset, after the General.

When the Civil War began, Swift remained loyal to the United States, but Louisa stayed in the South. The letter to deRosset asked for news of his "dear wife, whom he had not seen for a long time." The doctor was told that the letter could be answered, but he was warned that it must be "confined entirely to the matter of the inquiry." If the Swifts reunited after the war, it could not have been for long. General Swift died in July 1865.[10]

In November 1862 General William H.C. Whiting assumed command of the Cape Fear District from General Samuel G. French. The tenor of his command may be inferred by one of his first notices to the populace. It stated in part that, he "having been specially charged with the defence of the Cape Fear …should he be governed by his own inclination and judgment…he will prefer to leave the old and honored place in ashes, sooner than permit it to be occupied by the countrymen of Butler."

The general quickly began to suspect that not all Wilmingtonians were loyal Confederates. Early on he suspected Joe Neff of spying and had him placed under surveillance, but he could never find enough evidence to arrest him. As late as 1864, still wary of Neff, he penned a letter to his superiors enclosing "a copy of the report…relative to a spy." Naming Neff as the culprit, he described him as "A Northern & union man who has been residing in this city before and during the war. His brother and father, his partners, fled on the breaking out of hostilities and he himself…was lodged in jail…he was kept as a prisoner…finally released but always regarded as an enemy to our cause."

Whiting's letter pointed out Neff as one of two men in the city to be trusted by "Yankee spies to secure freedom from detection." There was "evidence which does not prove guilt but only justifies suspicion." All he could do was to have Neff watched.

There were others who also vexed Whiting. At the outbreak of war, a man named Piver fled to Union lines. Captured when he returned to visit his family at Masonboro Sound, he was lodged in the military prison. A few months later, he escaped and was again captured as he made his way to the coast in the company of a deserter. While Piver languished in jail, Whiting corresponded with the War Department, notifying them he wanted to shoot Piver as a spy. Cooler heads pointed out that the man would have to be tried first. Fortunately for Piver, Federal forces took Wilmington before Whiting could carry out his threat.

In another letter to Richmond, Whiting told Richmond, "There are several persons known to be disloyal living upon the sounds...It is well ascertained that they have been in communication with the enemy. The heads of some of these families have escaped to the fleet & are known to be on board. Have I the right...to order these people across the lines? They should not be permitted to reside where they are. We have just arrested two men belonging to these families with passes from New Bern on their persons. They were here as spies & will be so dealt with." Whiting asked if he could order the rest of the families across the lines into Union controlled territory.[11]

Just who was this man who controlled the destiny of so many in the Cape Fear? Whiting was described by one onlooker as "in stature rather under medium size...[with] a square forehead, high and intellectual, [with] a beautiful head of black hair, a small hazel eye – keen as an eagle – whiskers all over his face, but neatly trimmed, and a clever, plain, unpretending look that renders him very popular indeed with the soldiers...It has been said that for a general to be successful, he must have not only the confidence of his men, but their love also – if this be true, Gen. Whiting must have a bright future[.]"

William Henry Chase Whiting graduated at the top of his class from Georgetown College in 1840 and continued his education at West Point, class of 1845. At the Military Academy he was quartered with Fitz John Porter, who would rise to the rank of Union Major General, and met other future notables, including U.S. Grant, George B. McClellan, Ambrose Burnside and George E. Pickett. While there, he tutored a cadet by the name of Thomas J. Jackson "so regularly...in fractions and mathematical systems" that the Virginian became known as "Whiting's Plebe." When he graduated he set an academic record that would not be topped until Douglas MacArthur graduated in 1903. Upon graduation he was assigned to the Topographical (Engineer) Corps at Pensacola, Florida.

Although he did not see action in the Mexican War, Whiting had charge of constructing harbor and river defenses throughout the country. In Texas in 1849 he was given the daunting task of surveying a wagon road from San Antonio to El Paso. With 14 men in his party, they struck off across a virtually unknown and hostile land. At one point on the Texas plains, surrounded by nearly two hundred Apache Indians, Whiting exhibited a reckless fearlessness. After going with the Indians to their camp, the explorers were accosted by a particularly violent chief who demanded to know why the whites had not yet gathered wood and started cooking fires. This, of course, was the traditional job of Indian women. Whiting, cradling a Colt repeating rifle, responded that he and his men held enough wood in their arms! Tribal elders soothed the volatile situation. Whiting and his men were allowed to continue on their way.

His mission soon accomplished, Whiting went on to oversee improvements along the Cape Fear River. It was probably here that he met Kate

D. Walker, who would become his wife. The pair, married on 22 April 1857, remained childless throughout their marriage. Although from a New England family, Whiting always considered himself a Southerner, having been born in Biloxi, Mississippi in 1824.

When war came, Whiting decided to remain South. He wrote to his mentor, General Joseph Swift, of his decision, indicating that he believed there would be more opportunity in the new country. Swift responded by reminding him that he was of New England stock, was not "of the manor born," and would never be totally accepted by Southerners.[12]

As the hostilities began, Whiting assisted General P.G.T. Beauregard in setting up the defenses of Charleston. This was followed by a tour of duty as North Carolina's Inspector General and then chief of staff to General Joseph Johnston. He showed great promise in the early battles around Richmond, but fell into disfavor with President Jefferson Davis and was relegated, in November 1862, to Wilmington, then considered a backwater of the war.

Whiting approached his new task with vigor and the power of martial law was quickly felt in the region. When Whiting observed many men wandering about the streets, he suggested to the Town Commissioners that a chain gang might work wonders: "I respectfully call your attention to the propriety of instituting a Chain Gang for the city, to which vagrants, drunkards, disorderly persons, plug uglies, suspicious characters, &c...may be assigned for punishment...This regulation will materially add to the peace and security of the city."

Whiting seems to have inspired either outright admiration or hatred. He could be solicitous to his men, as shown when he directed that the sentries "that are obliged to stand in the sun" be relieved during the heat of the day (during business hours)." Yet when he suspected that the workers at the State Salt works were communicating with the U.S. Navy blockaders along the coast, he pushed to have the works removed from the sounds. He believed that the workers were disloyal and would, with a Yankee invasion, act as guides, cut telegraph wires and burn bridges.[13] He ordered that all boats along the river and sounds be seized and placed under guard to prevent them from being used by deserters or others seeking to escape by sea.

Further control over the populace came when all male citizens and female heads of households were requested to register so strangers could more easily be identified. This edict did not last long and the following week registration ceased. In its place a passport system was established. This system, which eventually encompassed all aspects of movement and travel by both soldiers and civilians, was originally meant to limit access to and from the front lines and military camps. One writer indicated that early on the passport system was found necessary for the Confederate capital. What he wrote of Richmond would hold true for Wilmington also: "The dramatic increase in population, the large numbers of transient soldiers and civilians…made passports essential for the control of movement. At first, only soldiers were required to produce some recognizable authority for their visits to the city…Eventually passports became mandatory for anyone leaving the city, even those who wished simply to go to their homes."

The local newspaper called for such precautionary action: "We are at war with a powerful and…unscrupulous nation, talking the same language…acquainted, many of them at least, with their manners and habitudes…let all Southern men traveling be prepared to give an account of themselves[.]" Women and children were, of course, allowed to leave the country, but any male citizen desiring to do so required a passport. A "Passport Office" was set up and an army officer questioned men wanting to leave town before a pass was issued. There were two sets of papers, one for "Strangers and other citizens" who were not known in town and "General Passports" issued to registered persons recommended by the town's Committee of Safety. To insure compliance, picket posts were situated at all points of egress: Smith's Creek, on the country roads and on the Plank Road leading out of town. The roads on the southeastern part of town were closed except for River Road and the road to Confederate Point, where the bastion of Fort Fisher was located. Both of these roads were closely guarded.

In addition, those desiring to leave the country were many times personally interrogated by Whiting. As early as January 1863, the general took an active role in issuing passes to the soldiers. One North Carolinian "complained that his regiment was bothered by the provost because so few could imitate the commanding general's signature." The time consuming process caused many travelers to miss their trains and was a continuing source of complaint, eased somewhat when the passport office changed their hours of operation. Regardless, many felt "the imposition of military authority over their right of free travel intolerable." As late as October 1863, the town still required registration with the military authorities, due to "the influx of many strange visitors, and among them those of bad character and of vicious and criminal intent[.]" Even with registration and passports, some managed to slip away. In July 1863, Whiting ordered a guard to be stationed at the North East ferry landing. It had been reported that the ferryman was secretly taking people without passports across the river at night.

It was found that travel to Wilmington from the islands also needed to be more closely watched. In the fall of 1863 Whiting ordered: "Improper or suspicious persons must not be taken as passengers to this port. They must be properly vouched for, and permission given to embark, by Major L. Heyliger, at Nassau, or Major Norman Walker, at Bermuda. Any passengers brought to this port, without proper credentials, will be sent back by the same steamer.[14]

That same year, 1863, it was suggested to the commanding general that detectives might prove useful around town to root out any deserters, spies or traitors. Major Thomas Sparrow, in command of the city garrison, thought such agents were needed both in town and in the Islands. As trade with the North was forbidden, detectives sent to Nassau and Bermuda were to verify the identity and homeport of the vessels clearing for Wilmington. There were three detectives in Wilmington and possibly as many in the Islands.

Those in town were instructed to visit the passport office at least once daily. On at least one occasion a detective in Bermuda reported his suspicions to Whiting concerning a traveler. Whiting relayed the information to Richmond: "My detectives in Bermuda report [the suspect] as very unsound & engaged in writing letters on reconstruction." But the results were mixed, for when two of the town detectives resigned in November 1863, Whiting wrote that he was glad to see them go as, "They have not made an arrest since they have been here & …are not likely to do so." The men were ordered back from whence they came: General John H. Winder's office at Richmond. The following year the local conscript officer asked to have detectives placed on board blockade runners, but Whiting thought this measure unnecessary as the "ships are thoroughly inspected in town, after that no communication is allowed with them. A guard goes down the river & remains till they put to sea." By early 1864, Whiting had all the agents he needed and applicants for the position were told they were not needed.

Regardless of how many agents Whiting employed, one who escaped detection was L.J. Sherman, who worked as a bartender for Benjamin Morrell at the Globe House, "No. 1 Granite Row, Front Street below Market Street." Thought at first to be a valiant fellow because he had remained at his post at the bar during the yellow fever epidemic, he was later found to be a spy. What better way to learn military secrets.

In 1863 the *Journal* reported: "Towards the close of last December…the police made a descent upon the 'little hell' of which Sherman was the presiding demon, and Sherman to escape capture and…very severe punishment …decamped and could not be found. How he got off we are unable to say. However, he did get off,…and…is now a Yankee spy and detective officer in Northern cities and on Northern rail roads, spotting Southern travelers."

Accused of operating a "disreputable establishment" and being a "fancy man," he was also implicated as a card shark! What the *Journal* failed to realize was that while Sherman was in Wilmington, he was spying for the Union. In April 1863, after his escape, he was sent to New Bern to see General John Foster and on his way there stopped to give information about Wilmington to the Union commanders of the blockade. Secretary of the Navy Gideon Welles told Admiral Lee: "I suggested that he should converse with you, as he is possessed of much information about Wilmington. He thinks he can procure three men who can carry vessels…into [the Cape Fear] River. The Department would give $5,000 for each vessel carried safely in." Admiral Lee, for his part, did not think much of the information Sherman provided.

As for the owner of the saloon, poor Morrell, himself of Yankee birth, ran an ad in the local paper stating that the hotel was now "entirely under my control and personal supervision." Throughout its wartime existence, the Globe House and its saloon was fined by the town for "retailing," which meant selling whiskey on Sunday. Morrell managed to stay in business for the entire conflict, even after a disastrous fire in December 1864. In May 1865, when under U.S. Army control, he advertised that the saloon would soon reopen with "the old banner thrown to the breeze!" [15] It did not remain open for long before it was sold to a new owner, L.J. Sherman.

Although many former residents of Wilmington had left to join the army, there were still enough people either living there or passing through to support the official twelve licensed bars. Unofficially there were many more.[16]

Endnotes

1. *Cases Argued and Determined in the Supreme Court of North Carolina at Raleigh*, January Term, 1867, 133-138, New Hanover County Public Library. See also June Term, 1868. The firm retained the name of Blossom and Company for most of the war.

2. *Official Records of the Union and Confederate Navies in the War of the Rebellion* (Washington: Government Printing Office, 1898) I:6, 198, hereinafter cited as ORN. *Daily Journal*, 28 November 1861. *ORA*, II:2, 92, 103, 155-156, 239, 269, 1368-1369. *Confederate Papers of the U.S. District Court of the Eastern District of North Carolina, 1861-1865*, National Archives microfilm no. 436. Hereinafter cited as *Confederate Papers*, these are records of persons accused of treason, mail robbery and harboring deserters, as well as those who were alien enemies. Stacy Van Amringe resigned his army commission in August, 1863; see *North Carolina Troops, A Roster, 1861-1865* (compiled by Louis H. Manarin and Louis T. Weymouth (Raleigh: Division of Archives and History, 1966), 4:715, hereinafter cited as *North Carolina Troops. Daily Journal*, 17 December 1863, 28 December, 21 May, 6 and 7 July 1864.

3. *Daily Journal*, 27 June 1861. *Confederate Papers*, deposition of Benjamin F. Grady, 18 December 1861, pages 1-12.

4. *Confederate Papers*, sequestration papers of Samuel D. Allen, frame 0311. As the Butler expedition failed, Reverend Grier would have to wait a few more months to return to Wilmington. Doctor Thomas Fanning Wood Collection, "Civil War Notes," 57, Special Collections, Randall Library, University of North Carolina at Wilmington, hereinafter cited as the *Wood Papers*. The Committee of

Safety ws a self-styled group of prominent secessionists and was modeld after the Revolutinary War patriots.

5. *Confederate Papers*, n.d., frame 423. *ORN*, I:8, 321-322, 579, 235, 237, 10:94, 443. See also the *Daily Journal*, 3 and 24 October 1861.

6. *ORN*, I:6, 283; *Daily Journal*, 24 October 1861. Eventually even Mrs. Bowen was spirited off in a daring night foray by Union sailors. See *ORN*, I:8, 334-335, 396 and I:9, 236, 300.

7. *ORN*, I:10, 94.

8. James Sprunt, *The Chronicles of the Cape Fear River, 1660-1916* (Raleigh: Edwards and Broughton Printing Company, 459-460. The [Wilmington] *Morning Star*, 20 and 21 November 1880. See also *ORN*, I:6, 177-178. The *North Carolina*, after going through several name changes, was renamed the *Victory* when captured by the U.S. Navy. Under the name *Gulf Stream*, she visited her homeport of Wilmington as late as 1880. She was "stranded Jan. 30, 1903, at Hartford Inlet, N.J." See Stephen Wise. *Lifeline of the Confederacy: Blockade Running During the Civil War* (Columbia: University of South Carolina, 1988) 288.

9. *ORN*, 5:663; Joyner Library, East Carolina University, Martin Smith Grant Collection, Diary of Ada A. Costin, entries dated 22-23 April 1861; ORN, 6:499, 726, 696. The following month (October 1862) the *Uncle Ben* was converted into a schooner and renamed the *Retribution*. In this role she made several captures, *ORN*, II, I:408.

10. *Confederate Veteran*, 24:494 (1916); *The Memoirs of General Joseph Swift, LL.D.,U.S.A.* (privately printed) [Worchester, Mass.: Press of F.S. Blanchard and Co.] 1890.

11. *Daily Journal*, 18 November 1862; 4 December 1862, *Whiting Papers*, Letters Sent, II:336, dated 2 June and 11 July 1864; Endorsements, II:336, dated 1 and 2 June 1864, 21 September and 13 October 1864.

12. James I. Robertson, *Stonewall Jackson: The Man, The Soldier, The Legend* (New York: MacMillan Publishing Co., 1997) 34. William S. Powell, *Dictionary of North Carolina Biography* (University of North Carolina Press: Chapel Hill, 1996) 6:189-190, hereinafter cited *as North Carolina Biography*; *Exploring Southwestern Trails, 1846-1854*, edited by Ralph P. Berger (Glendale, Ca.: The Arthur H. Clark Company, 1938) 270-273; Swift, 286.

13. *Whiting Papers*, Letters Sent, II:336, dated 27 October 1864, 10 August 1863. Whiting wanted to conscript the workers; there were nearly 300 men at the Sounds, many of whom were Quakers.

14. Kenneth Radley, *Rebel Watchdog: The Confederate States Army Provost Guard* (Louisiana State University Press: Baton Rouge, 1989) 77-79, 89. *Daily Journal*, 4 September 1863, 4, 5 and 12 December 1862, 12 October 1863. *Whiting Papers*, II:336, 2 September 1863.

15 *Daily Journal*, 11 February, 26 August 1863; *ORN*, I:10, 818-819. *ORN*, I:9, 14. The *Journal*, quoting the *New York World*, reported that Sherman floated "out sixty miles on the sea," before being picked up by a U.S. Navy ship. It was also said that he was appointed colonel under General Foster. "Colonel" Sherman was likewise reported to be the chief of the detective forces for the United States, see the *Wilmington Herald*, 19 and 21 August 1865, hereafter cited as the *Herald*. Morrell was from Massachusetts, see *Herald of the Union*, 6 May 1865, *Herald*, 29 August, 12 October 1865 and 23 February 1866.
16. In 1864, in addition to Morrell, the following were licensed to "retail spirituous liquors by the small measure": J.P. Sharpsteen, J.G. Beauman, Shemwell and McDonald, (of the City Hotel), S.R. Bunting, N.F. [Bourdeaux?], henry Webb, James H. Mitchell, John Thornton, Hamm M. Bremer, Joseph Meyers and [Runger?] and Kortland. See New Hanover County, *Court Minutes*, 1864, 318. Virtually all were constantly fined for failure to collect the proper tax or for selling liquor on Sundays.

Around Town

There were, of course, other businesses besides saloons in town. One could get a good meal at Harry Webb's restaurant on Front Street. Of English birth, Harry had enlisted in the18th North Carolina Regiment and served for a year and a half before leaving the army and devoting himself to his eatery. His oysters were said to be the best in the area. Another draw for customers was Webb's renowned cook, William Curtis. Fish and fowl were an important part of the port's food supply and by early March white shad were said to be "abundant and the delicate birdies now plump and juicy." Fierce competition developed among the restaurants during the war. The Globe House had the best turtle soup in town and advertised that meals were available "all hours, day or night." The Blockade House secured the services of the "celebrated cook and caterer," Allen Denton. C.F. Hopkins offered thirty-five dollars for the first pair of shad caught in 1863 but was outbid by Webb, who offered fifty dollars and got the fish, which had "patriotically run the blockade...that they may be taken and eaten."

Surely Hopkins made money when, in 1864, he offered oysters at sixteen dollars per gallon! The editor of the *Journal*, James Fulton, often freely advertised for those who left delicacies at his office; when Mrs. Hopkins dropped off some shad to him, he publicly thanked her and wrote that he would reduce them to a

A Civil War-era ad for Harry Webb's saloon. (NHCPL)

"shad-ow."[1] Indicative of the rampant inflation in Wilmington and throughout the Confederacy, in early 1865 shad sold for $1.50 in specie, with the value in Confederate currency unknown! Mr. Fulton often commented on the state of food in town and always seemed to be taken aback by the higher prices: "We noticed yesterday Mr. Webb's Shad as being the first of the season... About noon we happened to accompany a friend to the Globe Restaurant, on Front Street...It is really fitted up in a style that would be luxurious in any place or at any time...The indefatigable proprietor of the Palmetto, Mr. Bailey, also continues to serve up excellent meals...as also Mrs. McCaleb...and Mrs. Blaney at the Railroad Depot." Prices had risen to one dollar for a meal which, in 1861, sold for ten cents.

Inflation, according to the local newspaper, also affected the local fowls. An article which ran in June 1863 declared: "It is positively asserted that the hens refused to lay any more eggs at one dollar per dozen. They have struck for higher wages. It is also asserted that the roosters have refused to crow, until they are better paid – one dollar per pound being less than they can afford to coo-coo-coohadoodle for."

Before settling down to a fine meal, one might want to clean up first. A visit to Elvin Artis' "Eagle Shaving, Hair Cutting and Shampooing Saloon" were in order. Artis, nearly forty-eight years old in 1861, was a free mulatto carpenter who owned property in town and had opened his barber shop during the war. In the early years of the conflict, he shot and killed a man, but after two months in jail, and paying a twenty-five dollar fine, he was released. Although his main income was likely derived from his barber shop, he also put his carpentry skills to work. In October 1862, he was paid by the Quartermaster Department for

The Rock Springs Hotel, in the foreground of a 1914 photo of the Wilmington riverfront. (Fales Collection, NHCPL)

The Railroad Hotel, later renamed the Atlantic. (Fales Collection, NHCPL)

"making 2 coffins for deceased soldiers" and later that year was compensated for nearly three weeks labor, having built a "wharf on Cape Fear River" for the Confederate Government.[2]

If one needed to transact business, there was the Bank of Wilmington or the Commercial Bank, both locally owned. There were the branch banks: the Bank of Cape Fear and the Bank of North Carolina. There were also brokers who were willing to lend cash or to handle stock transactions.

If a visitor wanted to stay in town overnight (many did not want to, but were forced to) there were several places where a room could be obtained. Owned by the Wood brothers before the war, the City Hotel, also known as the Carolina Hotel, was a four-story brick building at Market and Second Streets and was one of the best places to lodge. By 1862 it had, like many other inns affected by the prevailing yellow fever epidemic, closed its doors. Reopened by Poindexter Shemwell early in 1863, it survived the fall of Wilmington and again reopened "under the old banner" late in 1865.

Another competitor, the Rock Springs Hotel, remained open for most of the war and was owned by Mrs. Mary Susan McCaleb. A thirty-six year old widow with five children, she ran the twenty-room hotel, located on Chestnut, between Front and Water Streets. It was a popular gathering spot for off-duty officers and was well remembered by a Captain Henry Chambers who attended a late-night party there in March 1863. Chambers appears to have been somewhat "taken" with one of Mrs. McCaleb's daughters and continued to write her for some time.

In early 1865, with the attack on Fort Fisher, several families from Confederate Point were given refuge at McCaleb's hotel, presumably rent-free. A room at that point of the war was very much out of reach for most of the area's residents.[3] In June 1864 Private Michael Turrentine, on leave from Fort Fisher, stayed for a day at McCaleb's and paid forty dollars for the privilege. Contrast that price with a stay in July 1862 at the Palmetto House: lodging with meals was $1.50, without meals, fifty cents.

The Farmer's House, run by Henry M. Bishop, was south of the railroad depot on Nutt Street. Containing about fifteen rooms, it could easily handle twice as many people by sharing rooms with two or three boarders each. Bishop eventually left the hotel business and enlisted in the Third North Carolina Regiment. Although wounded at Gettysburg, he continued to serve throughout the war.[4]

Other hotels included the Pilot House, which was still open even after an August 1861 shooting in which a drunken soldier killed a railroad engineer who asked him "to act like a gentleman." There was the Railroad Hotel, a three-story brick building containing 36 rooms, the Merchants Hotel and of course, the Palmetto.

The Palmetto, a 30-room establishment on Front Street across from the Bank of Cape Fear, "a few doors north of Market," was owned by James H. Bailey, who also performed with his troupe at Thalian Hall. A hack at the W&W railroad station was available to whisk a traveler to the hotel free of charge, but even this amenity couldn't stave off the hotel's closure in 1862. The Palmetto reopened early in 1863 and after the war was renamed Bailey's Star Hotel.

In addition to the hotels, many folks rented rooms. As Wilmington became more and more a military town and a center of commerce, even a room was hard to come by. By the summer of 1864, rents skyrocketed to unprecedented heights. In one case, the amount charged went from $1,000 per year to $13,500! General Whiting took a hard but necessary stance: if owners attempted to charge exorbitant rates for houses occupied by the army, he would simply impress the real estate. If the owner persisted, Whiting demanded assurances that the property would be used by the owner himself and not be rented at a high rate for profit.

If one desired exercise, the Confederate Billiard Saloon, above Carter's Shoe Store on Market Street was just the place. After all, they advertised, "Exercise was essential to Health."

Across Front Street, opposite the Globe Saloon, was the auction house of Wilkes Morris. A native Wilmingtonian and lifelong bachelor, Morris was hired before the war by auctioneer Michael Cronly. Said by many to have the finest voice in the land, he soon proved his worth and became a partner in the company. The partnership lasted until Cronly's death in 1898. Morris' obituary in 1901 recorded: "During the war Mr. Morris...served the Confederacy by appointment of Governor Vance as State purchasing agent of supplies for the army at Nassau, New Providence and at Halifax, Nova Scotia, an important position, every duty of which he performed with signal ability[.]"

While Morris did spend time abroad in 1864, he was more likely to be found at Number 2 Granite Row. It was here that the cargoes of runners were auctioned off. On auction day, the location saw large crowds gathered to examine and bid on clothing, whiskey, dry goods, hardware and nearly anything else brought in by the runners. The newspapers were usually filled with lists of items that were to be offered for sale.[5] State agents, speculators, merchants and average citizens vied for everything that was brought in. As the war progressed, the status of Wilmington, not only as a blockade running center, but as a commercial and financial emporium, grew steadily. Strange to say though, as more money flowed through town, the several military departments were quickly running out of funds to pay their debts and all work for the military threatened to come to a halt.

In the spring of 1863, when they were burned out of their Richmond premises, the Crenshaw brothers relocated closer to the scene of the auction action. They quickly established themselves in town on Water Street, able now to bid on goods as the runners docked at the wharves. Unfortunately, the gap between the upper and lower classes also grew, with many average citizens falling into the latter group. As more men were conscripted, more families were left without a livelihood and it immediately became apparent that a soldier's pay would not support a family in Wilmington. As more people fell into the poorer classes, quite a few of these unfortunates simply starved to death.

On the riverfront, at the south end of town, was the gas works. Prior to this, whale oil lit the few street lights about town, which did "little more than make the darkness visible." Chartered in 1851, the works were built on Queen and Surry, an extension of Water Street. The first public utility in Wilmington, the company manufactured gas "by a special process" from the resin of the long leaf pine. Soon afterwards, gas lines were being run to the homes of the more wealthy citizens, who were charged five dollars per thousand feet of gas.[6]

The town commissioners voted to install streetlights throughout the town, including all along Front Street and at the foot of all streets that ended at the river. This last was especially important to prevent people from walking off the docks into the water. The town's prewar budget included the cost of hiring a worker for the purpose of "lighting, cleaning and putting out public lamps." The *Journal* noted in the fall of 1860 that they had just received new burners in their office and "had a jubilee over the event. The light was much better than we were led to anticipate. It is not, however, as brilliant a light as the former gas produced." The paper noted that the company fully intended to make a better

Members of a black Wilmington fire company, circa 1898. (NHCPL)

grade of gas "when the coal comes down from the mines up on Deep River."
Even with that source, there would be problems with the supply of gas all during
the war, not the least of which was the increasing cost to customers.

Although there were laws prohibiting animals running free, many times
horses, hogs, cows and mules broke loose and wandered the town until captured
and returned to their owners. Dogs were then, as now, quite popular, with the
Newfoundland Labrador Retriever being one of the more preferred breeds.
Owners were required to purchase a "badge" or license for one dollar, but many
strays roamed the streets until someone complained about the nuisance. Then it
was Chief McGreal's job to check to see if the animal was licensed, as the law
stated. If it was not, the dog could be shot. Horses, of course, were the main
means of transportation around town as wagons, carriages and drays all required
horsepower. One of the most widely recognized steeds of the day was "Dan," a
large white stallion that pulled the Southern Express wagon. When Dan died on
the job, it was a newsworthy event.

With tongue slightly in cheek, the *Journal* also reported the death of
"Major Rogers," a horse belonging to Mayor Dawson. After extolling the
animal's speed, they went on to say: "The Major was something of a public
character, and therefore worthy of notice. We were not sufficiently acquainted
with his moral character or social habits to speak intelligently on these points,
but we have heard that he was, in addition to his other qualities, a gentle family
horse."

According to the rates set by the town, it cost three dollars to dispose of a horse's carcass, a bargain when for a dollar more, a pauper could be buried.

Slaves were required to wear badges. The town bell pealed for the breakfast, dinner and supper hours. When Elizabeth Bishop rang the curfew bell at nine o'clock at night, slaves were to be at home and not out on the street.[7] Merchants were warned against allowing Negroes to remain or loiter in their stores; slaves could be fined for smoking in the street.

Children, both black and white, were also restricted. Those caught throwing stones or brickbats were liable to a fine of $5. There was to be no flying of kites, which carried a $2 fine, nor firing of "Canton crackers," which could cost yet another $5 fine. "Canton crackers could be fired at designated times of the year" which included Christmas Eve, New Year's Day and probably also the Fourth of July.

Early in the war a citizen informed the Mayor that "certain boys were in the habit of shooting pigeons on Second and Third between Dock and Orange Streets to the annoyance of the neighborhood." It is likely McGreal was called upon to warn the boys to cease fire.

Younger slaves had additional restrictions placed upon them. An ordinance deemed: "That hereafter, all Negro boys found in the streets of this town, pitching cents or quoits, playing marbles, rolling hoops, playing ball or any kind of game, shall receive twenty lashes, or their owner pay a fine of five dollars for each and every offense."

There were four fire companies in town at the outbreak of war. Although officered by white men, it would appear that the members were mostly blacks. The companies had three steam engines: the Fire King, the Franklin and the Wilmington. Along with these was a Hook and Ladder company. The only time a citizen was allowed to ring the town bell was in case of fire or other emergency. Upon hearing the bell, the respective companies would race to get to the "Scene of conflagration" before other companies. A reward of five dollars was doled out to the company that arrived first and hosed the fire down. Church bells were also utilized to signal the danger, with sextons paid $1 for the service. Citizens were asked not to give alcoholic drinks to the men while they were fighting a fire, but many times this request went unheeded. Upon arrival, the chief situated himself so that he could see the progress, or lack thereof, in quenching the fire's appetite. To avoid confusion between the chief and his assistants, the chief could usually be located by looking for a "Stand" with a small flag attached to it. Fire was so feared that in the early 1850s, the town decreed that only fireproof buildings equipped with tin roofs could be erected in the center of town. If the hose wouldn't reach the engine, citizens formed "bucket brigades" to feed the steam engines, which then pumped the water through often leaky leather hoses to be played on the flames. The fire wardens were empowered to require the assistance of any citizen to remove merchandise from a building afire. Anyone not answering the call for help was fined. Being a member of a fire company bestowed no especial favors on slaves or free blacks. They still needed a pass to be on the street after hours. In wartime Wilmington, as the grip of the enrolling officer got tighter and the labor pool shrank, these firemen continued to fall out when needed, but there would be less and less help left in town.

As the need for labor became more intense, General Whiting eyed the fire companies and in 1864 agreed to send "five or six Negroes (both free and slave) belonging to the fire companies in Wilmington to Bald head." As for the white companies, there was a huge benefit in being a fireman: exemption from conscription.

William W. Holden

In 1863, William W. Holden ran against Zebulon Vance for Governor. Holden, formerly a Whig turned-Democrat, was the editor of the Raleigh *North Carolina Standard*. Interestingly, in the national election of 1856, Holden, then a radical Democrat, was all for secession of the South if Republican John C. Fremont was elected President. In 1862, it had been William Holden who persuaded Zeb Vance to run for Governor. After the military setbacks at Gettysburg and Vicksburg, a peace movement had gained strength in the state. The local paper wrote, "on the occasion of each reverse to our arms" many in the state fell despondent and began to yearn for an end to the conflict. Many of these "croakers," said the *Journal*, "are doing all that they can to defeat the cause...They are preaching us peace, when in fact, no terms of peace are open ...to us but those of absolute submission to Lincoln and Seward...[and] Beast Butler, Brute Milroy, Dog Rosecrans, etc."

The peace movement, however, gained enough strength to nominate Holden as their candidate in 1864. When the votes were tallied, Vance won overwhelmingly. The statewide count was over 44,000 for Vance and 12,647 for Holden. The vote in the army was even more lopsided: Vance received 13,209 while Holden garnered only 1,824. The vote in southeastern North Carolina was strongly in favor of Vance, although at Fort Fisher Holden garnered 125 of the 562 votes cast.

Holden getting more than 22% of the vote at Fort Fisher was due in large part to the efforts of T.S. Whitaker, who was a young Wilmington bookseller. He appeared at the fort prior to the election and distributed copies of Holden's newspaper to the troops. When General Whiting found out, he was incensed and immediately attempted to have Whitaker drafted. Whitaker claimed exemption because he was a member of a fire company, so Whiting tried using the tactic that being a member of a fire company was simply "an indulgence" and could be revoked "for misbehavior." Although the Conscript Office agreed with him, higher-ups pronounced Whitaker secure in his dodging the draft because he was a fireman. The fire companies were filled with those who tried to avoid conscription.

Joseph Strauss, a naturalized German-born citizen, was an early member of the German Volunteers, but when that company was called to active duty, he refused to serve. Arrested and put in jail, he was finally released upon joining a fire company. Another fireman who irritated General Whiting was the already familiar Joe Neff. Try as he might to have Neff placed in the army, he was thwarted due to the fact that Neff belonged to the town's Hook and Ladder Company and thus remained exempt from military service for the entire war. In April 1863, a fire broke out in town and the commanding general was on the scene. "I was present last night at the fire – The Engine companies did not make their appearance until nearly an hour after it broke out...and then in very small numbers."

In a letter to Mayor Parsley, Whiting informed him that he was ordering the men of the fire companies to muster, "preparatory to forwarding them to the camp of instruction at Raleigh." The duty, Whiting went on, would henceforth be assumed by soldiers detailed as firemen. Mayor Parsley resisted the idea of drafting the men and on July 22nd sent a letter to Governor Vance requesting exemptions for the fire companies. As if to add insult to injury, the bearer of the missive was Joe Neff. The Governor exempted the men, but they were required to form into Militia Companies and hold regular drill sessions. They were also armed with not only muskets, but had access to, and manned, the town's "two light field pieces."[8]

In March 1864, several businesses in town banded together to purchase a fire engine which was to be placed on the west bank of the Cape Fear River, "for the protection of the common property there." It probably did not arrive in time to assist the firemen when a terrific blaze broke out in the latter part of April. The fire spread quickly and soon engulfed "every building on the Western side of the river." Property damage was great, with more than 4,300 bales of cotton lost, as well as a quarter of a mile of wharves, sheds and buildings. When the total loss was tallied, it reached the astounding figure of more than six million dollars. The fire spread with such rapidity that the *Journal* "doubted that human power could have arrested the progress of the fire when it had once gotten under way." The paper then noted that "there was no fire department to be found." Upon further questioning, the paper was told that "white companies are on duty as home guard, and the colored companies, mustering 180 men in all, mainly free Negroes, have had their members either impressed or scared off by the fear of impressments."

The fire also destroyed the offices of the Wilmington and Manchester Railroad, damaged Beery's shipyard (then engaged in building an ironclad vessel) and burned several freight cars belonging to the Georgia Central Railroad. The following month, General Whiting communicated to his superiors that he needed more laborers because of the "heavy demands of the Q.M. Dep't. for the transshipment of supplies to replace the great losses in buildings & works arising from the late disastrous fire."

Also ruined in that conflagration were two Southern Express railroad cars and a warehouse used by the Express Company. Before the war that company had been known as the Adams Express Company, but in the spirit of independence the name was changed to the Southern Express Company. After the war the name would again be changed to the Adams and Southern Express Company.

As soon as war began, no freight south of Washington, D.C. was received, but packages could be mailed throughout the Confederacy. Packages containing liquor had to be plainly marked while those meant for hospitals were often sent without charge, leaving many to question why others did not follow suit. The question was directed to the railroad companies. The Express Company was widely used to send money and other items that one wanted to make sure got to the recipient. The value of the items was required to be marked on the package, as it was insured for loss, "acts of God or the enemy excepted."

James Macomber ran the Southern Express office in town and when complaints were received about delays, he pointed out that government freight had precedence. The company had their own freight cars which ran fairly regularly. By the summer of 1864, they had established regular service between Wilmington and Fayetteville via steamers that ran the Cape Fear River three times a week. Requesting that his clerks and messengers be exempted from military service, Macomber was not always successful. In 1864, so many workers were called out for home guard duty that many businesses, including the Express Company, found it hard to stay open and at times it was impossible to pick up or deliver freight. Macomber sometimes hired the wrong person. One of his employees, J.B. Davidge, was sought by the city commandant for desertion. It was said that Davidge was "in the employment of the Express Co. in this place."

One crate was not delivered because it attracted Macomber's attention. It was plainly marked, but he wasn't looking at the labeling. He noticed hair sticking out from a crack and when the box was opened, it revealed a man inside! Secreted and mailed at first to Florence, South Carolina, where he was unboxed, fed and recrated, the man steadfastedly refused to disclose who helped him along the way. The unlucky fellow, who obviously needed a haircut, was sent back to his unit where he possibly faced the death penalty.

The year 1863 brought yet another sweep of those not yet in the army. The order from Raleigh was to "Assemble all able-bodied men fit for military duty not yet conscripts, organize them into companies of 75 men each... Organize and drill necessary for the purpose of being prepared to repel an expected advance of the enemy."[9]

Endnotes

1. *Daily Journal*, 22 June 1863, 15, 27 January, 2 February and 13 May 1864.

2. Bill Reaves, *Strength Through Struggle: The Chronological and Historical Record of the African-American Community in Wilmington, 1865-1950* (Thomson-Shore, Inc.: Wilmington, 1998) 24. *Daily Journal*, 13 July 1863; 15 November 1861 and 2 November 1863. National Archives, Record Group 45, microfilm publication M346, "Confederate Papers Relating to Citizens and Business Firms," Washington, D.C., hereinafter cited as *Citizens Papers*, Elvin Artis file. For the two coffins, Artis was paid $24 and $54 for 18 days labor on the wharf. Artis died at age 66 on 7 June 1886 and was buried in Pine Forest Cemetery in Wilmington. See the Bill Reaves Collection, African-American Family files, "The Artis Family," I:1, 1-4.

3. Henry Judson Bleeker, *Wilmington During the Civil War*, thesis presented to Duke University, 1941, 5. A fifth bank, the Bank of Wilmington, was a savings bank. *Daily Journal*, 15 April 1861, 24 February 1864; [Wilmington] *Daily Dispatch*, 24 October 1865. Henry Webb was back in business at 20 Market Street after the war. He died on Christmas Eve, 1888 and is buried in Wilmington's Oakdale Cemetery. During the war a fireman from the blockade runner *Lynx* was killed at the Blockade House by the owner, Mr. Kelly; *Vance Papers*, 3:46, 5 March 1863. *Daily Journal*, 1 September 1864, 28 October 1864. Mrs. McCaleb took over the hotel in the early part of 1860. *Daily North Carolinian*, 1 January 1865. Mary died on 5 May 1896 and is also buried in Oakdale. The Rock Springs Hotel was on the south side of Chestnut Street. See also *The Diary of Captain Henry A. Chambers*, edited by T.H. Pearce (Wendell, N.C.: Broadfoot's Bookmark, 1983) 96. Michael Turrentine Papers, Perkins Library, Duke University, letter dated 15 June 1864; *Daily Journal*, 29 July 1862.

4. *The Morning Star*, 7 February 1915. The 1860 Federal Census listed sixty people boarding at Bishop's hotel. See also the *Daily Journal*, 27 December 1859, 18 February 1862.

5. *Morning Star*, 12 February 1901. Mike Cronly was born in New York and was buried in Oakdale Cemetery. Gordon B. McKinney and Richard McMurray, eds.,

The Papers of Zebulon Vance (Frederick, Md." University Publications of America, 1987) microfilm edition, 25:279, hereinafter cited as the *Vance Papers*.

6. *Daily Journal*, 15 May 1863. Phillip Lewis Hall, *Land of the Golden River*, (Wilmington: Wilmington Printing Company, 1980) 64; Sprunt, *Chronicles*, 163, 676.

7. *Daily Journal*, 13 October 1863. Andrew J. Howell, *The Book of Wilmington*, n.d., n.p., 92.

8. *Commissioner's Minutes*, 124, 158, 162, 180-181. *Daily Herald*, 25 February 1861; *Daily Journal*, 20 July 1863. For T.S. Whitaker, see the *Whiting Papers*, 2:236, letter dated 10 August 1864, 22 October 1864. For the results of the election see the *Daily Journal*, 30 July 1864. See also *Southern Claims Commission Disallowed Claims* Index, no. 758, hereinafter cited as *Disallowed Claims*. Strauss was seeking compensation for his house, but his claim was denied, the Commissioners decided that service in a fire company "rendered equivalent aid to the rebellion." *Vance Papers,* 18:933-934. Neff remained a thorn in Whiting's hide throughout the war, see the Whiting Papers, 7 July, 11 July and 17 July 1864. See also the *Daily Journal*, 19 August 1863.

9. *Commissioner's Minutes*, 159. *Daily Journal*, 19 February 1864. *Whiting Papers*, II:336, letter dated 7 September 1863. Macomber himself was a member of the 22nd N.C. Militia, see the *Daily Journal*, 29 January 1863.

A Stroll Through Town

any citizens in Wilmington were enrolled in either the Home Guard or militia. Although some of them did not like it and tried everything to get out of reporting for the usual weekly muster, they fell in as ordered, carrying their rifle and axe. Some who refused to obey the orders of officers were "put on double duty at the bridges." If they still proved obstinate, they were arrested and jailed. Local attorney Frederick J. Lord felt that as he was the representative or consul of Spain, he should be exempt. He went so far as to pen "Vice Consulate of Spain" on his letter to the Governor. Vance fired back, "When it is well established that Spain has any right to a consul in the port of a government she does not recognize…I will cheerfully comply."

Governor Vance was the recipient of many such letters. A dentist wanted to know if he was considered a physician and thus exempt. He was not.

Some militiamen were found shirking their duty. "Complaint has been made that the patrol in your regiment is of no service…that the patrol rides only on pleasant days & not out at night or in bad weather. Please report the facts to this office."[1]

At the intersection of Market and Eighth Streets, was the Confederate State's stable, housing about one hundred horse and mules. In 1864, Lieutenant Johns was in command at the stable. After giving Johns the necessary paperwork, a horse could be obtained for use. They were not, however, the best in the state. When the surgeons at General Hospital No. 4 received horses from the stable, they rejected them as "useless." By late 1864 there were no animals available, even when the request came from Richmond. The army began to seize both horses and wagons from citizens.[2]

There were also at least three, and probably more, privately owned stables in town. By the end of 1860, John K. Currie ran one of these on the corner of 2nd and Princess Streets. It was, he said, "fitted up in the most modern style, with secret and patented Racks, so that no dust can fall in the horse's eyes …which often blinds a good horse." Currie also owned a stallion, named "Lone Star." Before the war he had traveled around the country, charging a stud fee for the animal's services. Lone Star's pedigree stretched back to horses known to be worth up to $20,000. In October 1861 Currie, at the age of forty-four, joined Captain William Howard's cavalry company as a farrier. He spent only two months in the service and was discharged in December because of "a disease which unfits him from military duty."

While John never left town, his son Stephen enlisted and served throughout the war. John's business looked quite promising at the beginning of the war, but as hostilities progressed, businesses failed and new ones took their place. Hit hard by the yellow fever epidemic in 1862, in which he lost a young daughter, John never really recovered his own health. However, he continued to support the Confederate cause. In 1863 he sold 100 pine trees, at $1 each, to the authorities. The trees were used "on outer line of defences [sic] at Wilmington for revetment & magazines." After the government confiscated his horses, he retired, preferring to rent out the stables as a cotton warehouse instead. Currie survived the war, but just barely, dying in late 1866.[3]

Horses were not the only way out of town. Before the war, steamboat service had been established between Wilmington and such cities as Charleston, S.C., New York, Philadelphia, Norfolk, Baltimore and upriver to Fayetteville. One could also board a train and head into South Carolina or Georgia, or north towards Petersburg and Richmond. One of the main roads out of town was the Topsail Plank Road, or present-day Market Street. Originally a toll road, with the Toll House at Tenth and Market Streets, it was often in need of repair. There was a road to Wrightsville Sound, another to Confederate Point, known as Federal Point before the war, and several other sand tracks loosely labeled as roads.

The telegraph came to town in the mid-1850s; the office was on the second floor of the London building, at the corner of Front and Market Streets. Located in the center of the early business district, the office was run before the war by men of northern birth. With war, communications north of Alexandria were broken. A Southerner, David J. Greer, who before the war had operated a "Carbon Oil & Lamp" shop, became the cashier and manager of the Wilmington office. As the fortunes of war waxed and waned, it was the telegraph office that received the news first. People flocked to the office as rumors of battle circulated through town. Located down the street from the provost marshal's office, it was a favorite place for loiterers to gather as they awaited the latest news. Those that stayed in the office long enough could probably decipher the messages as quickly as the operators.

In the spring and summer of 1864, Major General Whiting ordered the lines from Wilmington to be kept open to Charleston, Magnolia, Goldsboro and Raleigh "day and night." This being done, the Telegraph Company later inquired who would be paying the operator's overtime. The military authorities paid up. When the war began, operators made about $50 a month, "chief operators $75 and superintendents $125." Salaries went up as inflation increased, but it was never enough to cover the cost of living in Wilmington.

To supplement the family income, Greer's wife, ever inventive, produced a first-rate "toilet soap" which had, according to the *Journal*, "a pleasant flavor and washes well." One could pick up a few bars at the telegraph office. One writer has stated that in February 1864, in "Wilmington... employees of the company were receiving monthly compensation of $150 a month, and paying out $200 a month for board alone."

In May of that year, the rates were increased 100 per cent. Later that year they went up another 50 per cent. The company had to be doing fairly well financially though, for when the Confederate government imposed a five per cent tax on all stocks, the company, like the railroad and steamboat companies, paid the tax for their shareholders.[4] As more men were conscripted, it was seriously suggested that women learn telegraphy and free a man for field duty. As with many occupations that provided exemption, the men resisted the change.

In October 1863, members of the newly-formed "Southern Telegraph Association," made up of employees, met at Augusta, Georgia and railed against the long hours and low pay. In the *Journal*, the following letter, addressed to "Members and Sympathizers of the Southern Telegraph Association" appeared: "The despotic action which the officers of the ... Company [have] chosen to adopt, has banished all hope of any recognition of our just rights; let us therefore imitate the manly example of our contrees at Richmond, Charleston and Wilmington, who choose dismissal rather than yield blind obedience... To the faint hearted I would say take cheer. We have the sympathy of the public and some of the highest military authorities. All that is now required is a firm stand[.]"

The owners of the telegraph company threatened dismissal if an employee did not resign from the Association. Dismissal, in many cases, meant the man would be conscripted. The strike collapsed and most operators returned to their posts after a week or so. It would appear that not all the men were taken back. A want ad in the Wilmington paper asked for "a suitable person to fill a situation that will exempt a man from conscription. Enquire at the Telegraph Office."

When Governor Vance complained of telegraphic delays between Raleigh and Wilmington in December of that year (1863), the President of the company, William S. Morris, apologized and informed the governor that the "subject has been called to the especial attention of the Superintendent of that division[.]" He also requested Vance to inform him if there were any more such occurrences, as he would "be glad to be informed of it." After the fall of Wilmington David Greer was removed as manager, but was reinstated after he took the Oath of Allegiance.[5]

Uriah P. Levy

Another who saw opportunity in Wilmington was Jonas P. Levy. Levy, a Commodore in the U.S. Navy was, as late as July 1860, Captain of the "sailing corvette" *USS Macedonian.* Seeing a more favorable business climate in Wilmington, he relocated there and secured his reputation by remaining to help the sick and dying during the yellow fever epidemic. By 1863 he was a commission merchant, later ran a dry goods establishment, owned a ship chandlery and even branched out into making vinegar.

Jonas' older brother, Uriah, was also a commodore in the U.S. Navy and was, at that same time, in New York awaiting orders. Uriah was well known in the Navy, having been one of the first Jews to attain high rank. He fought anti-Semitism for years and was instrumental in abolishing "flogging" aboard U.S. ships. Uriah had purchased Monticello, the home of Thomas Jefferson, for the sum of $2,700 some ten years after Jefferson's death. He did not live continuously at the home, so his mother Rachel moved in. She died in 1839 and was buried in the cemetery on the grounds.

Uriah spent the next thirteen years in New York, only occasionally visiting Virginia, as did other family members, including Jonas. He hired an overseer by the name of Joel Wheeler to attend the house. Wheeler moved his family into the home but did not take very good care of the premises. In that first fall of secession, Jonas left Wilmington and went to Monticello. Arriving at the plantation, Jonas proudly hoisted a Confederate flag "on the mansion," but was quickly aroused when it was hauled down by the plantation's obviously pro-

Monticello

Union overseer. Levy began to berate and denounce the fellow. He wrote to Richmond and charged Wheeler "with incendiary language toward the...government."

While Virginia's Governor, John Letcher, agreed with Levy and offered to have Wheeler arrested, the overseer got a small measure of revenge when he packed up Jonas' belongings and sent them to Charlottesville. Uriah died in New York in 1862. In his will he left the former Jefferson estate to the American people. In March 1863, the Supreme Court of the United States declared the request "null and void" and the estate "descended to & [was] vested in the heirs-at-law & next of kin."

Jonas quickly appealed to the Confederate courts seeking possession of the plantation. He swore, "I am the brother of the late Commodore Uriah P. Levy of the old U.S. Navy, he left no relations but myself in this confederacy." He asked to have the sequestration act amended so that title of the property was vested to himself, but Jefferson's home was auctioned off and sold under the Confiscation Act. In the winter of 1864, Levy, back in Virginia, intended to bid on the historic site. He stated that "He did not come there to interfere with or prevent the sale in any way and that...he intended to bid for the property himself."[6]

The cemetery on the grounds was to remain in the Jefferson family (Levy's mother would also remain interred there) but the remainder went for twenty thousand dollars to Lieutenant Colonel Benjamin F. Ficklin. Levy did

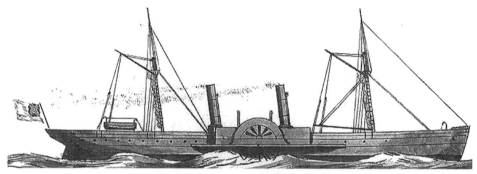

The blockade runner **Giraffe.**

come away with some mementos including a model of the *USS Vandalia* (at a cost of $100) and John, a slave ($5,400). Ficklin purchased items from the home which included a bust of Jefferson ($50), and "a Negro woman with seven children, one at the breast ($23,100)."

The home had been in disrepair for some time. "Visitors...defaced the walls of the house by scribbling their names over them...pieces of the bust of Mr. Jefferson were chipped off; chairs, tables, mirrors, vases, broken and destroyed[.]" In all, fifty thousand dollars was realized from the sale and many valuable relics collected by Jefferson had been sold. As a newspaper reported, "Shame, shame upon our thoughtless countrymen. Why should they be so disrespectful to the sepulchre of the great patriot of the Revolution?"

While in Wilmington, Levy began to purchase real estate in town, or actually what was then the outskirts of town. He bought several lots on both Dock and Church Streets and was soon renting out the premises to the Commissary, Quartermaster and Engineer Departments. Levy sold anything he could get at his store – clothing, "country produce," varnish, linseed oil, files, brandy, window sashes, blank note books, paint, soap and when he could get it, coffee. Some of the items, such as chain, shackles and rope, were sold to Captain William James of the Engineer Department. These were used to anchor obstructions placed in the Cape Fear River. Many other items purchased by James were for repairs on the river steamers and lighters used by the engineers.[7]

By May, 1863 Levy, while complaining to Richmond about "foreigners" (Englishmen) commanding many of the blockade running steamers, he suggested that the name of the recently purchased *Giraffe*, be changed from *Robert E. Lee* to *Thomas J. Jackson*, although there was already a runner with that name. Command should be given, he said, to "one who leaves no means unemployed to avenge his death." Jonas may well have had himself in mind, as a few months later he offered to take command of the States' steamer, the *Advance*.

Offering himself as captain of the steamer was no idle boast. Jonas Phillips Levy was of Navy "Blue Blood." Born in Philadelphia in 1807, the youngest surviving child of Michael and Rachel Levy, his ancestry stretched back to 1650 when the family emigrated from England. His maternal grandfather, Jonas Phillips, had fought in the American Revolution. Grandson Jonas was "one of the Americans, although then but a boy, who on July 4, 1824, escorted Gen. Lafayette...to this country." He would again meet General Lafayette when he rescued him from a sinking steamer and was given a signet ring by a grateful Lafayette.

When Hungarian revolutionary Louis Kossuth came to America in 1851, it was Levy, then in command of the steamer *Mississippi*, who carried him safely across the Atlantic to New York. He remained in the merchant service and owned and sailed West India clippers for many years and even continued his maritime career by joining the Peruvian Navy. After attaining the rank of Admiral in that service, he was granted the freedom of that country.

When the Mexican War broke out, he was given command of the transport vessel, *America,* and was "in charge of the landing of the troops at the capture of Vera Cruz." After the war, he began "corresponding with the President of Mexico...[about] constructing a line of communication" from the Gulf to the Pacific. This was in violation of an antiquated law, but when it was brought to the attention of Daniel Webster, then U.S. Secretary of State, it resulted in Levy's arrest. Webster's view was that Levy's correspondence would cause the Mexicans to think twice about signing the Gadsden Purchase, as Levy had an interest in transiting the Isthmus of Tehuantepec.

An ad from Froelich's arms factory.
(NHCPL)

In the winter of 1855, Levy was still in the Navy, and living in Washington, D.C. where he ran a dry goods establishment. By April 1858, still in the nation's capitol, he and his wife attended the "Grand fancy Ball at Mrs. Senator Gwin's Residence." It was a costume ball and many of the Capitol's notables were there: Anson Burlingame of Massachusetts (who came as Julian St. Pierre) and the Honorable Thomas L. Clingman (as a gentleman of the Twentieth Century). The *New York Times* commented: "If all those...who live in the twentieth century look as well as did the honorable and gallant member from North Carolina, the appearance of ballrooms will be improved."

Also in attendance was Mrs. Rose Greenhow (with her daughter), as she continued her reputation as a leading socialite. Levy came dressed as an English Country Gentleman of olden times, while his wife, Fanny, came as the Biblical "Miriam."

Alfred Moore Waddell

Levy was also active in prewar politics: in 1860 the *New York Times* charged him with attempting to set up a "Southern Jerusalem" by backing U.S. Senators Benjamin and Yulee, both Jewish and from the South. In memoirs penned some years after the war, Jonas wrote that he left his wife and four children and went to Baltimore where he remained until "the breaking out of the revolution with the South." He left Baltimore intending to go "to Mexico," but "got as far as Wilmington, N.C. until 1865[.]" By the winter of 1863, he was proudly advertising his store as "Levy's Grand Bazaar." That year he also bought stock in a blockade runner (probably the *SS Merrimac*).[8]

There were many other businesses in Wilmington, some employing quite a few workers. By November 1861, Louis Froelich's sword factory had about seventy workers, while the railroads and shipbuilders had many more. In an ironic twist, Froelich moved his business out of town because he feared not only yellow fever, but a Yankee attack. By March, 1863, he was safely ensconced in Kenansville, some sixty miles north of Wilmington. Four months later, Kenansville was raided by Union cavalry and the factory burned to the ground.

In Wilmington, merchants thrived. Even smaller enterprises such as James Wilson's harness establishment and Henry Lowe's stocking factory needed more people from time to time, as government contracts were secured. Wilson required fifty harness makers and coach trimmers when he got the contract to supply "military trappings" for troops in Florida. Lowe began round-the-clock operations. Young boys were hired to work nights preparing the machines for the next day's production, while one hundred women were needed as sewers. Ladies needing work came to the foot of Chestnut Street to pick up supplies, finished knitting the heels of socks at home and returned the completed product to the factory.[9] When a letter to the newspaper charged Wilson with speculating on leather (and on being a Yankee) he responded: "With respect to certain slurs thrown out by certain [people]...all that I have to say is that my business is open to the public...and I wish to state that I am not a native of the North and have spent the best part of my life in the South, and [am as] good a Southern man as any person[.]"[10]

The Confederate Navy Yard on the Cape Fear River at Wilmington.

Although of Yankee birth, another who prospered was Oran Baldwin. Baldwin had been a partner in the firm of Scott and Baldwin before the war and like many Southern merchants had "gone north" to purchase the latest clothing fashions. With war, he was determined to start a "Southern Clothing Factory" in town, but supplies of cloth and buttons were uncertain and the idea never got off the ground. He did quite well selling uniforms and providing Captain E.D. Hall's company with blankets when they moved downriver to "capture" the forts at the mouth of the Cape Fear. He also allowed his store at 38 Market Street to be used as a mail drop for packages going to the troops downriver.

One of Baldwin's competitor's, John Hilzinger, seeking a military contract, wrote to the state quartermaster, Major John Deveraux, to ask about prices and terms of payment. Apparently Deveraux rejected his request because shortly afterwards, he found employment with Baldwin as a tailor. Hilzinger was but one of about one hundred men and women working for Oran. When Hilzinger's young daughter died of yellow fever in the summer of 1862, John was devastated. Two months later he was stricken by the same disease and died.

Baldwin continued to prosper. At one time, it would appear that he had the market on uniform buttons, an item that was holding up production of that necessity. In March 1862 he sold Major Deveraux eighty gross (at $9 per gross) of buttons. After the yellow fever epidemic, Baldwin sold out to Horace Munson, but remained in town.[11]

Capitalizing on the state of affairs early in 1861 was "the Inimitable" Jesse Cassidey. He and his father, James, ran a grocery store. Although he purchased many of his goods from the North, he advertised, "To Arms! To

Thalian Hall circa 1900. (NHCPL)

Arms! All those who are opposed to the Federal coercion of a sovereign State, and who are opposed to the passage of abolition soldiers through North Carolina, for the purpose of subjugating a sister State, will buy their Groceries, Provisions, small stores and accoutrements of the patriotic [at Cassidey's.]"

It was Cassidey who suggested that the sick and wounded soldiers passing through town would much prefer hot coffee instead of the flowers that the ladies brought them. Cassidey closed his doors in 1863 and his son Jesse, went to work for his father, who operated a shipyard in town. Young Jesse would remain exempt throughout the war by virtue of being the only man on the river who could operate the company's "Marine Railway" machinery, used to haul vessels in need of repair up out of the water.

After the war, Cassidey joined the Republican Party and for a time edited the *Wilmington Post*. In post-war politics, he made Congressman Alfred M. Waddell, a former Confederate officer, a special target of his enmity via his virulent editorials, calling him a drunkard, a gambler and a liar. Waddell waylaid Cassidey in town and with the help of a few friends, "caned" him. Cassidey got his revenge in Washington when he attacked Waddell as he entered a hotel and struck him several blows with a heavy "stick." Waddell's bodyguards quickly subdued Cassidey but not before he kicked Waddell in the stomach.

Cassidey wrote: "He subsided with the seat of his pants in a large iron spittoon, among cigars, stumps and rejected tobacco quids, his heels flying in the air and his head thumping on the marble tiles of the floor...I had accomplished that for which I had gone to Washington...I struck him twice, besides kicking him."[12]

Regardless of Cassidey's change of heart in the Reconstruction era, during the war his father's shipyards did much work for the army, including the construction of at least two torpedo launches, in addition to marine repairs. Another shipyard, run by the Beery brothers, William and Benjamin, was located across the river on Eagles Island. Their yard contracted mainly with the navy. The iron works of Levi Hart and Joseph Bailey also dealt with the local naval commander, Flag Officer William F. Lynch, while Thomas Robert's Clarendon Iron Works was pretty well taken over by General Whiting for army work. The iron founders worked on Whiting's Torpedo Boat No. 1 and also repaired government steamers. This firm produced munitions for the town (twenty and thirty-two pounder balls, paid for by the Committee of Safety). The foundry also made iron bolts, gun carriages, "iron point spikes" for the tops of the log obstructions set in the river and "mushroom anchors" for the same. They also produced the hot shot furnace for Fort Fisher and cut up railroad iron for Fort Caswell's casemates.[13]

When not laboring, soldiers and citizens had some opportunities to escape the ravages of war. One was to attend Thalian Hall where various

WILMINGTON THEATRE.

At the earnest solicitation of many citizens

MR. HARRY MACARTHY

AND

MRS. HARRY MACARTHY

Have kindly consented to remain

FOR THREE NIGHTS MORE!

They will appear this evening in one of their

MIMIC ENTERTAINMENTS!

Dec. 17.   84-1t.

Traveling shows like that of Harry Macarthy relieved the tedium of wartime for the residents of Wilmington. This ad announces a three night run of shows. (NHCPL) troupes like that of townsman James H. Bailey performed plays. The theater, which was constructed as part of the Town Hall, had been built in the late 1850s and had a capacity of 1,500 theatergoers. Here musicals, comedies and many war-inspired dramas were produced. Some productions were good, others were not, but it was an avenue of escape for the war-weary populace.

On occasion there was more action in the galleries than onstage. One citizen recorded that "The play house is reeking with the foul crowd. It is difficult to say which is more farcical, the stage or the pit." On hand was a "Full and Efficient Police Force" to prevent rowdies from upsetting the crowd. Due to the danger of fire, guards were posted to insure there was no smoking in the theater. Because of the curfew enforced by the army, the curtain rose somewhat earlier than usual, at 6:30 precisely.

In 1863, an actor advertised that if the man "who threw a wrench at me while performing [would] please call the theater, it will be returned to him." Shows were varied, from the N.C. Ethiopians to the "Eutaw Band," members of the 25th South Carolina Regiment. The latter band played at the hall several times throughout 1863 and one of its final performances in the state was at Fort Anderson in February while that fort was under attack. The band dueled with opposing Yankee musicians.

The famous Harry Macarthy, known as the "Arkansas Comedian" appeared in Wilmington late in 1863 and again in 1864. After one show, he donated over one thousand dollars to General Hospital No. 4 in town. On stage, dressed "in a ruffled shirtfront, with a low set collar and wristbands studded with diamonds" he elicited howls of laughter from his audiences. At some of his shows, he played several parts, including "a Yorkshireman, Irishman, Dutchman, Yankee, Shrew and Ethiopian."

In September 1863, several "acknowledged leading members of the Dramatic profession...having by accident met in [Wilmington] decided to put on a "Star Dramatic Entertainment." They donated the proceeds to the various hospitals and other "Charitable Associations." Harry was there, as was another well-known actor, Walter Keeble, along with a Miss Ella Wren, Edmond Dalton and Frank Bates. The members dedicated their performance "to the brave soldiers who have nobly battled for Justice and Freeman's rights," and also to the city's defender, General Whiting, who was requested to appoint a committee to "resolve the gross proceeds."

One author has written that Macarthy "was unquestionably the South's best-known and most popular entertainer." Also known as the "National Poet of the South" for having penned the famous song "Bonnie Blue Flag," his reputation faltered when it was reported that he had fled to the North when it appeared that he would be drafted. Indeed, shortly after his appearance in Wilmington, he left the Confederacy. As early as 18 January 1865, he was in the Bahamas putting on a show at the Prince of Wales Concert Hall in Nassau.[14]

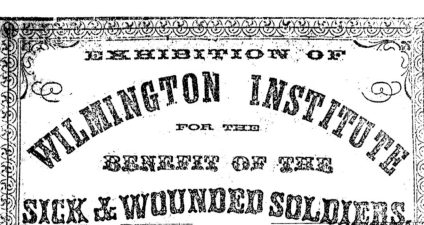

EXHIBITION OF
WILMINGTON INSTITUTE
FOR THE
BENEFIT OF THE
SICK & WOUNDED SOLDIERS,
JULY 1st, 1864.

The Maniac............Miss Emma Keen	Quarrel of Brutus and Cassius...Thos. Post and Jas. King
The Indian's Bride............Miss Mary Keen	Scene in the Roman Senate.......Thos. Post and Jas. King
The Soldier's Dream.......Miss Martha Bowden	Marco Bozzaris............Leighton Boon
What is Time............Miss Martha Bowden	Character of Napoleon Bonaparte............Ashley Gilbert
Richmond on the James............Miss Lucy Greer	Ricnzi's Address to the Romans............Henry Bauman
Battle of Waterloo............Miss Henrietta Eckle	Sailor Boy's Dream............James Post
The Lady Christabel............Miss Julia Jacobs	Gen. Johnston's Address to his Army......Henry Shulken
Home............Miss Mary Duguid	Crossing the Rubicon............Frank McMillan
The Sunbeam............Miss Addie Lyons	The Indian............Walter Coney
Casabianca............Miss Mary Bauman	The Two Robbers......Henry Bauman and James Post
Gelert............Miss Hattie Reeves	Sir Christopher and Quiz............L. Boon and H. Shulken
The Miseries of War............Miss Annie Hainey	Countryman and Lexicographer......H. Loeb and J. Myers
The Burial of Sir John Moore............Miss Laney Orrell	My Mother's Voice............John Tienken
Indolence will bring want......Miss E. Keen and L. Orrell	How to tell Bad News......Wm. Shemwell and John Riley
Foolish Habit............Miss H. Eckle and J. Jacobs	Death of Napoleon............William Alderman
Thoughtfulness and Honesty, Miss M. Bowden and L. Greer	Ruins of Time............Alvord Van Amringe
About School............Miss M. Keen and H. Reeves	The Sailor............George Parsley
	The Horrors of War............George West

WITH THE FOLLOWING
SONGS AND DOXOLOGY,
INTERSPERSED WITH OTHER PIECES OF VOCAL MUSIC:

CAROLINA'S SONS ARE READY.

Written for the Wilmington Light Infantry, by the Hon. GEO. DAVIS.

AIR.—Dixie's Land.

I.

Our gallant boys are going to battle,
See'ing fame where the cannon rattle,
March away, march away, march away, cheer the boys!
Oh cheer them on in the path of duty,
To fight for home, and love, and beauty,
March away, march away, march away, cheer the boys!
Carolina's sons are ready.
Hurrah! hurrah!
With heart and hand,
They'll by her stand,
With a courage true and steady.
Hurrah! hurrah!
Our own brave boys are ready.

II.

Oh, Mecklenburg! thy proud old story,
Never shall they dim its glory,
March away, &c., cheer the boys!
Their father's gave them freedom's blessing,
They will ne'er forget the lesson,
March away, &c., cheer the boys!
Carolina's sons are ready. &c.

III.

Oh, gallant boys, God's arms enfold you!

THE OLD NORTH STATE.

Carolina! Carolina! Heaven's blessings attend her,
While we live we will cherish, protect and defend her;
Tho' the scorner may sneer at, and witlings defame her,
Yet our hearts swell with gladness whenever we name her.

CHORUS:
Hurrah! hurrah! the Old North State forever!
Hurrah! hurrah! the good Old North State.

II.

Tho' she envies not others their merited glory,
Say whose name stands the foremost in liberty's story
Tho' too true to herself e'er to crouch to oppression,
Who can yield to just rule a more loyal submission.

CHORUS:

III.

Plain and artless her sons, but whose doors open faster,
To the knock of the stranger, or tale of disaster;
How like to the rudeness of their dear native mountains,
With rich ore in their bosoms, and life in their fountains.

CHORUS:

The show announced in this ad was a benefit for injured soldiers. (LCFHS)

There were other amusements offered to the citizens. Mozart Hall, on Front Street, over the Express office, put on dances and shows. To help bring in the New Year, a "Grand Military and Civic Ball" was held there on Friday night on the first of January 1864, with music provided by Allen's Band.[15] If a party was planned, it just wasn't a grand affair unless there was a band hired for the occasion.

Conscription and impressments also affected the free black population. Before the war, these men had comprised the musicians, barbers, blacksmiths and brick masons. Now during the war, many of them wound up working at the forts. Some, like Frank Johnson, may have been considered exempt; after all, it was said that "Dances were not complete without Frank Johnson's band."

But there were others, like the Rose Bud Band led by James Jackson, also a free black, who were every bit as good and always in demand. Of these musicians it was later said: "By the year 1853, all southern cities, and many good-sized towns, had black musical aggregations known as cornet bands, brass bands and string bands…These bands were usually composed of free blacks or house slaves who played European marching music, in imitation of white concert bands."

"Wilmington had the Rose Bud Band. According to the recollections of Thomas Fanning Wood…[bands] regularly entertained the Confederate troops during the Civil War and were present at all of Wilmington's finest dances and parties. This caused a dilemma for the local police, because a city code prohibited blacks to congregate after dark. More than once the police raided an unsuspecting party, and more likely the charges were dropped."

These musicians could be found leading the parade of troops as they marched through town on their way to their encampments, for "most military or fraternal organizations hired a brass band to lead their numerous parades."

F.D. Smaw's bookstore on Market Street offered a selection of not only books, but sheet music. The very popular "Lorena" and "Bonnie Blue Flag" could be purchased, as could other tunes such as "Rock Me to Sleep, Mother," "I'd be a Star" and "Let Me Kiss Him For His Mother."

For the soldiers in camp, there were different activities to ease the boredom. Some wrote, in addition to letters home, poetry or songs. There was music in the camps as well, using old or home-made instruments or simply singing around a campfire. Sports were played and sometimes hunting was a welcome diversion. Then, if one was lucky enough and one's time was due, there could be a furlough home. These were quite difficult to come by and, as the army's need for riflemen grew, furloughs became a thing of the past. There could be occasional trips to Wilmington from the many camps in the area and at least two soldiers from Fort Fisher found a different diversion. They paid for the following ad: "We, desiring to enter the connubial state, take this method of obtaining wives. One of us (Jerry) is dark complected, black hair and eyes. The other, light complected, grey eyes, light hair. Any of our lady friends who may wish to connect themselves with two soldiers, who have the reputation of being good ones, will direct their letters to...Tom and Jerry, Fort Fisher, C.F.L.A."

Such ads, although somewhat unusual, were seen fairly often in the papers. Jokes, played on the unsuspecting soldier, were a mainstay of camp life. Lieutenant C.S. Powell, of the 10th N.C. Battalion, was something of a jokester. He related a story about removing gunpowder from a magazine: "and [I] took a sample of powder...and dropped [the grains] in my trunk near my loose smoking tobacco. One of the officers taking my pipe reached in and filled it...Pretty soon there was a blow-out, sending the smoke down his throat and a cloud of sparks around his face."

After the laughter died down, the men thought it was such a good joke that they wanted to pull it on their company commander, Captain Charles McCauley. McCauley had enlisted in 1862 at the age of 44 and had, on more than one occasion, tendered his resignation. He usually withdrew it a few days later, but finally left the service at the end of 1864, citing "extreme ill health." Wiser heads prevailed and the men did not play the trick on McCauley.[16]

A high point for the citizens came in November 1863, with the visit of President of the Confederacy, Jefferson Davis. He had passed through town once before in 1861, on his way to the new capitol at Richmond. On Thursday, 5 November, Davis, together with a delegation sent to meet him at Florence, got off at the depot of the Wilmington and Manchester Railroad. There to greet him, at seven in the morning, was General Whiting, Mayor Dawson and several other prominent citizens. Upon debarking from the Market Street ferry, he was saluted by a volley from Southerland's artillery battery. After arriving at his lodgings, Davis was requested to give a speech, which he did from the front balcony, where he was staying with General Whiting in the Walker house on Market Street.

Davis "expressed his pleasure in being so warmly welcomed...He made fine reference to the fortifications in defense of the city and to General Whiting...He referred to the city as the ancient and honored town...[and] said he knew the importance of the harbor, which was then the only one through which trade was carried on with the outside world."

After a pep talk on the struggles through which the citizens were now passing, he finished by stating that North Carolina had "extinguished every bit of Union feeling and was loyal to the Confederacy." The crowd called for Whiting to speak also, but the general demurred. Davis, it was later said, spoke in a voice that was full, round and sonorous, his slightest accents being distinctly audible...by the large crowd." The following day the general and the president took a steamer downriver to view the forts and upon their return, Davis continued on to Richmond.

There were benefits and fund-raisers for soldiers held at Thalian Hall. In the summer of 1864, Levin McGinney presented his students of the Wilmington Institute. Schoolteacher McGinney was exempt and "unable to shoulder a musket" due to an old injury, but their benefit for the sick and wounded soldiers netted $1,275 which was given to the Ladies Aid Society for distribution.

"The eye deceived and the ear amused, the mind astonished" was how Guss Rich, billed as the "Southern Magician" was advertised when he appeared at the theater during the yellow fever epidemic. Born in 1833 in Forsyth County, William Augustus Rich had become famous for his trickery and was also known as "The Wizard of the Blue Ridge." Guss joined the 26th N.C.T. as a drummer and whenever the band was called upon to perform, his magical talents were also "not to be missed."

Thalian Hall closed its doors soon after the first attack on Fort Fisher in December 1864 and did not reopen until late in 1865. Many of Wilmington's prewar citizens never did get to see a wartime play. They were giving their all on the bloody battlefields throughout the South.

Endnotes

1. *North Carolina Confederate Militia and Home Guard Records*, abstracted by Dr. Stephen E. Bradley, privately published, Virginia Beach, 1995, 1: 64, 1176, 72. *Vance Papers*, 19: 274.
2. *Whiting Papers*, II: 338, letters dated 16 October 1864, 15 November 1864; *Vance Papers*, 25: 452. After the war, auctioneer J. Shackelford would sell off "11 splendid ambulances…also a lot of other articles at the Government Stables." These may have been Federal stock, not Confederate, see the *Herald*, 16 November 1865.
3. Manarin, 3: 714. In April 1864, he again provided the government with "312 poles @ 50 cts. each, for the Inner line of Infantry covers near Wilmington." *Citizen's Papers*, John K. Currie file, roll no. 7. Currie probably owned a wood lot as he also provided lumber, in January 1863, "for wood & building winter quarters for the 3rd N.C. Battalion by apprassment [sic]." *Daily Journal*, 5 October 1863, Currie's stable was "no longer open due to illness." His son Stephen ran the stable after the war.
4. J. Cutler Andrews, "The Southern Telegraph Company, 1861-1865: A Chapter in the History of Wartime Communication," *Journal of Southern History*, 30: 3, August 1964, 337-338.
5. It is probable that the wartime demands (the September 1863 movement of Longstreet's Corps for example) and the limited number of qualified non-conscripts able to work the telegraph lines, caused much dissension among the employees. *Daily Journal*, 31 May and 31 December 1864; see also 27 April 1864. The company also had a warehouse across the river on Eagles Island.

Daily Journal, 4 and 19 February 1864. See also the Wilmington *Herald*, 5
September 1865; *Vance Papers*, 21: 156.
6. The [Washington, D.C.] *National Intelligencer, Newspaper Abstracts, The
Civil War Years*, by Joan M. Dixon (Heritage Books: Bowie, Md., 2001), 518,
dated 31 March 1863, 523, dated 8 April 1863. *The New York Times*, 18 April
1971; Commission Claims, no. 135, Claim of Jonas P. Levy.
7. *General Index to Real Estate Conveyances, New Hanover County, North
Carolina*, deeds registered 1862, book RR, 492, 564; 1864, book SS, 422; 1866,
book TT, 181, 211. Levy also rented homes for "quarters of hired Negroes." He
also sold "wrought iron nails" for the construction of magazines. In August
1863, he sold "one field glass – for general use" for $130, as well as "one tea pot
– for use at hospital for negroes" for $4.50. See National Archives, *Citizen's
Papers*, reel 584, J.P. Levy; *Daily Journal*, 23 October and 6 December 1863.
For a time at least, Levy remained in Wilmington after the war, with a residence
on Dock, between 7th and 8th Streets, 1865-66 *Wilmington City Directory*, 49.
8. *The New York Times*, 4 and 5 February 1852. Jonas P. Levy died in New York
City in September 1883, see *The New York Times*, 15 September 1883; he left
three sons and two daughters. Internet website, http://muse.jhu.edu, has Levy in
Washington in December 1855. For Mrs. Gwin's party, see *The New York Times*,
12 April 1858. Robert N. Rosen, *The Jewish Confederates* (Columbia:
University of South Carolina Press, 2000), 35. Jonas sued the "legatees of
Commodore Levy" in 1868. When Uriah died in N.Y., his will effectively "cut
off his natural heirs without a dollar," *The New York Times*, 26 August 1868.
Daily Journal, 5 December 1863. Levy's son, Jefferson Monroe, became the
sole owner of Monticello and was coerced into selling the historic property to
the government. See *The New York Times*, 4 April, 11 August 1912 and 6
October 1914. Marc Leepson, *Saving Monticello* (New York: The Free Press,
2001) 90-92. Leepson suggests that Levy came South specifically to gain
control of Monticello.
9. *Daily Journal*, 7 June, 10, 13 and 14 May 1862.
10. Ibid., 3 April 1862. In the 1860 Federal Census for Wilmington, Wilson
listed his birthplace as New York.
11. *Daily Journal*, 14 March 1855, 16 July 1859, 13, 20, 21 and 25 May 1861,
13 October 1863; State Archives, Quartermaster records, box 44.5, letter dated 7
October 1861, 19 March 1862. Dawson Carr, *Gray Phantoms of the Cape Fear:
Running the Civil War Blockade* (Winston-Salem, N.C.: John F. Blair, 1998) 162.
12. *Daily Journal*, 1 January 1861; *Whiting Papers*, II: 348, letter dated 27
October 1864. See also the *Wilmington Post*, 19 May 1876; W. McKee Evans,
Ballots and Fence Rails: Reconstruction on the Lower Cape Fear (Durham:
Seeman Printing, 1967) 223-224.
13 National Archives, *Citizens Papers*, Thomas Roberts. For work done on the
Torpedo Boat, the foundry billed the government for a boiler and engine, "688

lbs. boiler plate" and 162 pounds of cast iron. The bill came to $7,075 and when labor costs were added, it soared to over $11,000.

14 *Daily Journal*, 21 December 1864, 26 January and 25 November 1863; *Daily North Carolinian*, 16 January 1865; Dr. Chris E. Fonvielle, Jr., *The Wilmington Campaign: Last Rays of Departing Hope* (Campbell, Calif: Savas Publishing Co., 1997) 367. *Daily Journal*, 1 and 7 July 1864. National Archives, *Citizens Papers*, reel no. 1126. See also E. Lawrence Abel, *Singing the New Nation: How Music Shaped the Confederacy, 1861-1865* (Mechanichsburg, Pa.: Stackpole Books, 2000) 59-63; *Nassau Guardian*, 21 January 1865. Macarthy continued on to England but returned to the United States in 1867. He again went on tour, but after a short burst of popularity, again receded into obscurity. He died penniless in Oakland, California in 1888.

15 *Daily Journal*, 29 December 1863.

16 *Daily Journal*, 27 July 1863; *Wood Papers*, book 4, 7. Reaves, *Strength Through Struggle*, 62. After the war, the Rose Bud Band broke up, but got back together again sometime in the 1870s. *Daily Journal*, 24 March, 1863. Bell Irvin Wiley, *The Life of Johnny Reb: The Common Soldier in the Civil War* (Baton Rouge: Louisiana State University Press, 2004)151-160. *Daily Journal*, 2 April 1862, see also 22 February 1864, on this occasion the "Rats" of General Hospital No. 4 sought companionship. *C.S. Powell Papers*, collection no. 610, Southern Historical Society, UNC-Chapel Hill, 8, herein after cited as the *Powell Papers*.

From First To Last

hen the tocsin sounded its war cry, many of Wilmington's finest citizens rushed to don the gray. There were "from the immediate vicinity of Wilmington twenty companies of infantry, two of cavalry, and six battalions of artillery, numbering in all nearly 4,000 men[.]" Quite a large number, considering the 1860 population of New Hanover County was nearly 22,000. Prior to the war there were several militia units, which included the Wilmington Light Artillery, the German Volunteers, the Cape Fear Light Artillery and the Wilmington Rifle Guards. These units were quickly filled up and offered for service to the Confederate Government. One of these volunteers was Alexander Duncan Moore.[1]

Alexander Moore faced an agonizing choice in the spring of 1861. A native of Wilmington, he had spent the last several years as a cadet at the U.S. Military Academy at West Point, N.Y. Other classmates included Patrick O'Rourke, Alonzo Cushing, George A. Custer and George A. Woodruff. While a cadet at West Point, Moore did "fairly well," ranking eighteenth in his class of sixty-two. He received demerits for such things as wandering off limits and being in officer's territory without permission. Once, on "a cold December morning Moore wrapped the cape of his overcoat about his head while marching from breakfast, and in January held his hands over his freezing ears…He was once quilled for wearing [a] watch chain…[and] had once 'introduced citizens into the barracks,' wore his dancing slippers at inspection, and was awarded a 2 for 'reading other than a prayer-book in church.' "

There were several other demerits received by Moore for various offenses, but he remained quite popular with his classmates and when he resigned, many of them "regretted his departure." In 1857, this class numbered eighty-four Plebes. Only thirty-four graduated. A large number of the Cadets resigned their commissions and headed South. Moore, together with classmates John Pelham, Thomas Rosser and James Dearing (Class of 1862) tendered his resignation on 22 April and left the Academy. Stopping in New York City, he and Pelham had their pictures taken. The photograph is said to be the only photo of Pelham in civilian clothing.[2]

Moore continued on to Wilmington where in March he was appointed a 2nd Lieutenant in the Artillery Corps, C.S.A. On 16 May he was promoted to the

Captaincy of Company E, 10th N.C. State Troops. This was the Wilmington Light Artillery, which was then often referred to as "Moore's Battery." At the end of the month, he wrote Warren Winslow, who Governor John Ellis had appointed as the head of his Military and Naval Board, about a problem that had developed when filling officer vacancies. Samuel R. Bunting had been elected an officer of Moore's company, but did not receive a commission.

John C. McIlhenny also applied for the position. McIlhenny promised "to bring with him into the service some ten or fifteen men, members of the Wilmington Light Infantry of which he is an officer. I was informed by…Mr. Baker (my 1st Lieut.) that Bunting would probably go with us and earnestly advising that his place

Alexander Duncan Moore
(photo from "An Unremaining Glory")

… be kept open as he can do more in filling our enlistment roles than any other. He is very popular."

Moore's problem was how to break the news to McIlhenny. He decided to come clean and tell him what had happened. After all, he noted, McIlhenny "is a gentleman and will not go where he is not wanted." Moore apologized for the "complication" and added in his report, "I never saw such a people for changing their minds & doing everything that they should not do, in my life, as some Wilmingtonians – *Entre Nous*."

Apparently minds were changed once more, for Second Lieutenant McIlhenny was enrolled in Moore's outfit, Company E, while Samuel Bunting went to Company I of the same regiment. As a Lieutenant, McIlhenny commanded a section of artillery and was noted as a "fine officer." In March 1862, he was authorized "to raise a light artillery company." Quite successfully, he "secured a fine battery with the assurance of horses and all necessary arms and equipments." Unfortunately, while in Raleigh, John was thrown from his horse and suffered such serious injury that he was subsequently discharged.

McIlhenny would face more difficulties after the war. In September 1873, while working at his brother's drug store, he was taken ill and died suddenly. He was only thirty-seven years old at his death.[3]

As for Company E, after being sent to Coosawatchie, S.C., the men were returned to Wilmington where they remained until 1863, when they were dispatched to Richmond. Upon the organization of the 66th N.C. Regiment, Alex Moore was promoted to Colonel and placed in command of the new regiment.

When he took over there were, at first, some hard feelings among his subordinate officers: "The appointment of Colonel Moore caused, at the time, some friction among the officers, as he was unknown to all of them, but he had not been long in the regiment before they recognized him as a good soldier, a fine disciplinarian and as brave an officer as ever fought for the cause of his country... shortly afterwards, he became the idol of his regiment."

After its organization, the 66th spent time back in Wilmington. By March 1864, they were on the move once again: Plymouth, Tarboro, Washington, N.C. and

Thomas Rosser

thence to Petersburg. Assigned to Kirkland's brigade in Hoke's Division, the unit was bloodied at Walthal Junction. They took part in the fighting at Bermuda Hundred and on 20 May, were ordered to move on the Federals. Moore, it was later reported, led the charge of his regiment "through a field of small grain into a pine thicket where the enemy was strongly entrenched and supported by his artillery." When told that his regiment was moving too fast, he took hold of the colors, lifted his sword in the air and "halted, dressed on the colors" until the other regiments reached them. The men continued their advance and swarmed over the enemy's works. The following day the men marched to Cold Harbor and it was there on 3 June, when a Virginia Brigade "broke and ran away" that the men of the Sixty-Sixth "boldly held their ground and fired hotly on the enemy on front and on the right...It was a great victory from the start, but deeply saddened by the death of Colonel A.D. Moore[.]" Shot in the neck, Moore died within a few minutes.

Another of Wilmington's heroes had fallen. When word was received of his death, the city mourned once more. Of the cadets who paused to have their picture taken that fateful April day, only Thomas Rosser would survive the war. "The Gallant Pelham" had fallen in March 1863 at Kelly's Ford. Rosser, who, during the war had risen to the rank of brigadier general, would return to active duty in the Spanish-American War, this time wearing a blue uniform, also adorned with the star of a general.

A young John Decatur Barry.

John Decatur Barry was yet another who offered his services to his country. Enlisting as a private in November 1861 in the Wilmington Rifle Guards, which became Company I, 18th N.C., he was sent with his company to South Carolina when that state was threatened with invasion. Sent back to Kinston, N.C., Barry was soon elected captain of the company. In May 1862, the regiment was ordered to Virginia and was soon embroiled in the worst of the fighting. They were at Hanover Court House, the Seven Days Battles (where Barry was wounded), Cedar Mountain, Second Manassas, Harper's Ferry and Sharpsburg.

In October (1862) Barry was elected major of his regiment. At Chancellorsville, General "Stonewall" Jackson maneuvered his corps into a flanking position and launched a successful attack against the Union XI Corps commanded by General Oliver O. Howard. The rout was complete and the Yankees fell back in disorder. As dusk was fast approaching, the attack began to falter. The 18th N.C. was placed across the Plank Road, in line of battle with General James K. Lanes's other regiments. Lane received orders to push ahead with the attack, but before he could begin moving, an artillery duel began, with federal artillery firing straight down the Plank Road, forcing the men of the 18th to lie down and seek cover. When the artillery fire

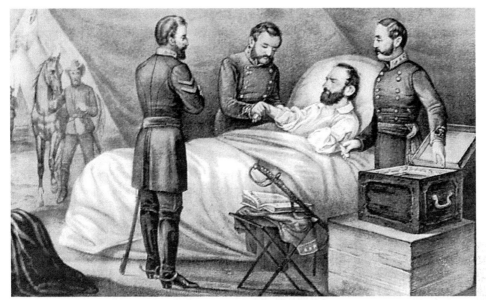

The death of "Stonewall" Jackson, mortally wounded by John D. Barry's men.

ceased, Lane sought to question his order to continue the attack and was told by General Jackson himself to "Push right ahead, Lane." In the dark, after warning his men to be wary of enemy activity, Lane's brigade moved forward, but immediately spotted Union troops off to their right. Desultory fire began between the forces, but unknown to the Confederates, Jackson had gone out in front of his own lines to reconnoiter. When he heard the gunfire, he turned and rode back towards his lines, hoping to avoid being out front when the troops opened up. The 18th, already skittish with all the firing, heard horsemen racing at them from the direction of the enemy. Major Barry, in command at that section of the line, gave the order to fire. After the first fusillade, one of Jackson's staff shouted, "Cease firing, you are firing into your own men!" Barry responded, "Who gave that order? It's a lie. Pour it to them boys!"

Jackson and his staff were only about seventy-five feet away when "a blaze of fire exploded from the infantry line." It was later determined that: "Bullets had struck Jackson not once, but three times. One bullet lodged in his right palm while two others struck his left arm."

Jackson was severely wounded and would die a week later. There was never any doubt that Barry and his men fired the shots that hit Jackson. Barry himself "always thought that...Jackson and [General Hill] were both wounded by his command." Lee and others in the army never blamed the regiment for Jackson's death. Stonewall, as close-mouthed as ever, told no one where he was going and it was an exceedingly dangerous position for a commander to place himself.

When the battle ended, Barry was the only one of thirteen regimental officers who had not been either killed or wounded. Even the 18th's commander, Colonel Thomas Purdie, was killed. Major Barry would assume command of the 18th and lead them throughout 1863 and 1864. When, in June 1864, General Lane was wounded, Colonel Barry took over the brigade. His division commander, General Cadmus Wilcox, was so impressed with Barry's leadership that he recommended him for promotion to general.

On 3 August, he was promoted to the temporary rank of general, but just a few short days later was himself badly wounded. He was shot in the hand and lost the second and third fingers of his right hand. He returned to Wilmington to recuperate and due to his disability was soon mustered out of the service.

After the war Barry went into the newspaper business and with a partner published the *Daily Dispatch*. The partnership soon dissolved, but Barry continued publishing the paper, even though his wounds still affected his health. In 1867, due in part to his wounds but also, according to family lore, to the depression or melancholia from which he suffered, he passed away. He is buried in Wilmington's Oakdale Cemetery and on his tombstone are the following words: "I found him a pygmy but left him a giant." The inscription refers to his meteoric rise from private to general, in less than three years. Those words were uttered by Napoleon in praise of yet another shooting star, French Marshal Lennes. Family tradition states that Barry's mother was not at all happy with his epitaph.

John S. Van Bokkelen was another young Wilmingtonian who enlisted in the Third North Carolina early in the war. Appointed a second lieutenant at the age of nineteen, he was quite popular with both officers and men. He was promoted to captain of company D after the battle of Sharpsburg and after surviving several major battles, was badly wounded at Chancellorsville, 3 June 1863. He was sent to Richmond's General Hospital No. 4. Known as the Institute Hospital, it was formerly the Baptist Female Institute and was used mainly for officers. Visited and cared for by his father, it was here that the young man lingered until death took him a month later. It was said that when the unit was apprised of his passing, "grief...without alloy" was widespread. He was "universally popular and almost idolized by his men...full of youthful ardor, intelligent, with...an indomitable energy." It was also said that the high morale exhibited by his men was due almost entirely to him "more than any officer of the company." The Third Regiment, which contained many from New Hanover County, lost thirty-nine killed, one hundred seventy-five wounded and seventeen missing in action at Chancellorsville.

There would be other battles and others would struggle vainly for their country. Some would return with shattered bodies. Some would not return at all.[4]

Endnotes

1. Sprunt, *Chronicles*, 273.

2. Mary Elizabeth Sergent, *An Unremaining Glory: Being a Supplement to They Lie Forgotten* (Middletown, N.Y.: Prior King Press, 1997) 47.

3. North Carolina State Archives, Military Collection, box 36, file 11, letter dated 30 May 1861. Wilmington *Morning Star*, 26 September 1873; Walter Clark, *Histories of the Several Regiments and Battalions From North Carolina in the Great War, 1861-'65* (Wilmington: Broadfoot Publishing Co., 1996) 1:581, 3:685-687; Stewart Sifakis, *Who Was Who in the Civil War* (New York: Facts on File Publications, 1988) 556.

4. Powell, *North Carolina Biography*, 1:104-105; *The Wounding of "Stonewall" Jackson*, National Park Service publication, Fredericksburg and Spotsylvania National Military Park. William K. Goolrick, *Rebels Resurgent: From Fredericksburg to Chancellorsville* (Time-Life Books: Alexandria, Va., 1985)138-139. Robertson, *Stonewall Jackson*, 728-729. Robert W. Waitt, Jr., *Confederate Military Hospitals in Richmond* (Richmond: Richmond Independence Bicentennial Commission, 1979) 11-12. The *Vance Papers*, 23: 390-391; Clark, I:212, 216; Manarin, 3:483, 522.

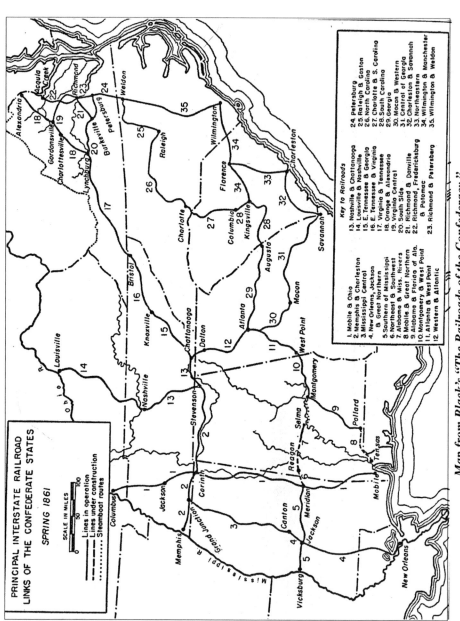

Map from Black's "The Railroads of the Confederacy."

7

Iron Transportation

olonel Sewall Fremont sat at his desk in the depot at Wilmington that cold December of 1863. He was writing a response to Governor Zebulon Vance's aide-de-camp, Colonel George Little. Since the war had begun over two years before, supplies for his railroad, the Wilmington and Weldon, had become harder to obtain. Iron had become so scarce that portions of non-essential railroads, so-called secondary lines, were torn up and the rails distributed to the more important lines. In addition to roads needing "T" rails, the Confederate Navy was also in the market for iron. They had begun building ironclads and desperately needed the iron rails to be melted down into plating to finish the vessels and send them against the Union blockaders. Old, worn out rails were given to the navy in exchange for newer rails, in a kind of two for one deal.

As he wrote, Fremont heard a " 'shriek' or 'scream' as of some one in terror." He ran to his window, which looked out on to the passenger depot, and saw several soldiers firing their weapons down the street. After determining what had occurred, he penned yet another letter, this one to General Whiting. Such scenes were becoming more common in the bustling blockade-running center. The town hosted a large contingent of soldiers, sailors and "speculators" as well as others of a lower class. "Thieves, rogues and prostitutes" roamed the streets, driving away many of the town's decent citizens. Frequent gunshots were heard as fights broke out.

In the summer of 1863, General Whiting ordered that "any soldiers, sailors or marines found in town after tattoo without passes were to be arrested." This led to nearly everyone walking the streets being questioned. In April of that

The Provost Guard were keen to capture army deserters found in the Wilmington area.

year, a native of the town reported, "The military have a guard placed at every crossing of the streets picking up all that are not in the service...I looked across the street and there was Mr. Reston coming along with a soldier after him to come to the bank to get his papers; and after that kept my seat for some time amusing myself seeing the different ones being taken up, and the guard themselves quite enjoying it, as if it were fun for them."

Many men were swept up and put in jail. With the new conscription law in effect, squads of soldiers from the provost guard were on the lookout for deserters who might be trying to use either the railroad or a blockade runner as a means of escape. The terminal was a good spot to catch these "sculkers." As the war dragged on, some deserters attempted a getaway by hiding in a coffin and having it loaded aboard the waiting train. When they heard the depot bell ring, they knew " ...they were moving away from the conscript officers, from whom they dreaded so badly...Draft dodger after draft dodger essayed the role of the dead until their trains reached a point north of the Mason and Dixon line, where the 'dead' would arise from their coffins and walk, at long last free from the conscript chasers."[1]

When Fremont described the incident to Whiting, he asked that the soldiers patrolling the streets be kept away from the depot. Later that month, in writing to Colonel Little, he described a second occurrence that had taken place on Market Street. He was told that in both instances, the provost guard had killed men who were attempting to evade the patrol.

Another who heard the gunfire that December day was William Mondonville Poisson. Before the war, William had been Secretary of the Cape Fear Marine Total Abstinence Society and was employed as a bookkeeper. He decided to write to Governor Vance about the incident: "I write to you confidentially because as I am an exempt, but liable to conscription, I might have some difficulty with the military authorities for reporting the [incident.]"

Poisson had gotten a wartime job as ticket agent at the depot, after resigning his position as the army's commissary officer at Fayetteville. He escaped the draft in August 1863 only after the W&W's agent, Stephen D. Wallace, wrote to the Secretary of War requesting his exemption.

Poisson later wrote directly to President Davis offering to become: "A detector for the Government. I could have an eye to stragglers, deserters &c. who come to purchase tickets. Besides this, I have the advantage of being raised here and could soon discover an unfamiliar face. Frequently soldiers hang around our depot or passenger shed because there are some rooms where they can sleep free. I have no doubt that frequently deserters &c. might thus be arrested...I have a family to support and...a small compensation is all I expect."

Earlier, while stationed in Fayetteville, Poisson had written to Vance informing him of the high prices being charged by "the factories in and near [Fayetteville]." He also wrote, "I write this *confidentially* because I am somewhat of a stranger here[.]" Poisson, it would appear, had a poison pen.

Others felt the military presence necessary. One writer reported that he "heard several citizens utter the word 'humbug,' in application to the demands, 'halt' which were made at the corners of our streets." He spoke of many strangers who filled the streets and made mention of an attack on an "inoffensive Negro" the preceding evening. The man's throat had been cut, but it was

At one time, the Wilmington & Weldon Railroad had the longest rail line in the world. It would play a vital role for Robert E. Lee's Army of Northern Virginia.

WILMINGTON AND WELDON RAILROAD

Longest railroad in the World when completed in 1840. Length 161-½ mi. Terminus was 4 blocks W.

thought he would survive. The dastardly act was committed by a sailor from one of the vessels then lying in the harbor. When General Whiting was informed of the attack, he issued a "stringent order" forbidding seamen to be in town after sundown. The writer then suggested that the town would be a "fine field for conscript reapers. May their harvest prove full."[2]

An early 1800s train.

Perhaps it was Colonel Fremont's military background that prompted him to report the shooting on that December morning. Perhaps Fremont, a Northerner by birth, wondered how things had come to this. When he had taken the reins of the Road back in 1854, it had been running for nearly fifteen years and the future looked bright. The company had come a long way since that first locomotive, the *Brunswick* (now used as the Superintendent's personal engine) pulled a train of cars from Wilmington to Weldon, located on the Roanoke River, near the Virginia border, on 7 March 1840.

At that town, a connection could be made to the Virginia railroads which would carry a traveler to Petersburg and Richmond. From there prewar travelers could continue their journey northward to Washington, Baltimore and New York. Passengers desiring to go south from Wilmington would board one of several company steamers, which would whisk them to Charleston, provided the mail train from the north was on schedule.[3] When it was completed in 1840, the

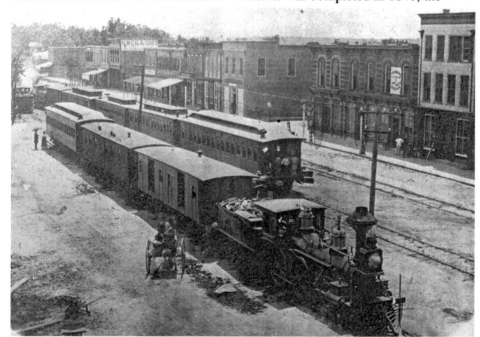

A train of the Wilmington & Weldon Railroad meets one of the NCRR trains in Goldsboro.

single-tracked W&W stretched 161.5 miles, making it for a time at least, the longest road in the country.

Originally incorporated as the Wilmington and Raleigh, the name was changed in 1854 because the backers in Raleigh failed to raise their share of the needed capital. (By 1840 they had their own road, the Raleigh and Gaston.) That failure made the burden of such local backers as Alexander MacRae, Platt Dickinson, Armand deRosset, James S. Green and Edward B. Dudley much more difficult. But state aid made the difference and the Road was completed in three years.

"The entire road was constructed under the following supervision: Walter Gwyn, chief engineer; Alexander MacRae, superintendent; Matthew T. Goldsborough, principal assistant engineer of the Southern Division, and Francis N. Barbarin, principal assistant engineer of the Northern Division."

James Sprunt would later write of that fateful rainy day when the celebration of the line's completion was held: "A large number of gentlemen assembled in the town from various parts of the State and from Virginia and South Carolina at an early hour of the morning. The bells gave out sonorous peals and the shipping in the harbor came up, their flags waving. Cannon were fired every fifteen minutes throughout the day [the *Daily Journal* would later report that almost miraculously, no one had been injured] with a national salute at meridian. At 2 p.m. a procession, composed of invited guests and citizens, including the president, directors, and officers of other roads, the Literary Board [from whence the money to finish the road came!], the president, directors, engineers, agents and others in the employ of the Wilmington and Raleigh railroad…marched thence to the dinner table, escorted by the Wilmington Volunteers with their fine band of music."

Quite a spread awaited them and it was said that well over five hundred people were fed. There were also a lot of toasts made – nearly seventy in all. There had to be a lot of wet, happy inebriates in town that day. There was at least one romance that blossomed on the rails. In 1852, a young gentleman boarded the cars at Richmond, headed to Charleston. Upon boarding, he noticed a young lady nearby. She was "one of the fairest daughters of the Old Dominion" and he soon began conversing with her. He became enamored and she returned the feeling and before they arrived at Wilmington, he had proposed marriage. Receiving the consent of her mother, she accepted and upon reaching Wilmington they engaged a minister and were united in matrimony at the Carolina Hotel. In the morning they boarded the steamer for Charleston and began their honeymoon. A writer, who witnessed the entire proceedings, wished that "… their sorrows be as brief in duration as their courtship."

If the couple were off to a good start, the W&W was not so fortunate. The road began operating with twelve engines, eight passenger coaches, fifty freight, four mail ("post office") cars and four steamboats. It soon ran into trouble. In those bleak days, the road's credit was so bad that "the principal merchant of Wilmington, Mr. Alexander Anderson, had refused to fill an order for one hundred dozen shovels to clear up the rubbish of a burnt building in the company's yard." The shovels were needed because a fire had destroyed some of the road's buildings and equipment.

The road proved, however, to be a good investment for its shareholders. It was also a good investment for the State. One historian wrote: "The railroads cut in half the old wagon freight rates…This encouraged the production of surplus crops for market, increased the farmer's profit on what he sold, and reduced the price of goods which he purchased. Land values and farm productivity increased. There was a marked growth of towns, trade factories, wealth and state revenue."

Additional benefits were increased travel, "more frequent mail service and a higher standard of living for many people."[4] Rip Van Winkle was astir! The road was something of an engineering marvel; the steepest grade on the entire line was 30 feet per mile and many sections were built in a straight line. One section, running south from Faison to Rocky Point, was forty-seven miles without a curve. The "sleepers," or crossties, were of white oak, the rails of yellow pine with strips of iron, two inches wide by almost a half inch thick, nailed to a "stringer" of wood. This "strap iron" could not stand up to even light traffic and was in constant need of repair. In addition, when the joints worked loose it became a danger. The wheels of a passing train would catch the loose end and force it up into the cars.

The directors realized that the newer, stronger (52 pounds to the yard) "T" rail was necessary. In 1849, Dr. Armand deRosset was sent to England on behalf of the W&W to exchange railroad bonds for new rails. He was able to make a very good deal because the English market was saturated and they had begun "dumping" on the American market. By 1850, most Southern manufacturers, unable to compete with the British, had ceased producing rails. This would have a disastrous effect on the South during the Civil War. However, by the end of 1851, most of the W&W had been relaid with the new rails.

The W&W was different than most Southern roads of that era, for while many south of the Mason-Dixon line used a five-foot gauge, the W&W was built as a standard-gauge, 4' 8" road. This gauge difference complicated the transportation of goods and people; it necessitated a change of cars at the southern terminus.

Several cities in both the South and the North, were not physically connected by rail. At Petersburg, travelers got off one train and took a hack to the next segment of rail. Hotel owners, draymen and the hacks, in search of profit, all exerted political pressure to keep the railroad tracks apart. Back in 1848 the W&W had more than 460 employees. In 1858-59, the state legislature examined their operation and noted: "It [the road] is under the general management of a president and ten directors, seven on the part of the individual stockholders and three on the part of the State. It has in its employ a secretary and treasurer, an assistant secretary and general ticket agent, and seven executive officers, embracing an engineer and superintendent, depot agent and yardmaster, general freight and transportation agent, master machinist, and a road master. In addition to these, there are six persons connected with the department of transportation and

A bale of cotton.

repairs; nineteen station agents; some of whom give their services in consideration of riding over the road free of charge; and twenty-four conductors and engineers."

The legislative committee which examined the books commented unfavorably on the number of people that had traveled the line without paying. The Road granted such passes to "All Presidents and General Superintendents of Railroads, who exchange passes with this company[.]" All employees on duty were also granted the privilege, as was "General Alexander McRae [sic], Ex-President, and his family," who were allowed to ride free, "indefinitely." Also allowed to ride the trains were the agents of the post office, Adam's Express and Magnetic Telegraph Companies, but only when on duty.

The lawmakers, sorting through reams of paperwork, noted that some sixty passengers had ridden the road for free and although the custom of granting free passes was well established by this time, they indicated that $180 per month, or more than $2,000, was lost per year by continuing this practice. Fremont likely pointed out that he had tried to curtail this loss by eliminating "deadheading" as it was termed, but had encountered "…considerable feeling against" it and so continued the practice.

In addition to the employees listed above, there were those who maintained the rolling stock, worked in the shops, on the steamers and at the depots. Most of the laborers, fully half of those employed, were African-American, either free blacks or slaves, leased from their owners. By 1860, the Road itself owned a dozen slaves. Many of them worked at maintaining the right-of-way, or as "train hands." These workers were required to load and unload the freight or to pick up a barrel or two of tar or turpentine left alongside the track.

By 1860, the W&W's cargo consisted less of pine products and more of cotton. Indeed, by that year, the cotton crop hauled nearly doubled to 145,514 bales, up from 73,845 in 1850. The bales, usually weighing five hundred pounds, were brought directly to the terminals, thus eliminating the need for train hands.

Train crews could not be eliminated. Without a doubt, the most dangerous job on the road was that of brakeman. These were the men who, when signaled by the engineer's whistle, clambered up on a rocking car and, because there was no central braking system, applied each car's brakes by hand. This was not easily done in inclement weather. The engineer had to estimate the stopping distance because the trains could take anywhere from 1,500 to 1,800 feet to stop. The brakeman also coupled and uncoupled the cars and it was said that one could tell an experienced brakeman by the number of fingers the man was missing.

The engineer was positioned in the right seat of the cab, while the fireman fed the insatiable fire of the boiler. Coal was expensive, so wood, especially pine, was the fuel of choice. Passenger trains ambled along at about thirty miles an hour, although during the war, that speed was cut by more than half. The engineer was responsible for the engine and, like the conductor, was required by the company to own a dependable timepiece and to have a timetable at hand. Strict rules governed the engineer: there was to be no smoking or undue talking and no one but the engineer and fireman were allowed in the cab. On occasion slaves were trained as firemen and once trained they commanded more money when leased back to the company. The engine had to be kept clean, all required tools (jack screws, head lamp and signal lights) were to be checked. The spark arrestor and the wire netting over the smoke pipe and by the ash pan were also checked. Another basic regulation was that when he pulled out of the station, he had to make sure the train was still attached. Passengers could usually pick out the engineer. He was the one with the oilcan, since he had to frequently lubricate parts of the engine.

So the crew and conductor could communicate with the engineer, there was a rope which ran through the cars, connecting to a bell in the cab. Aboard a train, a conductor's word was law. These men were indeed the "Captains" of their ship and, as such, the job was one of the most prestigious on the line. It was also the most demanding. The company would sometimes test their employees by sending agents aboard. A beautiful young lady, who worked for a detective agency, would board and sobbingly tell a tale of woe. If the conductor was taken in by her story, she noted the time and date and the man would soon be taken to task for his seemingly humane action. After a while, conductors trusted no one, not even clergymen!

In 1854, the new president of the road, former Congressman William S. Ashe, long a proponent of internal improvements, especially those that benefited his home district, had been chosen to run the company after a bitter contest. His election by the board of directors was something of a surprise as it was thought that someone connected with the railroad, like board member William A. Wright, would assume the position. As matter of fact it was reported that Ashe had, "Never owned a share of stock…until recently, when a transfer of a sufficient number of shares was made to qualify him the office…[he] has had no acquaintance with the…management of Rail Roads; and so far as the duties of a President is concerned, was disqualified; is yet, in direct opposition to the wishes of a large majority of the…stockholders, forced upon the Company as its chief officer."[5]

William S. Ashe

Governor David S. Reid was a Democrat. So was Congressman Ashe. It was the proxy voting power of the state that swung the election Ashe's way. It would turn out that Ashe was an excellent manager and led the company through difficult times. He had served three terms in Congress (from 1849 to 1854) and during that time " …acted with the ultra-southern men in opposition to the compromise measures of that sectional crisis." The Compromise of 1850 had been passed during his time in Congress, but he had little to do with it. He felt then that secession was the best course for the South.

Not content to be merely a figurehead, he took an active role in the running of the railroad. Two items that many roads paid scant attention to, safety and passenger comfort, were on his priority list. In talks with Florida's Senator David L. Yulee, "sleeper car" service was discussed and several cars of this type were run on the W&W night trains, but it would not be until after the Civil War that this refinement became permanent.

In an effort to promote business, Ashe arranged with the North Carolina Railroad to have freight trains run directly from Charlotte to Wilmington, eliminating the offloading of freight from the N.C.R.R. cars to those of the W&W. It helped that the N.C.R.R. track was also of standard gauge.

A writer once said of Ashe, "He sought to eliminate as far as practicable all breaks at terminals and to relieve travel of its inconvenience and tedium, and in conjunction with Senator Yulee...he developed Florida travel until it reached large proportions and became a highly remunerative business."[6]

For the safety and comfort of females, a "Ladies only" coach and a designated smoking car were established. Some coaches of that time were gas lighted, fed by a bladder-like tank that ran horizontally across the undercarriage of the car. It is likely that the lamps on the W&W were oil fed. Although there was a "gas works" in the shops, it was probably for lighting the buildings. In 1859 it was reported that the two burners in the cars gave "very nearly enough light to read in all parts of the car[.]"

The telegraph (1851) was an important innovation which increased not only passenger comfort but safety. For a single-track road it was very important to know where the trains were at all times. Derailments, breakdowns or other delays could cause a collision. By the mid-1850s, there were telegraph operators at both the Wilmington and Weldon terminals, and at selected stations along the road. When two trains approached each other on the main track, one would be required to back off into a siding. In the early days, the most senior conductor had the right-of-way. By 1859 this situation was regulated by timetables issued infrequently. At the stations where there was no telegraph, the station master adjusted his clock by the conductor's timepiece.[7]

Constructed in 1856, the depot at Wilmington was a rather large affair, some 280 feet by 80 feet, able to accommodate several trains at once. The dining room, in which the food was kept warm by means of steam heat, seated 200 people. In fact, the entire building was warmed with steam. There were waiting rooms, separated by the ticket office, for both ladies and gentlemen. Either sex would have the opportunity to avail themselves of the dressing and bathing rooms, which contained hot and cold water and shower-baths. Also located within were a hotel and barbershop. The entire premises was lighted by gas.

One visitor reported: "More than once we have had an opportunity of testing the arrangements of the table and the quality of the viands...at the Wilmington and Weldon Railroad Depot, by Mrs. Brothers...but until recently we were unaware of the...airy and commodious sleeping rooms[.] We can now say...that such rooms have been fitted up. They are just a little the nicest and most nicely arranged and furnished...to be found anywhere[.]"[8]

Another favorable report came from a reporter who noted the "efficient board of directors" and wrote: "We have passed over this road a few times and we pronounce it the best running Road between the north and south. Everything connected with it moves like clock work. The trains run with such precision, that the people along the road regulate their watches by them...Finally, this road is in excellent condition and...[it] must be regarded as the finest Railroad in the United States."

Superintendent Fremont was in overall charge of the day-to-day running of the road. This transplanted Yankee controlled quite a large operation, for he was responsible to see that the trains kept to their schedules and arrived at the stations safely. There was no such thing as Standard Time; different roads used different clocks to schedule their trains. "Railroad" time was ten minutes ahead of town time and delays were an inherent part of the system. In addition, before the completion of the Wilmington and Manchester railroad, the W&W had been tied to the very flexible schedule of steamers which brought passengers northward from Charleston. Different flags flown from the roof of the Commercial building indicated what was coming, train or steamer, but by 1856, with the W&M Railroad now completed and the steamboats to Charleston no longer needed, they were sold. The W&W had pledged to purchase $100,000 of stock from the W&M and this money came from the sale of the steamers.

Travelers headed south would detrain at the Wilmington depot, unless the tracks were blocked by ice, snow or sand, walk down a step incline to the railroad's wharf and there board the ferryboat *Harlee* for the short ride across the Cape Fear River to Eagles Island. The Manchester Road's shops, offices and terminals were located there and by boarding that line, the journey would continue to Florence, S.C. From there, it was on to Charleston, Columbia, Augusta, Atlanta, Savannah and points further south.

In March, 1861, after an unusually heavy snowfall, the newly constructed iron-roofed roundhouse of the Manchester Road collapsed due to the weight of the snow. The house was estimated to be 170 feet in diameter and some of the equipment was damaged, but within twenty minutes, the entire workforce was out working to clear up the mess so that there would be no interruption in service.

Northbound from Wilmington, trains passed over Smith's Creek and the first of six covered bridges on the line. From there the tracks continued north for ten miles to North East Station at present-day Castle Hayne, then crossed the North East Cape Fear River and ran through Marlboro to Rocky Point.[9]

It was near here, at Ashton, that William Ashe lived. As a courtesy to the president of the road, trains made unofficial stops at the small shed which served as Ashe's own depot.

Continuing north through Burgaw, South Washington, Leesburg and Teachey, the iron monster would soon have to stop for wood and water. Passenger engines of the 1850s consumed a cord of wood about every 40 miles. Freighters used nearly a cord every 29 miles. During that decade woodsheds and water tanks were located along the line, but in the beginning, when the boiler ran low, the train would simply stop by a stream and everyone, passengers included, would get out and lend a hand toting water to the tender. Because it was so plentiful, and a lot cheaper than coal, the engines burned pine wood, which after time, fouled the flues and decreased the engine's performance.

Four hours after leaving Wilmington, the junction with the North Carolina R.R. at Goldsboro was reached. That road ran west to Greensboro,

Gov. John Ellis

through Salisbury to Charlotte, where it connected with the South Carolina roads. Eastward from Goldsboro ran the Atlantic and North Carolina Road, to New Bern and Morehead City. Along the W&W line there were several bridges covered to protect the structures from the elements, thus increasing their life expectancy. Unfortunately, it increased the danger of the bridges burning due to the sparks from the engines. Watchmen had to be stationed at the bridges to prevent such catastrophes.

A passenger train usually consisted of the locomotive and its tender filled with wood and water, a baggage car, followed by two passenger coaches. One of these last was a first-class car, which naturally cost a little more to ride in. The common folk (and slaves) rode in the second-class car. There were no cabooses as such, but there were "conductor's cars" on some of the roads. The train hands along with the conductor would usually be found in this car. With the cars coupled together with links and pins, there was a great deal of bumping and jostling as the train pulled into and left the station. Before and during the war there were complaints of no ventilation or the cars were too hot or cold, too crowded or too slow. Those complaints increased during the war, but soon soldiers and civilians alike grew accustomed to the evils of railroad travel.

Soldiers riding in boxcars were wont to kick out a few boards for ventilation, or to get a better view of the countryside. Delays were rampant. One young soldier, stuck aboard an unmoving train, took the time to pen the following verse:

> *Vanity of vanities*
> *Climax of vexation,*
> *Waiting on the cars*
> *At a RR station.*
> *Thinking every moment*
> *That the train will go*
> *Waiting hour after hour*
> *In a small depot*

By 1860, when the Democrats held their national convention in Charleston, S.C., war clouds had long been on the horizon. Many of the delegates traveled by rail there and back and many of them stopped at the Griswold Hotel in Goldsboro. There one member of the convention, Benjamin F. Butler of Massachusetts, gave a speech, "as he stood on a chair in the dining room addressing the delegates who were in the greatest state of excitement as he shouted, 'It is Stephen A. Douglas or War!' "

It is said that at the Charleston convention, Butler voted 157 times for Jefferson Davis for President! When war came to Goldsboro, Mr. George V. Strong made the statement that "he would guarantee to wipe up all the bloodshed in the war with his pocket handkerchief."

When the troops were called up, the following scene took place at Goldsboro: "The station, the hotels, the streets through which the rail ran was filled with an excited mob...A man in a large wide awake...with a red sash and a pair of cotton trousers thrust into his boots, came out of Griswold's Hotel with a sword under his arm...[waving] enthusiastically, swaying to and fro on his legs, and ejaculating, 'H'ra for Jeff Davis – H'ra for Sothern E'R'rights and tottered over to the carriage...Just as he got into the train, a man in uniform dashed after him, and caught him by the elbow, exclaiming, 'Them's not the cars, General! The car's this way, General! The military dignitary, however, felt that if he permitted such liberties...he was degraded forever, so screwing up his lips and looking grave and grand, he [bellowed:] 'Sergeant, you go be —, I say these are my cars! They're all my cars! I'll send them where I please-to-if I like, sir. They shall go where I please—to New York, sir or New Orleans, sir! And sir, I'll arrest you.' " Losing track of his thoughts, the general continued to mumble, "I'll arrest you!" as he tottered back into the hotel.[10]

Two other visitors later that month were Jefferson Davis and Alexander Stephens. Both were on their way to Richmond and stopped briefly at the hotel.

War Comes to the Railroads

In April 1861, with the firing on Fort Sumter in Charleston Harbor, many knew it was only a matter of time before North Carolina joined the seceded states. That month former army Captain Fremont led a party of concerned citizens (including many of the town's Committee of Safety) on a tour to the river's mouth and together they scouted out locations to construct fortifications along the river and on adjacent islands. One of the first spots selected on Confederate Point would soon see a large earthernwork fort erected. This was the beginning of Fort Fisher, "the Malakoff of the South."

Fremont's expertise was called upon to help in constructing Fort Fisher and he gladly offered his services to his "adopted state" and was offered the position of Adjutant and Inspector General.

In the latter part of May, Fremont was invited by the president of the Petersburg Railroad, Mr. C. Sanford, to attend a conference of the Virginia railroads. While en route, he was given a telegram from President Ashe, who ordered him not to make the connection with the train at Weldon.

On board the train with Fremont were several others who had pressing business in Washington and points north. Lieutenant J. Pembroke Jones had just resigned from the U.S. Navy and was on his way to the capitol with dispatches. He informed Fremont that he was anxious to get there. As he was in a hurry to meet Sanford, Fremont detached the locomotive and went on ahead, allowing Jones and two others to come along.

At Weldon, they were met by an excited crowd who demanded that the spy who held Federal dispatches turn them over to Confederate authorities. It seemed that the dispatches carried by Jones concerned the movements of the Africa Squadron, of which Jones had been associated.

Fremont later reported: "Lt. Jones was then surrounded, and the dispatches demanded and…given up, and as I thought, the matter was at an end." When he tried to secure passage for himself and the others to Garysburg, where he was to meet Sanford and the others would continue on to Washington, he found the train delayed.

He decided to eat dinner: "While dining, a party of about 200 soldiers came in and arrested me. After a short time my friends…procured my release. A short time after another party arrested me again, and the officer commanding released me. Mr. Jones and myself had no further annoyance until about 8 p.m., when I was about leaving for Wilmington, when Lieut. Jones and myself were again arrested – at that moment a telegram from Major Whiting was received directing my instant release[.]"[11]

The Superintendent bore it all with good grace, writing that no one had done him any harm and explained away the action saying that it was because the troops, who were Georgians, were angry at not having obtained transportation. Unknown to the troops at the time was that Fremont had recently been appointed a colonel in the North Carolina militia. North Carolina voted to leave the Union on 20 May 1861. Even before secession there was heavy military traffic all along the line, highlighting the importance of the railroads.

Fremont actively sought a position in the N.C. militia and telegrammed Governor John Ellis: "Though the Board of Directors [of the W&W] have not yet acted on the question…I accept the office [of Adjutant General]…Please send the appointment and…a letter that I can lay before the Board asking for a leave of absence to serve the state."

He did not get the position he had hoped for, but, being given a commission in the regular Confederate army, was delegated to head the artillery arm for the state. He began fortifying Confederate Point and established Camp Wyatt, about one mile north of Fort Fisher, as an artillery training base.

All summer, troops and munitions of war arrived in Wilmington. Troops from Louisiana, Alabama, Georgia, South Carolina and Florida streamed through town. The *Daily Journal* reported: "Last night a company from Eastern Alabama and Western Georgia passed through here on their way to Richmond. They are called the Border Rangers, and number one hundred and twelve men... They were a fine looking body of men, indeed."

The former Mrs. William Reston, whose husband was the cashier of the Bank of North Carolina, as well as a member of the militia, penned a description of one of her husband's duties: "To meet all the troops that passed through Wilmington on their way to Richmond, and furnish them with all the money they required. After the troops were safely landed from across the river on Ferry Boats and the Companies drawn up in line (some days as many as 10,000), each company was marched down Front Street and halted at the corner of Front and Princess Streets in front of the Bank of the State...I shook hands with many of our Confederate Generals...The impression left in my mind of those days and of those brave soldiers, some tall men over 6 feet with tiny grey beards, little drummer boys not 10 to 12 years, young men, middle aged men, drums beating, bands playing and even the horses dancing and prancing all so eager to march to duty."[12]

Although exact numbers are hard to determine, from August to November of that first year of war, the W&W sent an invoice to Richmond for ferrying 12,489 soldiers across the Cape Fear. The company charged $936.67 for that service. The troops were transported on the railroad at the rate of two cents per mile, that being half the normal rate. Most soldiers boarded night trains, which were used mainly for troop movements, while others encamped in and around town. Heading southward, the soldiers were met at the depot by the Ladies Aid Society, who distributed foodstuffs to the men.

The first major battle of the war was fought at Manassas on 21 July 1861 and from that time onward, the majority of troops camped near town were sent on to Virginia.

In addition to contributing to the success of the battles by transporting troops, the W&W would soon provide one of the first ambulance cars to carry the wounded from the Richmond hospitals. The cars, fitted up with "easy lounges and hammocks" could handle about twenty patients. The greatest advantage to the wounded was not, however, the accommodations, as soldiers preferred straw-filled boxcars, but the fact that the cars ran all the way from the capital to Wilmington.

Col. Charles Fisher

As the local paper noted: "When the pulse throbs with fever or their mangled frame is torn with torture at every turn, the changing of the cars and the forced necessity of maintaining an erect position is agony unendurable[.]"

In September 1862, the Confederate Congress approved an act which authorized the army to make arrangements with the several railroad companies whereby wounded and ill soldiers, with their attendants, would be placed in a special car reserved for their use alone. Surgeons discharging wounded men were ordered to have "some competent person" accompany the soldier to the depot to ensure that "all such are properly cared for."

One of those killed at Manassas was Colonel Charles F. Fisher of the Sixth N.C. Regiment. He was formerly the president of the North Carolina R.R. and had been a friend of Colonel Fremont's. He had known Fisher before the war, both socially and through their railroad connection. In honor of his deceased associate, Fremont named one of the casemated gun batteries located at the mouth of the river for him. The name would endure and soon encompass the huge fortress which was said to be the largest earthenwork fort in the Confederacy.

By virtue of his rank and experience, Colonel Fremont was given charge for several months of the coastal defenses of the state. He remained in this capacity until returning to his railroad duties early in 1862. He retained the rank throughout the war, as it was felt that he would have to deal with army officers of equal rank.

As superintendent, Fremont realized there was a lot of work to be done. Men and munitions were still being rushed to Virginia. The sick, wounded and dead were being sent home, many of them by way of the W&W. Many of those soldiers that expired on the train or in the several hospitals in town were interred in Oakdale Cemetery.

Besides men, war materiel flowed in, so much so that the W&W refused to take any more freight at the depot because: "The warehouse and wharfs are all full, and [there is] no room to receive any more at present."[13] Wounded soldiers, prisoners and civilians still filled the cars heading south.

While his superintendent had been busy, President Ashe had not been idle. With the tensions of the times, he found it hard to stay away from politics

Machinists of the Wilmington & Weldon Railroad who lived in the city.
(photo courtesy of James Burke)

and was chosen as a delegate to the Democratic National Convention where he was to be nominated for vice president, but "the course of events at Charleston rendered it inexpedient...and in the crisis that followed he became one of the most urgent secessionists in North Carolina." Indeed, it was a telegram sent from Washington, D.C. by Ashe, to Wilmington's Committee of Safety that prompted the early capture of Forts Caswell and Johnston, at the mouth of the river. As their taking was premature, the forts were returned to the Federal government, only to be retaken when the state officially seceded.

Ashe offered his services to the Confederate government and was appointed a major in the Quartermaster Department. In 1862, with an office in Richmond, he was placed in charge of all rail transportation east of the Mississippi River. He traveled throughout the South, trying to solve existing problems and head off potential ones, using his expertise, both of politics and of the railroads. As unofficial field agents, he selected railroad men of known ability. At least two of these men, William Shaw and Stephen D. Wallace, were W&W employees. He sorted out a tie-up with the Virginia Central Railroad, suggested better ways to transport the wounded and again went south to try to obtain much-needed rolling stock (boxcars, flatcars and passenger coaches). He was not always successful. In Georgia, he came up against Governor Joe Brown who was incensed when Ashe attempted to seize some stock from the Western and Atlantic Road. As the State of Georgia owned the line, Ashe was turned down. Infuriated to think that the rolling stock would be impressed, Governor

Brown wrote to Richmond: "I shall certainly resist the impressments by force if necessary." Ashe's orders were quickly altered by his boss, Quartermaster General Abraham Myers, and he was instead sent on an inspection tour of Southern railroads. He continued to make recommendations and cost estimates for various connections.

Ashe now saw things from a different view. He advocated the building of the Piedmont Railroad from Danville, Virginia to Greensboro, N.C., something he had long fought against. North Carolina's Governor Zebulon B. Vance was the stumbling block against which the builders of the road had to contend. Vance felt that if it were built, Richmond would be more prone to abandon North Carolina's eastern line, the W&W. Most of Ashe's recommendations and requests went unheeded and he soon tired of the frustrations of his position. By the summer of 1862, he resigned from his Quartermaster duties in order to take a more active role in the war, desiring especially to drive the Yankees from their bases along the North Carolina coast.

Gov. Henry T. Clark

In a letter to President Davis, Ashe reiterated: "The imminent danger of our affairs in North Carolina requires that I should be at home…Therefore with your consent I will be absent from Richmond until the enemy ceases to give us alarm." He concluded, "I am willing to contribute to the defense of our State and our common country by raising a command of one or two Regiments…if the Government will arm and equip them."

Before he left Richmond, he visited General Robert E. Lee, who authorized Ashe to canvass the state in an attempt to acquire more arms for the troops in training camps. Lee wrote to General Theophilus Holmes: "I am informed by Major Ashe…that large numbers of country rifles and other arms can be collected in that State and I have directed him to get all that he can."

Upon his return to Wilmington, Ashe advertised in the local paper: "At the request of President Davis, I have been invested with authority to borrow, purchase, or, if necessary to impress them…I have also been requested to purchase old scrap iron."

Ashe's notice created quite a stir not only in Wilmington, but in Raleigh as well. A member of the N.C. House called upon President Davis to inquire if he had authorized "any person…in the State of North Carolina…to seize the private arms of the citizens."

Governor Henry T. Clark advised Ashe that: "Any attempt to seize the arms of our citizens is directly at variance with the Constitution…which makes it the duty of every citizen to keep and bear arms[.]" He continued: "To disarm a Country is the first step towards its subjugation. The spirit of a freeman is gone when he is not allowed to keep his arms…I want it understood in North Carolina that private arms – one for each man, cannot and shall not be seized."

Once again, Ashe was in hot water. Some firearms were gathered, but nothing near what General Lee required. One writer desired to contribute to the war effort by offering "about 100 lbs. of old castings, which I would like very much to have returned to the Yankees, in the shape of something different from their form at present."

In September of that year Ashe was at Wrightsville Sound where he was examining salt works he had just purchased. He received word that one of his sons, with Jackson's army, had been wounded and captured. He quickly made his way back to the depot at Wilmington where he commandeered a hand car. In company with several workers, he made his way up the track to his home at Rocky Point. He knew the southbound mail train had left Weldon some time before, but he was certain they could reach the North East siding before the mail train did. What he didn't know was that the train had experienced engine problems and had switched to a faster one recently purchased. Neither the new engine nor the hand car had headlights. Just south of the siding, the mail train smashed into the hand car, "picking it up on the cowcatcher."

Ashe's thigh was "dreadfully fractured" and his right foot literally crushed with the heel and toes torn away. Dragged nearly two hundred yards on the cowcatcher, his head was smashed against the ground and it was thought that he was surely dead. He was not.

"The others who were with Mr. Ashe…got off and escaped. He alone was hurt[.]" The next day, when he was finally found, he was unrecognizable. He was returned to Wilmington and was ministered to by the town's physicians, but to no avail. He lingered for several days but succumbed to his injuries on 14 September.

The war went on. At its inception, a naval blockade was hastily put together by the U.S. Navy. Flimsy and full of holes at first, it tightened with every ship placed on station. Most blockade runners got through in the early part of the war, but as more seacoast towns came under siege, it became more difficult for a runner to reach a Southern sanctuary.

Wilmington became a haven for blockade runners during the war: "Wilmington served as the port not only for the Ordnance Bureau vessels but for all east coast blockade runners operating under contracts with the Confederacy. It was also used by the vessels owned by the states of North Carolina, Virginia and Georgia, as well as private companies."[14]

The port was also the closest one available to the Army of Northern Virginia. By the summer of 1863, with it's three rail lines, Wilmington was probably the most important city in the southeast. The W&W was the most direct route to the fighting in Virginia. The Wilmington and Manchester ran into South Carolina through Florence to Manchester, near Kingsville, and connected with roads going south and west. The Wilmington, Charlotte and Rutherfordton, unfinished as it was, also contributed to the war effort by supplying food for Wilmington's denizens.

While it is dangerous to generalize, and realizing that at one time or another all carried cotton, naval stores, troops, shot and shell as well as passengers, the freights and cargoes of the three lines might be summarized as follows: the WC&R brought in cotton and food not only for the townspeople, but also fodder for the animals. The Eastern Division of the line ran west to within twelve and one-half miles east of Rockingham, but was then "broken" or incomplete. The Western Division picked up again at Charlotte, ran thirty-one miles to Lincolnton and was graded all the way to Shelby.

In December 1862, trains left Wilmington at six in the morning and arrived at Laurenburg a little after four in the afternoon. There the crews had dinner and then reboarded the train. They passed through "Old Hundred," so named because it was the one hundred mile mark from Wilmington and continued on to Rockingham.

One observant soldier complained in a letter: "Will some official of [the WC&R] explain why it costs more generally to go to any given point on the Road from Wilmington, than it does to return again from the same point to Wilmington."

The writer went on say that it cost $4.40 to go to Lumberton, but $4.30 to return. He questioned the discrepancy and ended by saying that he believed he had found the answer: "the Road must not be level, and that it requires a greater volume of steam to run up the Road than it does to return." Regardless of the difference in pricing, the road remained in business right up until General William T. Sherman came calling.

Interestingly, this road contained the longest, straightest stretch of track in the country: "A short distance west of Wilmington, a ruler must have been placed on Lumberton and for 78.86 miles, through a land of scrub oaks, pine barrens, forests and swamps, the rails were laid in a straight line. Recognized as the longest stretch of track without a curve in the United States, the nearest to it is a straight line of 71.94 miles on the Rock Island Lines[.]"

This road, which was intended to reach the rich cotton belt, would not be completed until after war's end. Towards the end of the conflict, the line became one of the few Southern "iron mines," with its rails taken up for use on other more important iron arteries. The road's president, war hero Robert H. Cowan, backed by Governor Vance, as well as Wilmington's Mayor John Dawson, thwarted the Confederate authorities several times in their attempts to confiscate the iron. In February 1864, Dawson penned a letter to Cowan, in which he said that the supply of provisions to the citizens of Wilmington, then on "short rations," did not come via the W&M, for that road was "almost entirely absorbed by the Confederate Government," while the W&W "runs through a section of country from which supplies are drawn for many other places besides [Wilmington]."

It was the WC&R that fed the town: "If your road is stopped it will be ruinous to the town. If it's capacity is diminished to any extent, to that extent the town is injured."

Regardless of the objections raised, Richmond finally prevailed. As the road fell within the definition of a "side line" because it did "not connect at one end with either a rail road, a navigable river or a densely settled place," laborers removed about ten miles of the much needed iron. The depot at Old Hundred became the end of the line. Thus the line had the rare distinction of being destroyed by both armies.

The second line, the W&M, ran westward from Eagles Island on the west bank of the Cape Fear, through Columbus County, through Florence, South Carolina, terminating at Kingsville, south of Columbia. This line brought in cotton from Georgia, South Carolina and states further south and shuttled troops southward when points further south were threatened.

The W&W carried troops, munitions and food for Lee's army, cotton and imported goods for the state, passengers and private freight. If blockade running is considered "the lifeline of the Confederacy," then surely the W&W must be considered an extension of that lifeline.[15] In the W&W annual report (November 1861) at the end of the first year of war, Superintendent Fremont touched upon a subject that would eventually erupt into a major problem. Friction was developing between the military authorities and the employees of railroads.

Fremont pointed out that: "if military officers…could for a moment appreciate the responsibility they assume, and the risk they take of crippling the operations of the government, as well as the extreme danger to life they are incurring by interfering with the regular running of trains, they would certainly leave that duty to the officers of the Companies, to whom it properly belongs."

In March 1862, General Lee issued an order making it clear that only railroad employees should operate trains "in accordance with the regulations and timetables of the company." It was perhaps Fremont's letter (4 February 1862) to Secretary of War Judah Benjamin in reference to a train commandeered by Colonel Wharton J. Green that helped set Lee's order in motion. Green, in command of the Second N.C. Battalion, had been ordered to Roanoke Island, which was being threatened with attack. After some delay in moving the battalion, Green ordered his men to board the train especially prepared to carry them toWeldon, where they would meet a train of the Seaboard & Roanoke Railroad, which would haul them to Portsmouth. From there they would board steamers for Roanoke Island.

Superintendent Fremont also took "the precaution, knowing the quartermaster would not do his duty, to telegraph to Portsmouth to have a train from that Road ready at Weldon for them. An accident to the wires delayed the

dispatch several hours, so that the train was not yet at Weldon when my train arrived."

Fremont continued: "Colonel Green compelled the train of this road to proceed onto Portsmouth without any notice to the trains on that Road and with an engineer and conductor that knew nothing of the timetables...of that Road... Fortunately the train that I had telegraphed for...was met at a station...Had these trains met in a curve both engines would have been ruined and many cars... destroyed."

Colonel Green arrived at Roanoke Island too late to help, but "quite in time" as he later said, "to be captured."

Col. Thomas Clingman

Later that month Fremont reported yet another instance of an army officer taking charge of a train. Colonel Collet Leventhorpe of the 34th N.C. had "on his arrival at Weldon ordered our agent...to open every coach for his men to sleep in or he would break them open. To save violence [the conductor] complied with the demand and the next day the cars were only fit to carry live hogs in beside various damages...Weldon is bad enough...but when men with arms in their hands and their skins full of whiskey are allowed to do what they please I must be excused from going there[.]"

He might have expected action from this missive as it was addressed to the then-Government Quartermaster at Richmond, Major William S. Ashe. The problem, however, would continue throughout the war.[16] The situation of army officers commandeering trains was but one of the myriad woes to beset the railroads of the Confederacy.

The following August (1862) Special Order No. 15 was issued by Brigadier General Thomas L. Clingman. It authorized his transportation agent take "the first R.R. Transportation, not already in the public service, that comes under his observation." That very month, President Davis addressed the Confederate Congress and hinted of a government takeover of the roads when he spoke of "the necessity for some legislation for controlling military transportation on the railroads and improving their present defective condition[.]"

Much of the "defective condition" of the roads was caused by the shortage of "T" rails. The shortage of iron became acute, as did a shortage of labor. The lack of an overall transportation system severely hampered the South, while the oft-times provincial and narrow-minded viewpoints of many of the railroad directors only exacerbated the problem. Interior lines of communication, whereby men and materiel could more quickly be shuttled from point to point, helped somewhat. The ingenuity of the South to compensate for equipment and materiel that was unavailable also helped, but in the end, neither could sustain the war-torn nation.

By 1861, North Carolina contained slightly less than 900 miles of track and came in fourth in mileage among Southern lines. Virginia had the most trackage of all the Southern states, with over 1,800 miles. The entire South had about 9,000 miles, some of differing gauge, which required unloading and reloading boxcars or troops. Added to this were the serious gaps between important lines.

Their Northern adversary boasted over 22,000 miles of lines. They had more engines; one northern road, the Pennsylvania Railroad, possessed 220 locomotives, which was more than the entire state of Virginia. The Federals had more of everything from boxcars, (one road had more than 4,000 cars, another 2,500) to employees.

The railroads of New York had nearly 7,000 workers. This figure is only slightly less than all the railroad men in the South.[17] The Confederate States of America had its work cut out for it, merely to sustain a war.

Early in 1862, with the Federal capture of Hatteras Island, the coastal town of New Bern was endangered, and fell in March of that year. This led to a mass exodus from that section of the state. Refugees flooded into Goldsboro, some remaining there, others continuing on to Wilmington or more distant points of safety.

Confederate troops made their stand at Kinston, holding firm until the end of the war, but the eastern sections (those near the rivers and sounds) continued to fall under Union domination, with the lands between them becoming a "no man's land." The Atlantic and North Carolina Railroad, which before the attack on Carolina's shore was one of the busiest lines in the state, was now much reduced in size. Unable to run into occupied territory, the road was fortunate enough to have evacuated much of its equipment and rolling stock. According to the line's master mechanic, "six locomotives and 57 box cars were sent up the North Carolina Railroad." Left behind were equipment and machinery which would be utilized by the Yankees as they rebuilt the road and strengthened their hold on the region. By 1862, now almost a railroad without a road, they were eyed as a source of iron when the Confederate Navy began to look around for the necessary plating for its ironclad program. Even Governor Vance suggested the Navy get its iron from the road and with about fifteen miles of track left, he proposed they take "all the iron on the railroad from Kinston to New Bern." The Road would continue to run trains east from Goldsboro to Kinston, but with an excess of coaches, boxcars, flat and cattle cars, the company made more money renting out the stock to the Confederate government and to other roads.[18]

Endnotes

1. Louis T. Moore Collection, Wilmington *Evening Post*, clipping dated 11 October 1947, New Hanover County Library, hereinafter cited as NHCPL. Fonvielle, *The Wilmington Campaign*, 19. See also the *Vance Papers*, 3:33-34, letter dated 23 February 1863, 21: 400-401, letters dated 18 and 28 December 1863; *Whiting Papers*, II:336, dated 25 July 1863. Much of the information about Sewall Fremont comes from the Dorothy Fremont Grant Collection, North Carolina State Archives, P.C. 1436. See also *The Papers of Zebulon Baird Vance,* ed. Frontis W. Johnson (Raleigh: State Department of Archives and History, 1963). It is doubtful that many men made their escape from conscription all the way to the enemy as the railroads were no longer connected.

2. *Daily Journal*, 1 January 1861; *Vance Papers*, 21: 339, letter dated 22 December 1863. Poisson remained with the W&W for some twenty years and was active in the local Masonic Lodge. He died on 15 August 1900, see the *Morning Star*, 16 August 1900. National Archives, *Citizens Papers*, 107: 345-346, letter dated 20 August 1863, also 107: 431-432, letter dated 9 October 1863. *Daily Journal*, 9 September 1863.

3. The steamers were named the *North Carolina, Governor Dudley, Gladiator* and the *Vanderbilt*. The *North Carolina* was sunk in 1840 when it rammed into the *Governor Dudley*, while the *Governor Dudley*, renamed the *Nellie*, saw service as a blockade runner. See Sprunt, *Chronicles*, 195.

4. *Daily Journal*, 4 November 1852. Sprunt, *Chronicles*, 150-152; Hugh Talmadge Lefler and Albert Ray Newsome, *North Carolina: The History of a Southern State* (Chapel Hill: UNC Press, 1963) 349.

5. Before the war, almost two-thirds of all turpentine manufactured in the United States came through either Fayetteville or Wilmington, Lefler and Newsome, *The History of a Southern State. Morning Star*, 19 July 1925. This article was

one of a series by Howard D. Dozier. Before "T" rails, the road installed "U"
rail. These too, gave out after a short time. See also Howard D. Dozier, *History
of the Atlantic Coast Line* (New York: Hart, Schafner and Marx, 1920) 86. *New
Berne Weekly Progress*, 6 December 1859. *Documents of the States of the
United States of America, 1860-1868*, hereinafter cited as *Documents of the
States*, Report of the Joint Select Committee on the Wilmington and Weldon
Railroad, Document no. 79, 2. Newsmen were especially favored for receiving
free passes and were expected in return, to give the road a favorable write-up.
"Deadheading" went on throughout the war; Governor Vance received such
treatment. See also *Tri-Weekly Commercial*, 29 December 1857, *New Berne
Weekly Progress*, 24 January 1860. The writer thanked "Col. S.L. Fremont...for
a complimentary ticket to pass over that road[.]" *Herald*, 10 November 1854; a
candidate for the presidency of the road was required to own at least twenty
shares of stock. For many years a share sold at $100. At war's end, the value
dropped to $45 per share (*Daily Dispatch*, 22 February 1866).
6. An 1856 attempt to include the N.C.R.R. in the "Through" passenger travel
network was rejected by that road. See the *Daily Journal*, 10 March 1856.
While in Congress, Ashe had eased the Road's import duty on "T" rails by
spreading the payments over several years. The money was deducted from "the
amounts due from the Post Office department, for carrying the mails." The duty
was eliminated before it was paid off, Sprunt, *Chronicles*, 152, 156.
7. Robert J. Cooke, *Lower Cape Fear Historical Society Bulletin*, hereinafter
cited as *LCFHS Bulletin* March 2001, "William Shepard Ashe." See also the
New York Times, 13 June 1859; *Proceedings of the Stockholders of the
Wilmington and Weldon R.R. Co.* (Wilmington: Fulton and Price, 1858) 3,
hereinafter cited as *Proceedings; Daily Journal*, 10 April 1854. Eugene Alvarez,
Travel on Southern Antebellum Rail roads, 1828-1860 (Mobile: University of
Alabama Press, 1974).
8. *Daily Journal*, 17 May 1860. Mrs. Brothers probably came from Flemington,
South Carolina, along the line of the Wilmington and Manchester Road, *Daily
Journal*, 21 March 1863. With war, the shed hosted quite a number of rallies as
troops passed through, "the depot shed...has become quite a grand reception
room[.]" See the *Raleigh Standard*, 1 May 1861 (quoting the *Wilmington
Herald*.)
9. *Tri-Weekly Commercial*, 29 December 1857, it is likely the writer also
received a few free passes for his article. The covered bridges were at Smith's
Creek, North East, Goldsboro, Rocky Mount, Contentnea Creek and Fishing
Creek. See *Proceedings,* 1858 and 1888.
10. "Frank Patterson's Diary," Pender County Historical Society, Burgaw, N.C.
Bob Johnson and Charles S. Norwood, *The History of Wayne County, N.C.*
(Goldsboro: Wayne County Historical Association, 1979) 144-146, 162. See

also William Howard Russell, Eugene H. Berlanger, ed. *My Diary, North and South* (Louisiana State University: New Orleans, 2001) 77-78.

11. *Daily Journal*, 11 May 1861. As the soldiers were from Georgia, it is possible they were the same troops that almost lost their lives in the attempted sabotage at Tossnot Creek several days earlier.

12. *Herald*, 24 April 1861. Mrs. Bolles' [Reston] memoirs are located in the N.C. State Archives, Raleigh, N.C., box 44-5. In 1864, Mr. Reston, a lieutenant colonel in the militia, tried to get out of drills due to his bank duties, see Bradley, *North Carolina Militia and Home Guard Records*, I: 110, entry no. 1426. Berlanger, *My Diary*, 79. As Russell passed through Wilmington, he saw at the wharf: "quantities of shot and shell. 'How came they here?' I inquired. 'They're anti-abolition pills,' said my neighbor, 'they've been waiting here for two months back but now that Sumter's taken, I guess they won't be wanted.' " *ORA*, I: 47, 200.

13. *Daily Journal*, 8 June 1861. *The Papers of John W. Ellis*, Noble J. Tolbert, ed., (Raleigh: State Department of Archives and History, 1964) II: 603. Angus James Johnson, *Virginia Railroads in the Civil War* (Chapel Hill: University of North Carolina Press, 1961) 32. One ambulance car remained at the Richmond depot for a time as an early "war bond" effort and was hailed as "most complete and elegant." It had been completed in Wilmington in August 1861, see the *Daily Journal*, 27 July and 14 September 1861. Throughout that summer, Fremont was wiring news of troop movements to President Davis. See *The Papers of Jefferson Davis*, Lynda Laswell Crist, ed. (Baton Rouge: Louisiana State University Press, 1995) 7, 192. Fremont resigned his command of the eastern defenses 27 February 1862. Cargo was again being taken by early October, see the *Daily Journal*, 19 September and 2 October 1861.

14. *Encyclopedia of the Confederacy*, Richard M. Current, ed. (New York: Simon and Shuster, 1993) 1726. *Wilmington Journal*, 23, September 1862; *Raleigh Register*, 17 September 1862.

15. The W&M was built with a five-foot gauge, hence W&W cars could not be sent over that road. North Carolina State Archives, *Papers of John D. Whitford*, Private Collections, box 89-4, "Circular" 12 September 1862. *Daily Journal*, 4 march, 23 December 1863; *Vance Papers*, 22: 145, letter dated 10 February 1864; "Robeson County's First Railroad", author unknown, copy in the Wilmington Railroad Museum. Dozier, *History of the Atlantic Coast Line*, 110-111.

16. *ORA*, IV: 127 and 1011. National Archives, "Letters Received by the Confederate Secretary of War," microfilm no. M437, 3:108-110, letter dated 4 February 1862, 29:47, letter dated 26 February 1862. *Confederate Veteran* (Wilmington: Broadfoot Publishing Company, 1989), 18:484 (1910).

17. North Carolina State Archives, Whitford Papers, box 89-4. William J. Miller and Brian C. Pohanka, *An Illustrated History of the Civil War* (Alexandria:

Time-Life Books, 2000) 48. Robert C. Black III, *The Railroads of the Confederacy* (Chapel Hill: The University of North Carolina Press, 1998) 3, 20-21. The date of Davis' address was 18 August 1862. Even the State of North Carolina threatened to take over the railroads, see the *Daily Journal*, 4 December 1862.

18. *ORA*, I:9, 472. The day after New Bern fell, the W&W prepared to haul over one thousand men, several pieces of artillery and a few hundred horses. Unfortunately, it was a case of too little, too late. See the Whitford Papers, box 89-4. *Crossties Through the Carolinas*, compiled by John W. Gilbert (Raleigh: he Helios Press, 1969). Gilbert mistakenly identifies E.J. Clayton as the Master Mechanic, it is more likely he was an engineer; T.J. Hudson was the Master Mechanic of this road, see *Documents of the States of the United States of America, Session of 1866-67*, document no. 24, page 218. From January 1863 to 31 May 1864, the A&NC made nearly $130,000 transporting troops and government freight.

A Civil War-era lathe

An engine of the type the Wilmington & Weldon Railroad would have used.

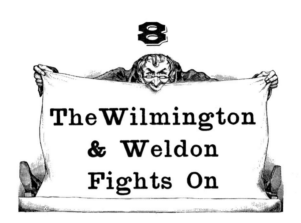

The Wilmington & Weldon Fights On

The Wilmington and Weldon Railroad was among the first to rent the rolling stock of the almost-defunct Atlantic Road, but it was not only rolling stock that was needed. In mid-June 1863, Major General Whiting, District Commander in North Carolina, borrowed (seized might be a better term) a lathe for the use of the mechanics reinforcing "the very defective guns which constituted the armament of this very important place." The lathe, taken from the Manassas Gap Railroad, was used by Whiting to band cannons which were to be emplaced in the defense of Wilmington. Superintendent Hugh Rice of the Manassas Gap Road had relocated his company's workshops to Raleigh, then to Clayton and finally to Greensboro. Shortly after settling in to his new location, he requested the return of his "all important" lathe, but Whiting, not quite done with it, turned down his request.

Rice then began a letter-writing campaign to Governor Vance and to the War Department in Richmond. Vance contacted Whiting about the equipment, who responded by informing the executive that the lathe had been impressed by the order of the Secretary of War and that several weeks had been consumed in simply "supplying the deficient parts of the lathe and the machinery to make it… the difficulty of procuring bands from Richmond delayed us." This answer is somewhat dubious, since when the lathe was taken, it was described as "One large Driving Wheel Lathe with counter-shafting Pulleys, etc., complete."

Whiting also informed the governor that he had ordered a new lathe from abroad, but it had not yet come through the blockade. As soon as it did, he would return Rice's lathe. In October, Confederate Quartermaster General A. R.

Lawton, wrote to Whiting that the lathe had originally been requested for only six weeks and was now needed by the Navy Department, the Quartermaster's Department and the Piedmont Railroad. As late as January 1864, Whiting still possessed the machine, and was now fending off the Tredegar Iron Works, which also sought the lathe. Presumably after a delay of more than six months. Rice got his lathe back, for there were no more letters to Richmond or Raleigh.

The year 1861 brought war and want to North Carolina.[1] 1862 brought little relief. While there had been an initial drop in regular civilian passenger travel, it was more than made up by transporting troops and war materiel. In his 1861 report to the stockholders, the superintendent pointed out that in 1860, receipts from "through travel" garnered over $133,000. By 1861, it was up to $195,000. Much of the increase was, of course, from moving troops for the Confederate government. As Confederate currency had not yet lost its value to inflation, this was one of the most profitable years for the Road in terms of buying power. The board of directors declared an eleven percent dividend. Profits, on paper at least, would continue to climb through the war years: in 1864, gross receipts reached a startling $3,010,039. Even though expenditures continued to rise, the profit for that year was still more than one million dollars in depreciating Confederate currency.

But many problems remained. With conscription in 1862, fewer men were available for work. Eventually the government would only allow one man per mile of track, which was the bare minimum.[2] As early as the end of 1861,

Maintaining railways was a labor intensive task made harder by the scarcity of men to do it.

the Road advertised for: "Laborers, Train Hands, Firemen, Blacksmiths, Strikers and Carpenters." The men were to be "Able bodied Negroes of good character," and owners along the line were given preference in the hiring of slaves.[3] The problem of laborers, both skilled and unskilled, vexed all Southern roads throughout the war.

Worn out, or "laminated" rails that became slick with wear was a major problem as well. There was an arrangement with the Tredegar Iron Works of Richmond whereby that company would also repair the rails of the W&W, but even Fremont realized, "The iron works of the South are too much occupied with army work to admit of such improvements at this time." Part of the problem of the Southern foundries stretched back to pre-war days when much of the manufacture of iron ceased due to "competition with richer areas in Pennsylvania."

The W&W was a little better off than most roads, because of a judicious purchase made in 1857 of a machine for repairing rails. This machine would prove invaluable during the war. Fremont acknowledged this and added that four forges were thusly kept busy. In his 1861 report, he indicated that the motive power of the Road was sufficient for passenger traffic in the upcoming year and felt that the freight engines, "when fully repaired and in good order," would suffice. He did, however, make a request for thirty additional boxcars, the number necessary to carry them through 1862. In reality, the Road could have used one hundred more cars. That is the number the Road asked for at a railroad convention at the end of 1862.

In 1861 the cost of lubricating materials, the oil, tallow and waste, had gone up. By war's end these products would become virtually nonexistent throughout the Confederacy, or were priced so high as to make them unavailable to many railroads.

Still, the W&W was slightly more fortunate than other roads. Take for example the Tennessee roads. They suffered depredations at the hands of Unionists who burned bridges and tore up track. The W&W had minor incidents, even before the state left the Union. In anticipation of secession, sabotage was attempted on the line. Fremont noted that at Tossnot Creek "some miscreant attempted to precipitate a train containing Confederate troops [from Georgia] into the Creek...by cutting down in part the trestle culvert at that point; fortunately the train passed over without accident."

The telegraph wires had also been severed and one young citizen of Wilmington recorded: "There is a rumor in town...that the up train...containing troops for Virginia in crossing a bridge near Wilson, produced such an effect that the engineer and passengers were induced to make an examination, when it was discovered that some cold-blooded scoundrel had sawed one of the timbers of the trestle-work...entirely through, and that it was barely sustained by the iron bolts on each side."

The writer went on to say that tracks had been discovered and followed to a nearby home. The occupant was questioned, found guilty and hung on the spot. Such actions might have been expected at that section of the line as many Quakers lived in the area and some homes were thought to be stops on the Underground Railroad.

It was unexpected when sabotage struck closer to home: "[A] similar attempt was made at Smith's Creek Bridge, by boring the stringers in two; this

Capt. John Lucas Cantwell, CSA

also failed…and though a reward was offered for the discovery of the fiend who was thus willing to trifle with human life, yet no certain information of the perpetrator has been received."[4]

The concern about bridges was real. In addition to watchmen at the bridges, the W&W Railroad Guards were mustered into service to guard the vital line. The guard company, numbering about 100 men, was originally raised by Stephen D. Wallace as early as August 1861, and by the end of the year was commanded by Captain John Lucas Cantwell. Most of the men came from the counties bordering the rail line. They were officially mustered into the army on 25 January 1862. They had the responsibility of guarding the railroad bridges from Weldon south to the South Carolina border, which included several bridges of the Wilmington and Manchester railroad. Designated the 13th Battalion and headquartered at Wilmington, small units were sent out along the line. Quite often consisting of nothing more than a Corporal's guard, certainly never more than ten or fifteen, the men were really simply watchmen paid by the state. As the war progressed, some of the men were transferred to the 51st N.C. Regiment. By mid-1863, the unit's existence was threatened when it was ordered to Virginia. Lieutenant Eugene F. Gilbert responded by reminding Richmond that the men had been enlisted for "local defense and special duty." That issue was gotten around by having the men mustered out and then reenlisted. By October 1863, the company was transferred to the 66th N.C. Regiment, with their bridge-guarding days long behind them.

In July1862, with the resumption of fighting around Richmond, the railroads again carried troops to and from the battlefields. As many wounded soldiers made their way from the carnage in Virginia, a "Wayside" hospital was established at Wilmington. Part of the W&W's huge depot, built on the wharf in 1856, was converted to accept the sick and wounded passing through town. The depot was the logical place for a hospital. A change of trains was necessary at this point and it minimized moving the men: "Cots have been fitted up, baths arranged, with all the other appliances of cleanliness and comfort, and a proper person engaged to take care of the establishment. We further learn that many – very many – of the ladies of Wilmington, deserve more than praise for their kind and generous attention to the wants of the soldiers…The soldiers say that this is the first point where such provision is found on the whole route from Richmond[.]"

The onus of caring for the troops was thrust upon the citizens of Wilmington. Most of the soldiers were transported at night, passing most stations in the wee hours of the morning. Telegrams from Weldon alerted the ladies of the "Soldier's Aid Society" to prepare for a certain number of soldiers and what time they would arrive. Here they would get a good meal, be bathed, have their wounds checked and bandages changed. Many of the town's citizens

Southern ladies offered comfort to war-bound soldiers along the rail lines.

came to the depot upon the arrival of a train, the ladies to help feed and nurse the wounded, the men to assist in carrying the men from the cars, while the army doctors and town's physicians attended to the injured. Troops being shuttled from one point to another sometimes found that their train from town had been cancelled. This meant that Wilmington had to feed and house them until they could continue on their way.

In winter, with a lull in the fighting, the Wayside Hospital was returned to the use of the Road and was even used as troop quarters. When the battle season began, it was again reopened as a hospital.

As more and more fighting went on, the W&W announced that it would send to Richmond, "each and every Thursday," one additional boxcar filled with "all manner of supplies for the relief of our sick and wounded soldiers[.]" The WC&R also offered solace by sending a car to Wilmington to join with the W&W effort. The train would stop at several depots along the way to pick up all kinds of donations, from farm products to clothing. Aboard the train, to ensure the items got to where they were supposed to, was usually a minister or other esteemed citizen.

The first train was an overwhelming success. Many of the items donated had to be left for a later train. Loaded with fruits, hospital supplies, clothing, wine and livestock, which included pigs, sheep and lambs, the cars made their way to their intended recipients. As the man who rode with the train, Mr. Patrick Murphy quickly found it was a mistake to put chickens and other livestock in the same car as the vegetables. It was suggested by the Reverend Mr. J.L. Pritchard, who accompanied the next shipment, that another car be added to accommodate the donations.

Rev. John Lamb Pritchard

This being done, there was still not enough room for all the supplies donated. In July, the *Petersburg Express* noted: "We observed...at the Southern depot, a car load of fowls, eggs, etc., which had been brought in from North Carolina and destined for the hospitals in Richmond. For yards around we could hear the crying of the chickens and singing of the hens and crowing of the roosters. What a treat they will be for the invalid soldiers." The donations continued into August, but were soon halted because Wilmington itself needed medical supplies.[5]

In the summer of 1862, yellow fever struck Wilmington. Everything quickly shut down and the town became isolated. The telegraph office was moved out of town because an "immune" could not be found to operate it. Many businesses were forced to close their doors, including virtually all the druggists. No visitors were allowed in and train service was severely curtailed. To avoid needless deaths among his workers, Fremont moved the shops and offices to Magnolia, about fifty miles above town.

By the end of November, when the disease abated, things were almost back to normal, but until then there was only one daily train. Probably a mail train would have also brought a freight car along, but there were no workers to unload the cargoes. Freight began to build up at the depot and as the crisis worsened, even the mail train ceased to enter the town.[6]

To help, the Road announced it would not charge for any "contributions for the sick and needy[.]" In addition, the Superintendent requested agents at the various depots to "exert themselves to send in fresh vegetables, chickens, eggs and the like, either as donations or for sale." Surrounding towns refused admittance to any one from the afflicted city and trade ceased. Cargo began to pile up at the worst possible time. The crops of the eastern counties were being harvested and it was imperative that they be gotten out of that section before Yankee raiders could desolate the area. The pileup of freight and consequent complaints began at this time and lasted throughout the war.

Other complaints were registered against the railroad. It was said that corn and cotton, among other things, were being delayed. Answering his critics later that year, Fremont admitted that his Road could not handle the needs of both the military and civilians. In a letter to the *Journal*, he indicated that the Road had carried 100,000 troops throughout the year and at times foodstuffs took a back seat when it came to transportation.

The forwarding of corn and cotton would present major problems to the Road, problems which many times took the form of complaints from high Confederate officials, including Governor Vance. Fremont insisted that the Road had not been insensitive to the town's plight and pointed out that they had given free space for medical supplies and food, as well as having collected donations from the Road's agents.

In June 1863, when General Whiting learned that the North East Railroad, which ran from Charlotte into South Carolina, was said to be carrying "the cotton of private parties engaged in running the blockade, in advance of, & to the exclusion of the government cotton," he wrote to that Road's president and warned him that if "a single bale of [government] cotton" remained at Florence, he would not permit any cars of that Road to come to Wilmington. He further stated that if any rolling stock was found to be in town "in violation of the above order" he would take it and use it to transport government freight.[7]

Also delayed that winter was the annual W&W shareholder meeting. Usually held in November, the directors pushed the date back to December, because there was no quorum of stockholders left in town. Rescheduling would allow more time for the shareholders to return, as well as letting the epidemic run its course. One soldier traveling on the rails at this time reported that he "returned to Wil. N.C. to find almost a deserted town…[and that he] came in train…with only S.D. Wallace, President W&W RR."[8]

It is likely that Stephen Wallace was returning to attend the shareholder's meeting. At that meeting, he was officially elected president of the Road to succeed William Ashe, who had been killed in September. Elected Treasurer was J. W. Thompson, to replace James S. Green, a long-time officer who had succumbed to yellow fever. The report to the stockholders, issued 11 December "congratulated the company that its road so far had been free from the incursions of the enemy. This cause for congratulations was removed two days later when the enemy attacked the road." Earlier that year, in November, Union General John G. Foster, in command of the Federals at New Bern, led 5,000 men, along with nearly two dozen artillery pieces, in a raid from Washington, N.C. through Williamston and Hamilton to within ten miles of Tarboro.

Hearing locomotive whistles throughout the day, Foster was led to believe Tarboro was being reinforced and withdrew to New Bern. What he didn't know was that it was a hoax. The whistles he heard were from only one train, being repeatedly run back and forth into town.[9] Very little was accomplished by the raid, although the green Federal troops got their first taste of combat.

The next month, the general left New Bern once more, this time with 10,000 troops, 40 pieces of artillery and 640 cavalrymen. The target this time was the W&W railroad bridge across the Neuse at Goldsboro.

Foster's raid was coordinated with General Ambrose Burnside's attack at Fredericksburg, Virginia. A naval attack on Wilmington by the U.S. Navy, it was hoped, would pin the forces there and prevent aid from that quarter. Destroying the bridge at Goldsboro would also prevent help from the Army of Northern Virginia. In any event, it was determined that the monitors that were to take part in the attack drew too much water to pass the sand bars at the mouth of the Cape Fear River.

Foster, after moving out on 11 December and following the Trent River, pushed on to Kinston. At Southwest Creek he met resistance, but after a short skirmish, drove the Confederates back towards the Neuse River.

Confederate General Nathan G. ("Shanks") Evans took command and dug in a few miles before Kinston. Another battle ensued, this one lasting for several hours, with the result of Evan's men retreating beyond Kinston. The town was now at the mercy of the Federals, who thoroughly devastated the place. Early on the morning of 16 December, Foster was at Whitehall, where he received news of Burnside's defeat in Virginia.

At Whitehall, another fight began, with almost the same results. Union troopers routed the Confederates and after partially destroying an ironclad, the *CSS Neuse*, advanced towards their final objective, the W&W railroad bridge.

After leaving Whitehall, Foster detached several companies of the Third New York Cavalry down the track to Mount Olive and Everettsville. They later reported: "On leaving the main column we pressed rapidly on...and after a gallop of over four miles, came out at the station at 3 P.M. This action was a perfect surprise to the people of the place. The agent was selling tickets; passengers were loitering around waiting for the cars, the mail for Wilmington lay ready on the platform, and a few paroled prisoners were in readiness to go to Wilmington, probably to fight again."

Charging into the depot at Mount Olive, the raiders surprised the stationmaster, Lemuel W. Kornegay, along with other citizens who were awaiting the southbound train. The telegraph wire was cut and everyone unfortunate enough to be at the station was placed under arrest and tied up to prevent their escaping and sounding the alarm.[10]

Gen. John G. Foster, USA

Detachments of cavalry and pioneers (colored troops) were sent further south to tear up as much track as they could. The *Journal* reported: "The enemy burned the two culverts on each side of the Goshen Swamp trestle work... seriously damaged the trestle-work itself, and tore up some two hundred yards of the track in one place and about seventy yards in another, or rather they made the railroad negroes do it."

The southbound mail train, with conductor E.D. Browning in charge, had left Goldsboro, and while making its way towards Mount Olive, according to the *Journal*, "the fact of something being wrong was noticed and the train was rapidly backed to Goldsboro where the alarm was given."

Actually what Browning saw was a column of bluecoats waiting in ambush. They had unlimbered a fieldpiece and began firing at the train, "and put three shells into [it] before the engineer could back it out of range."

The Federals remained in the area for two days, making further forays to Dudley Station, where they burned the water tank and tore up yet more track. Upon their return to Mount Olive, they lit large bonfires upon which the rails were thrown. After setting the depot aflame, "outside Mount Olive, they burned a plantation house and then moved on."[11]

Foster's main column had, on 17 December, almost reached their goal. The bridge across the Neuse was defended by three Confederate regiments, but the Union army was quick to attack and pushed back one of the regiments, the 52nd N.C. They now had a toehold on the approach to the bridge. Artillery on both sides raked the area, but Lieutenant George Graham, of the Twenty-Third New York Battery, was able to reach cover behind the structure and coolly set the bridge afire.

"Just as the bridge began to catch fire, cheers were heard from the rebel side of the river. A train had just arrived, bearing part of General James J. Pettigrew's brigade as reinforcements…The Union battery…quickly repositioned itself…the Confederate train was the most tempting target they had ever seen…The rebel train carried not only troops, but also an iron-plated 'monitor' car that began lobbing shells [at the Yankees.] But on this occasion the Yankee gunners were better, and their third shot blew up the train's boiler."[12]

When he saw the bridge burning fiercely and heard the report of fresh rebel troops arriving, Foster decided he had pushed his luck far enough. Another deciding factor was that his men were fast running out of ammunition. By 21 December, Foster's men were safely ensconced back in New Bern. Foster considered the raid a great success; after all, he had accomplished his main goal. The railroad bridge was out of service and in addition they had burned a few railroad buildings and torn up track in several places. They had also brought back many "contrabands" (freed slaves) and had destroyed much of the crops throughout the area.

The *Journal* reported: "During the recent raid of the enemy…their conduct was gratuitously evil and wantonly barbarous…Many plantations were stripped of servants, horses, pigs, cattle, meat, and, in fact, everything that could be either carried off or destroyed. The number of negroes taken off is estimated at 500…With the single exception of the burning of the Neuse bridge, the injury to the Wilmington and Weldon Railroad is very slight, and the attempted destruction of the track was done in a most bungling manner. Even the burning of the Goshen bridge and trestle was not half done[.]"[13]

Colonel Fremont was quick to ride to the scene and pronounced that the damage to the road could be repaired in two days, while the bridge would be

rebuilt in about a week. Fortunately for the Confederates, a new unit of
Pontiliers (bridge builders) had recently been formed and these men were
quickly put on the job, building a pontoon bridge across the gap. Travelers were
run up close to the temporary structure and walked across the pontoon bridge to
board a waiting train on the other side. The Road was back in normal operation
before the new year. The *Richmond Daily Dispatch* summed up the feeling by
reporting: "The cars are running on the Wilmington Railroad to Neuse
River...Foster came far with a large force to accomplish little." [14]

One unforeseen result of the Union raid was the effect it had on the local
populace. Citizens began to question whether the Road could be defended
against such forays. It was realized that the railroad guards were not up to the
task of preventing enemy cavalry from striking at nearly any point on the Road.
More troops were desperately needed if the railroad was to be protected.

At a meeting of the North Carolina railroads, held in Goldsboro shortly
after the fall of New Bern in 1862, it was resolved that the several lines would
all contribute enough rolling stock to enable "a large body of troops...in the
shortest possible time" to be transferred to any endangered spot in the state.
Some ten thousand troops were to be kept at Goldsboro, ready to be sent either
north or south, as needed. Most of the companies promised to send at least one
engine and several cars. The W&W was to provide two engines, as was the
A&NC, and 40 cars, while side lines, such as the WC&R could only afford to
contribute one engine.

Relegated to state service, these trains were often used to transport more
than troops. Governor Vance used them to move cotton and corn from various
points of the interior to wherever they were needed. Also included in the
Goldsboro resolutions were the charges (.03 cents per mile for each car) when a
"foreign" train was run on another company's tracks. The last resolution was an
important one. Every attendee, which included the Virginia roads of the
Seaboard and Roanoke and Petersburg, had to "pledge itself to return to the same
Road to which it belongs, with the most convenient dispatch" any borrowed
stock. It became readily apparent that any borrowed stock was not being
repaired or maintained and indeed, was sometimes used as movable warehouses.

While Confederate troops may have thwarted yet another foray in April
1863, the men assembled at Goldsboro were not available when the Yankees
struck Warsaw in July. While the Battle of Gettysburg raged in Pennsylvania,
about 650 Unionists, comprised of cavalry and artillery, were dispatched from
New Bern on 3 July. Again their target was the W&W railroad. Dividing his
force after scattering enemy pickets at Hallsville, the Union commander,
Lieutenant Colonel George Lewis, sent one column on rapidly towards

Kenansville. Taking the town by surprise, the horsemen "completely dispersed a company of cavalry," captured quite a few prisoners and "nearly all their horses and equipment and arms[.]"

It was to Kenansville that proprietor Louis Froelich had relocated his sword factory from Wilmington early in 1863. The move was made in large part because the latter town was thought to be the next target for a major Federal assault. Lewis later reported proudly: "The Confederates had established an armory and saddle manufactory at [Kenansville], both of which I destroyed, burning the former, with a large quantity of sabers, saber bayonets, knives, and all kinds of arms of that description[.]"

Lewis also laid waste to any stores found, including bacon, flour and corn. After resting his troopers for the night, they arose before dawn and moved on to the "nearest point on the [W&W]," Magnolia. Being informed that the place was garrisoned by no less than a brigade with some artillery, Lewis opted to shift the focus of his attack to the depot at Warsaw. Arriving at the depot in the early morning, the men of the Third New York Cavalry cut the telegraph wires and began tearing up the track. Led by Captain H.W. Wilson, this work was again performed by pioneers, men of the First N.C. Colored Regiment. The depot and warehouses were completely demolished, as they too were filled with about 15,000 pounds of bacon, flour and corn. Also caught in the destructive path of the cavalry raiders were nearly 1,000 barrels of tar and turpentine and at least one passenger car.

Withdrawing and making his way back to New Bern, in his official report Lewis wrote that his men had torn up "between 3 and 4 miles in both directions" but engineer Wilson reported that "the cavalry gangs were not properly organized...the result of which was getting only four gangs to work... twisting less than 50 rails...breaking up less than one-quarter of a mile of track." Wilson's men were using new tools designed by Union Colonel Herman Haupt. Just to bend the iron wasn't enough. It could be straightened and reused. These special tools rendered the twisted track unusable. To be used again the rails would have to be melted down and recast.

Except for the loss of stores, the damage to the railroad was minimal. Superintendent Fremont visited the site and reported, "The track will be repaired today, as I have a large force. The train will pass as usual to-morrow morning." Still, Fremont had cause to worry. He had moved not only his office and shops of the road to Magnolia, just a short distance from Warsaw, but his family was there as well. The very next day, Confederate Major John Whitford was telegraphing the Governor Vance that a "train of cotton left [Goldsboro] 10 A.M. for Wilmington."

Even as Whitford was advising the Governor, U.S. General Foster was notifying Secretary of War Edwin M. Stanton that, as soon as his raiding party returned, he intended to send them out again "to cut the railroad farther north,

between Goldsboro and Weldon." This he did towards the end of July.[15]
Citizens along the road began to realize the road could never be successfully
defended.

One writer asked: "How is it that the Abolitionists, with five or six
hundred men, are allowed to make raids through Eastern Carolina…without
receiving [a] check, or no demonstration…to impede their progress."

That was the question on everyone's mind when Union forces made
another raid on 20 July. As outlined by General Foster, the force, this time
consisting of at least two infantry regiments, several cavalry companies and
"two sections of mountain howitzers," hit Greenville and then split up, with one
column going for the railroad bridge over the Tar River at Rocky Mount.
Another moved on to Tarboro, where "an iron-clad on the stocks was found" and
burned. Also consigned to the flames were some boxcars, at least 100 bales of
cotton, quartermaster and ordnance stores. Intrepid Major Jacobs of the Third
N.Y. Cavalry volunteered to move on to Rocky Mount and attack the bridge.
Advancing swiftly, he captured a train of cars on the track. The credit actually
went to Private George A. White of the 3rd N.Y. He "sprang from his horse, and,
jumping upon a passenger train in motion…placed his revolver at the head of the
engineer, reversed the engine, and brought back the train."

Several Confederates aboard were taken prisoner and Jacobs
successfully completed his mission by firing the railroad bridge, trestle-work
(over 750 feet he estimated) and the county bridge. The bridge guards, said by
one account to number between fifteen and twenty, were no match for the Union
cavalry and, it was hoped, "retired in good order." At least one Federal was
injured when he tried to put out a fire on a boxcar. The car exploded and he was
blown from the car and badly burned.

Jacob's men also destroyed the cotton mill owned by William S. Battle.
The mill, six stories high and located at the falls of the Tar River, was said to be
the second oldest in the state. It supplied yarn to the people of eastern North
Carolina and South Side Virginia. In addition to the mill, the gin and gristmill
were demolished, but when the raiders started to apply the torch to the Battle
residence, the superintendent of the mill appealed to the commanding officer.
Because the superintendent was a northerner, the officer was persuaded to spare
the home.

The overseer of the Battle plantation, surmising that the Yankees would
relish in destroying farm property, organized a caravan of some thirty-four carts
and wagons, loaded them with meats and other provisions and sent them into
hiding. They were nearly all hidden when suddenly Union cavalry galloped into
view and captured the entire convoy.

"[T]he mules were cut from their traces, the vehicles with meat and
other supplies piled into a huge heap and burned…The drivers were taken off by
the troops and carried to New Bern."

The Union cavalry was hotly pursued and "a considerable number of Negroes[,] horses and other plunder & a few prisoners" were taken. The main force was able to effect an escape back to the safety of their coastal enclave.

By this point of the war, Superintendent Fremont kept a large work force on hand. He had applied to General Whiting to exempt nearly one hundred black laborers from working on the surrounding fortifications and likely used these men to immediately begin the necessary repairs. By 21 July, the day following the raid, Fremont had re-laid the track to the ruined bridge and was awaiting a shipment of pontoon boats to construct a temporary span. The Governor was informed that: "this afternoon will see connection again over the river but not for trains."

Again the cry was heard "Have we not any security that any point... may [we] not be raided upon at almost any time?"

Governor Vance heard directly from William Battle: "I feel constrained by my feelings to a few lines to express to you my deep mortification at the... Yankee raid on Rocky Mount on Monday. The loss to this portion of the state is at least two millions of dollars, burnt up & carried off. Can no arrangement be made with the Confederate or by the State Government to arrest such raids?"

Battle went on to advise the Governor that: "I have in my own mind raised the Black Flag & intend fighting on my own hook, & will ask no quarter & show no quarter. I will not take prisoners nor be taken prisoner. I need not say more[.]" If the line could not be defended, Battle suggested it be abandoned.

The superintendent had some semblance of service restored by the following week. Trains were again brought to the river's edge, passengers disembarked and walked across the bridge to board another train waiting for them. An ad run by the W&W advised that only light freight could be sent via this route, heavier freight would have to be transshipped at Goldsboro to the North Carolina Road. By 1 August, the bridge was fully repaired and trains once more rumbled up and down the line.

By this point of the war, Fremont had seen enough of Union cavalry raids. He told General Whiting: "It seems to me General, that the time has fully arrived for the Government to take some efficient steps to defend the line of this road, if the road...is to be maintained...We want 1,000 cavalry along the line... and then we can maintain our line; otherwise not."[16]

The pontoons that had been pressed into hasty service were originally intended for Richmond and at least one quartermaster, Major Mason Morfit, was quite upset with Fremont. He wrote to President S. D. Wallace that "your Supt. Mr. S.L. Fremont has again shown himself in small colors. Last Sunday he had the effrontery to ask the Adjt. Genl. to order a Petersburg train to go forty miles on his road for pontoons, for which he had no excuse for not hauling on his own cars[.]" Morfit continued his diatribe, stating that Fremont, after shipping the rest of the boats in his own cars, "had the meanness to get Genl. Whiting's order not to send [the cars] further" than Weldon.

Fremont, it must be supposed, fumed when he read Morfit's letter. He sent it on to Quartermaster General Alexander Lawton, along with a letter of explanation. He thought Morfit's words "ungentlemanly and unofficer-like," that he would not "submit to such slanderous official communications" and closed by asking for an official investigation into the matter. He added that the major's interference had caused a delay in sending ordnance to Charleston.

In his response, Lawton noted "the tone and temper of Major Morfit's letters or such as, cannot be permitted and he will be informed of the intemperance of his conduct." Lawton also noted: "the attention of the Secretary of War is...called to the serious consequences which may result from the control which General Whiting assumes over the Rail Roads in N. Carolina." Differences of opinion would surface many times during the war between quartermasters and railroad men.

There was at least one more repercussion of the Union raid. The W&M railroad was transporting a quantity of heavy guns from Charleston to Richmond, but had run "off the tracks somewhere between Florence and Wilmington. Depot quartermaster Styron, at Wilmington, was notified of the accident by the messenger who had been traveling with the cargo. He tried his best to get things moving again, but, as he reported, it was difficult to get space on any trains due to the "heavy accumulation of government Goods...arriving through the blockade...The means of transportation being limited," he was forced to break up the shipment. While "one or two of the guns" got to Weldon, most of them remained at Wilmington. It was at that point that the Yankees struck the road, forcing a halt to all freight. When the road was repaired, the guns in Wilmington were immediately forwarded, but the guns at Weldon were unaccompanied and were sent back to Wilmington.

Confusion, or the "fog of war," was hard at work.[17]

Endnotes

1. The information on Rice's lathe can be found in the *Vance Papers*, 18:850-851, letter dated 20 July 1863, 19: 137, letter dated 11 August 1863; *Whiting Papers*, II:336, entry dated 28 October 1863 and 14 January 1864. See also http://www.csa.railroads.com, letters dated 16 June and 22 October 1863. The Piedmont Road was to be built between Greensboro and Danville, Virginia.
2. *Daily Journal*, 28 November and December 1861. The *Journal* of 28 November reprinted the Annual Report. During the war, private travel actually increased when compared to pre-war numbers.
3. *Daily Journal*, 18 December, 1861.

4. Lefler and Newsome, *The History of a Southern State*, 377. Ada Amelia Costin, diary entry 25 April 1861, Martin Smith Grant Collection No. 73, J.Y. Joyner Library, East Carolina University. See also the *Herald*, 24 April 1861. It is apparent that Miss Costin copied the newspaper article verbatim. *Daily Journal*, 24 August 1861. Later in the war, yet another attempt was apparently made at Weldon, but the saboteurs ran after being fired upon.
5. In early 1862 the government established Wayside Hospitals throughout the several railroad lines. S.L. Fremont had anticipated this somewhat by calling upon the town's doctors and ladies to assist the wounded as they changed cars. See the *Daily Journal*, 17 August 1861, 8 April 1862, 6 August 1862 (and several dates in July 1862). (Salisbury) *Carolina Watchman*, 7 July 1862. Much of the monies for the hospital were diverted from the "Gunboat Fund," a project that never got off the ground. There was also a magazine for storing explosives located near the depot, *Whiting Papers*, II:335, dated 1 May 1863.
6. Yellow fever was new to most doctors in Wilmington. See *The Lonely Road: A History of the Physics and Physicians of the Lower Cape Fear, 1735-1976*, Diane Cashman, et. al. Eds. 27, hereinafter cited as *The Lonely Road*. Even the provost marshal's office shut down.
7. *Daily Journal*, 7 October 1862. The Road also donated 1,000 pounds of bacon, 30 barrels of flour and 50 bushels of meal to help the needy, ibid., 2 October 1862. *Vance Papers*, I: 397-398, 422. The fever caused a great deal of freight to be left in town, "there were at Wilmington & Weldon Rl. Rd. Sundry lots of Flour, Hides & etc…it was impossible to obtain means of forwarding." See also the *Daily Journal*, 17 November 1862. *Whiting Papers*, II: 336, 11 June 1863.
8. *The Schenck Diary*, indexed by Bill Reaves, New Hanover County Library, 6. Virtually all businesses shut down, but Mayor Dawson ordered at least one drugstore to remain open; even this last closed when the apothecary became ill.
9. John G. Barrett, *The Civil War in North Carolina* (Chapel Hill: The University of North Carolina Press, 1963) 138.
10. *History of Wayne County, North Carolina* (Winston-Salem: Wayne County Historical Association, 1982) 13. Kornegay was well-known in Mount Olive. He was a merchant "and became a prominent figure in the town's history." His troubles did not end there, for when Union General Hugh J. Kilpatrick occupied Mount Olive in 1865, he commandeered Kornegay's home for his headquarters. See also Samuel J. Martin, *Kil-Cavalry: The Life of Union General Hugh Judson Kilpatrick* (Mechanicsburg, Pa.: Stackpole Books, 2000), 225.
11. William R. Trotter, *Ironclads and Columbiads: The Civil War in North Carolina, The Coast* (Winston-Salem: John F. Blair, 1989) 185. *Daily Journal*, 18, 20 and 25 December 1862. *The History of Wayne County*, 17. See also David Norris, "Foster's March to the Sea," *Civil War Times Illustrated*, August 2002. The depot at Everettsville was also burned.

12. Trotter, *Ironclads and Columbiads*, 186.

13. *Daily Journal*, 25 December 1862.

14. Ibid., 1 January 1863, *Richmond Daily Dispatch*, 30 December 1862.

15. *Whitford Papers*, box 89, folder 4, "Proceedings of a Convention of Rail Roads Connecting with the Wilmington and Weldon Rail Road, Held at Goldsboro, April 1, 1862," 4-7. In September 1862, one of the Western N.C.'s cars was held at Goldsboro for 32 days by order of General Holmes. The government reimbursed that road at $3 per day for a total of $96, *Whitford Papers*, box 89-4, 30 September 1862. *Daily Journal*, 10 April 1862. ORA, I:27, 859-863; *Daily Journal*, 6 July 1863; *Vance Papers*, 18:562. The army maintained a telegraph station at Magnolia, *Whiting Papers*, II:336, letter dated 2 July 1863.

16. *Daily Journal*, 18 July 1863; *ORA*, I:27, 965-976; *Raleigh [Weekly] Register*, 29 July 1863; *The Battle Book*, 179-181; *Vance Papers*, 18:918, 959, 26:730. *Daily Journal*, 20 July 1863. General Whiting had to respond to the impressment of the pontoon train which was originally headed to Richmond, see the *Whiting Papers*, II:336, letter dated 31 July 1863.

17. National Archives, Citizens Papers, Wilmington and Weldon Railroad, 114:410-430. *Whiting Papers*, II:344, entry dated 1 September 1863.

The Men of the Railroads

The Wilmington and Weldon Railroad was but one of many industries that needed more laborers. The Road constantly required hands throughout the war. In November, 1862, Richmond appointed Colonel William M. Wadley to replace William Ashe. Wadley supervised and controlled all government transportation on southern railroads. He was probably the best available choice for the job. A long-time railroad troubleshooter, he had first-hand knowledge of the problems many of the roads faced.

Shortly after assuming his new position, Wadley called a conference of railroad presidents, to be held in Augusta, Georgia. There were two objectives on his agenda: "To take into consideration a tariff of charges for Government transportation" and to set up a schedule for trains to run from Richmond to Montgomery, Alabama.

At the convention, he recognized many of the problems of the roads: "The…most important is the disregard many army officers have for the…property of the railroad companies…for instance, ordering rolling stock from one road to another without making any provision for returning it…Impressing cars and engines has been a common occurrence…This involves the Government in much additional expense and causes the demoralization of railroad employees."

He also spoke of the need for more trained workers, hinting that Richmond might exempt mechanics from conscription. Iron, much in demand, might also be made available to the roads, he said. He ended his talk by reminding all present that these problems had to be overcome or the transportation system might soon grind to a halt.

The Confederate blockade running steamer **Advance.**

Sewall Fremont was at that meeting and was appointed to a committee to look into existing railroad rates. When his committee returned from their deliberations, Wadley was shocked to find that they had raised the rates. Soldiers would now be carried at .025 cents per mile. The government was still getting a break as civilian passengers would pay five cents per mile. Freight was divided into five classes, depending on its importance to the war effort. Left unclassified were "the bodies of soldiers killed in battle or [who] die in service," although if it was requested that the body be transported by coach, the full fare was charged.

In the fall of 1864, the W&W again raised its rates. In addition, those items most subject to loss (cotton, liquor, coffee and tobacco) were specifically cited that they were to be "carried at the owner's…risk of fire, water leakage or stealage[.]"

A fire in January 1864 had caused alarm when cotton bales stacked in the depot began smoking. Some "15 to 20 bales" were burned and it was reported that the cotton "was in very bad condition and the fire no doubt was caused by sparks from the yard engine." Destined for the blockade runner *City of Petersburg*, the cotton was moved to an adjacent wharf where it again broke into flames later that night. Another twenty-five or thirty bales were consumed by the flames.[1]

As the Union blockade along the southern coast tightened, Wilmington became the favored port for the runners. It was also the closest major port to the fighting in Virginia and even General Robert E. Lee recognized its importance.[2] North Carolina's governor, Zeb Vance, jumped into the blockade running trade by purchasing, in 1863, the *Advance*, a ship that would make many successful runs into Wilmington before she was captured in September 1864.

Not to pass up an opportunity, the W&W requested space on the state's new steamer for "30 or 40 bales of cotton." This request was apparently not complied with, for in August, Superintendent Fremont penned another letter to Raleigh. This time the W&W asked permission to ship only five bales on each

trip of the vessel. Both requests spoke
of the urgent need for "tools, machines
and machinery of transportation,"
without which the "company can not be
successfully operated." After reminding
the governor that the state owned quite a
bit of stock in the Road, Vance agreed to
carry the cotton.

Fremont also notified John D.
Whitford, president of the Atlantic and
North Carolina, a major in the C.S.A.
and Richmond's man in charge of rail
transportation in North Carolina, about
his arrangement with Vance. Soon
enough, the A.&N.C., Wilmington and
Manchester, W.C.&R. and the N.C.R.R.
sought the same favor of the governor.
Even a contractor working on the

Gov. Zebulon B. Vance

W.C.&R. found it necessary to ask permission to send out a bale to purchase
shovels, which "cannot be obtained in the Confederacy." As for the W&W, the
cotton went out and with the profits the road bought equipment that could not be
found anywhere in the new nation.[3]

One bale of cotton, with an average weight of around five hundred
pounds, could bring profits from $150 to $250. Several factors determined the
price. Seeds of "Sea Island" cotton were easier to remove and it made a more
durable fabric. It sold at a higher price than did "Upland" cotton.

Many times cotton arrived in poor condition for shipment. It was
strongly recommended that the cotton be compressed by the state cotton press,
located on the west bank of the river, and
should be secured with metal ties, which
cost $1 each. On the dock were cotton
inspectors, there to ensure that the bales
were as labeled; sometimes inferior
cotton was stuffed inside bales
tagged as Sea Island. If a bale
was damaged, it would bring less
money and of course, fluctuations
in the London market also
affected prices. The cargo could
be sold in the islands or sent on
to England, where it would also
bring a higher price.

A cotton press

The W&W purchased scarce railroad materials and had them imported through the blockade right up to the end of the war. In this manner, Fremont was able to import T-rails, "Tyres" (locomotive wheels), shovels and axes. The W&M was also able to import not only badly needed car wheels, but on at least one occasion, a locomotive. Throughout the war, various steamers brought goods of all sorts for the railroads but it was never enough. As the blockade tightened, it became harder to obtain the necessary materials from abroad.[4]

When the *SS Advance* came to port in February 1864, she grounded on a sand bar at the mouth of the river. Fremont had to be distressed to learn that sixty pigs of lead had been thrown overboard to lighten the vessel. All over the Confederacy, railroads were suffering the same fate. Men, rails and equipment were wearing out and could not be replaced quickly enough.

The scarcity of trained machinists and mechanics were severely felt in Wilmington. Men "detailed" from the army eased the pressure somewhat, but the different companies in town often vied for the services of the scant few good workers who were also exempt from the military.

Charles R. McQuestion is an example of how the war took its toll. Charles was a W&W employee before the war, running passenger trains and earning eighty dollars per month. Still engaged by the W&W in 1864, not feeling well, and believing that a sea voyage would do him good, he obtained a "certificate" from the War Department agent to allow him to leave the country.

Charles desired to go to sea for his health, but approval was denied by Superintendent Fremont, who later wrote to the head of the Railroad Bureau: "I had refused him permission to go the very day we left Wilmington [for a railroad convention in Columbia, April 1864] but with an old certificate … the gov't. agent Seixas had promised to get him on as an Engineer – for a few trips for the benefit of his health. With that paper he obtained a pass from General Whiting – Much to our regret as he was one of the best machinists we had."

Perhaps if the suggestion made by General Whiting had been followed, Charles McQuestion would have been compelled to remain in town. Whiting asked if the managers and owners of the various foundries, railroad and iron works could review all passenger lists. Any known mechanics found would be denied passage.

At the time McQuestion was sailing the high seas aboard the *Advance*, many detailed men were being recalled to their units and at least one foundry owner went to Richmond to complain not only of the lack of labor, but that a trained railroad engineer (McQuestion) had been let go. Fremont's letter explained that, "the President and Superintendent of this Road did not consent to his going."

McQuestion went to England and back on the state's runner. Upon his return to Wilmington he was grabbed by the conscript officer. As he was a trained engineer, both the officers of the *Advance* as well as the railroad desired him back. Letters to General Whiting and Governor Vance asked that he be returned to their employ. Such was the dearth of trained men that three different entities sought the man. As for McQuestion himself, he seems to have disappeared. He did not return to the railroad and was not conscripted. If he did return to the *Advance*, the chances are good that he wound up in a northern prison. The runner was captured on her very next trip.

It was not only the lack of employees that hampered the southern transportation network. When the superintendent of the W&W needed to have two of his engines repaired, he realized that, as the shops in Wilmington would not be available, he would have to send them to Raleigh. As it turned out, those shops were also unavailable, so he was forced to send the engines to the Navy Yard at Charlotte. He was appalled when the chief engineer there reported that the locomotives would need a lot of work, necessitating more time and expense. It cost $1,000 just to get the engines there and in addition, the Navy Department had to agree to allow the work. Fremont offered to send a mechanic to Charlotte to help with the repairs, but even with the extra help, it was not enough. Chief Engineer Ramsey at Charlotte wrote that he needed at least seven machinists and even more blacksmiths to finish all the work he had on hand.[5]

At the outbreak of the Civil War, there were quite a few northern workers who chose to remain and work in the South. One of the strangest occurrences had to be a train load of northern women who had been allowed to pass through the lines to visit their husbands who were working in the South. In a quid pro quo action, women and children were also allowed to travel northward. General Whiting added his own twist, requiring those alien enemies to take an oath before leaving the country. Some objected to this, but as one citizen "present…at a conversation…between a lady of Wilmington and a member of the Government" recorded: "At first the subject was retaliation, and how far it could be carried out…and then turned on General Whiting and his course in exacting a certain obligation from parties returning to abolitiondom. The lady warmly praised the general's course…The gentleman heard her…and remarked, 'you are right…' The lady observed that a great deal of righteous indignation had been expressed regarding the course adopted by General Whiting[.]"

The gentleman opined that "Such an expression would be a sure test of disloyal feelings and would never be uttered except by those who sympathize with our enemies." The refugees going north were not limited by the amount of baggage they could take, unlike those going south. Those folks were informed: "No person will be allowed to take more than one trunk or package of female wearing apparel, weighing not over one hundred pounds, and subject to inspection; and if anything contraband be found in the trunk, or on the person, the property will be forfeited and the pass revoked."[6]

One writer to the paper suggested that not all the northern ladies who came through the lines had relatives in the Confederacy. It was supposed that some were spies.

Another likely source for spies was the Confederate government attempt to utilize POW labor. It would appear that prisoners were used in the workshops of the W&W Railroad, the Fayetteville Arsenal and at the Egypt Coal Mines. These men, it was quickly determined, were next to useless and usually stirred up trouble among the slaves. They were quietly sent back to the Salisbury prison. When the Union army raided Rocky Mount in July 1863, a black Union soldier was wounded and captured. It caused a quandary for General Whiting. The man was identified as a former slave and the owner asked for his return. Whiting said that it would be better if the man had been shot instead of being taken alive, because the general did not know what to do with him. Indeed, he stated that his standing order was "to take no negro prisoners nor any white man with them." The soldier was finally sent off to a POW camp.

Other prisoners presented different problems. Some Union deserters, not wishing to be repatriated, refused to serve the Confederacy. This led, for a time at least, to Yankees wandering the streets of Wilmington. These few were usually put aboard the next available blockade runner and sent to the Islands, although, in the case of August Miller, a deserter from the U.S. Navy, Whiting had the man put on the railroad and sent to Lynchburg, Virginia, "to the frontier." There he was sent across the lines to Union controlled territory.[7]

It is probable that the railroads of North Carolina and the Confederacy as a whole could have done more to aid the war effort. The closest the system was administered with a "will to win" might have been the September 1863 movement of General James Longstreet's Corps from the battlefields around Richmond to the slaughterhouse called Chickamauga. Longstreet conceived the idea of moving some twenty thousand troops of his command to aid General Braxton Bragg's struggles in the western theater. It was not until he withdrew from Chattanooga that Richmond finally answered Bragg's pleas for reinforcements.

Utilizing interior lines of transportation showed the importance of the rail network and also highlighted the necessary assistance of the various railroad involved. On 6 September, General Lee "directed Quartermaster General Lawton to proceed with the arrangements." Lawton delegated Major Frederick W. Sims of the Railroad Bureau to handle the details.

Major Sims worked in the bureau under Colonel Wadley and took over in June 1863, after that officer was discharged. "Frederick William Sims was a man of parts. Unlike Wadley, he was no Yankee. Born in the north Georgia village of Washington on October 18, 1823, he passed the greater part of his childhood in Macon, where his father was Mayor...During his young manhood he served as 'transporting agent' on the Central of Georgia and became acquainted with Wadley[.]"

A former prisoner of war, captured at Fort Pulaski, he was barely forty years old, but "had already displayed marked administrative ability. All things considered, Sims represented the administrative branch of the Confederate Army at its best." Although he had only a small staff to work with, the men selected were the best. Major John Dalton Whitford, president of the almost-defunct Atlantic and North Carolina Railroad, was chosen to be Richmond's Transportation Agent in North Carolina. It would seem that wherever Whitford went, his able Superintendent William H. Harvey also went. It was Whitford who made the final arrangements for the troop movement (at least the North Carolina portion) which was about to begin.

Whitford, a native and one-time mayor of New Bern, was born in 1825. He was elected to the helm of the A&NC at its first stockholder's meeting in 1854. As a member of the New Bern Light Infantry, he was one of the first to enlist in the Confederate Army. After taking part in the Battle of New Bern, in March 1862, he was given charge of rail transportation in the state. Just before New Bern fell to the Federals, his road managed to bring off most of their rolling stock and much-needed equipment. Left behind for the occupiers were only three hand cars and two "pole" (platform) cars.

As the Yankees advanced inland, several bridges of the road were burned and track torn up. This left the A&NC a railroad virtually without a road; what was left ran from Goldsboro to Kinston, a distance of less than thirty miles. Most of their rolling stock was converted to Confederate use; indeed, a railroad circular issued from Richmond in October 1862 indicated that all government rolling stock could be identified by the markings "C.S.A., R.&O.R.R., A.&N.C., & U.S."

Sims' Railroad Bureau had four main tasks: "the expediting of Army shipments by rail, the apportionment of rolling stock and supplies among the several lines, the coordination of major troop movements, and the negotiation of tariffs for government business."

The bureau was about to coordinate one of the largest troop movements of the war. Whitford knew his job well. He notified all railroads involved as to time and numbers of troops. He requested that the telegraph lines be kept open between major depots. The following day, he was notified that the operators at Charlotte, Raleigh, Weldon, Wilmington and Company Shops (Burlington) were standing by. Placed at these strategic stations were men who were best suited for the work about to be undertaken. S.L. Fremont was at Wilmington, William Harvey was stationed at Goldsboro, at Company Shops was T.J. Sumner (Superintendent of the NCRR), while P.A. Dunn (A&NC) was at Weldon and

J.R. Sharp of the South Carolina R.R. was at Charlotte. Not to be left uninformed was Henry Drane, superintendent of the W&M. These men would see to it that things went smoothly, although they were not in charge. Whitford made sure the military authorities were kept informed. Whitford was to receive reports every few hours, as trains left their stations. Except for a few bruised egos, the movement went well.

Not completely able to relinquish control, and quite possibly looking to make more of a profit for his Road, Superintendent Fremont wired Whitford: "Will you please inform [me what] P.A. Dunn has to do with the Atlantic Rail road. He ordered one [train] to go by Raleigh yesterday[.] Of course it is for the interest of the Gov. to send all the troops this way[. They] can do it about two dollars less by this [route.]"

It was at Wilmington during this movement that several of General Hood's Texans found their way to Paddy's Hollow, where they soon became drunk and boisterous. When the town guard came to quiet them down, a fight ensued. The police (three older exempts), outnumbered, were severely injured, with one suffering a knife wound. No one was arrested and the men made their way back to their units and were soon ferried across the Cape Fear and entrained southward.

By 15 September, "the last of Jenkins' Brigade left" Weldon and Sims wired Whitford from Richmond that the brigade "closes the movement." One who complained bitterly about the transportation network was former Virginia Governor Henry A. Wise. Now a brigadier general, he had been ordered to Charleston in the middle of the troop movement. Leaving Weldon with some of his troops, his train soon broke down.

He wrote to General Samuel Cooper (the Adjutant and Inspector General): "On the Weldon R.R. 45 miles from Weldon and 115 from Wilmington…I deem it my duty to report through you to the Secy. of War the utter deficiency & neglect of transportation on this R. Road…The engineer very openly and ingeniously confesses…that this [breakdown] is owing to willful and very culpable neglect on the part of the chief machinist of the Road at Wilmington."

One of the engine's drivers had broken apart, completely disabling the train. Wise was quite upset about the delay, but more so because he could find "neither the conductor nor RR Superintendent to have the matter remedied." Two days later, having reached Wilmington, he again penned a missive to Cooper. His anger had not at all abated as he wrote: "A few minutes after I reported to you the day before yesterday, the Superintendent of the R. Road… S.L Fremont made his appearance. I stated to him the report of the Conductor… He, Fremont, behaved very badly, replying with insolence, showing a guiltiness or dereliction of duty and bad temper for making it known. He defied all interference…and went off with the damaged locomotive…leaving me with the 59th, the baggage and the horses[.]"

Both men were having a very bad day. Wise's comments to General Cooper were correct when he described the deplorable state of transportation, but he did not perhaps realize that his mobilization was of a lower priority than that of the men headed to Chickamauga. Now a colonel, Sims was asked to investigate the incident, but nothing came of it.

Major Whitford had some writing to do. Mortified to learn that Governor Vance held him partially responsible for not preventing a riot in Raleigh, he had to explain himself. Georgian troops had passed through that city during the troop movement and had targeted William Holden's newspaper, the *Raleigh Standard*, for destruction.

Vance's letter condemning Whitford appeared in the *Standard* and was directed to President Davis. In it, he related that Whitford had prior knowledge of the men's intent to wreck the office and did nothing to prevent it. Vance wrote: "In my letter to the President I said that General [Henry L.] Benning remarked to Col. Whitford…some hours previous to the mob that he should not be surprised if some of his men did not tear down the *Standard* office as he heard it threatened."

Responding from Hillsboro, Whitford was quick to deny any such knowledge and replied that "not a word was said to me on the subject by Gen'l. Benning or any other officer or soldier of his Brigade either before or after the outrage was perpetrated."

For his part, the Governor accepted Whitford's explanation, admitting that "your recollection is perhaps better than mine having less on yr. mind at the time than I had." Not willing to let it go though, he added, "I am perfectly confident however that such a statement was made to me by someone. You were the author of it as alluded to…the next day after the occurrence in my private conversations on the subject I always mentioned your name as the author, and never doubted it for a moment until the reception of your note. Even now I can not fix upon any other possible person who could have told me…Still Colonel, I repeat that I accept your denial."

Another who felt Vance's anger was Lieutenant Colonel W.S. Shepherd of the 2nd Georgia. He was named as a leader of the mob, but was cleared of any wrongdoing by General Benning. Benning wrote to Vance on his behalf since Shepherd had been wounded in the recent battle. Shepherd himself later wrote the Governor to remind him that it had been Shepherd who accompanied Vance in an attempt to arrest the mob and to thank him for "kindness [shown] to members of my command while in Raleigh." During the disturbance, Vance had personally appealed to the mob in a vain attempt to quell the riot. As the *Journal* recorded: "[He] reached the spot after the work of destruction was nearly over, and addressed the crowd, begging them to desist. He rebuked them for the act, telling them that no such example had been set in Lincoln's dominions."

In a somewhat apologetic letter, Vance wrote to Secretary of War James Seddon: "As to Lt. Col. Shepherd...I suppose I must have fallen into a very great mistake concerning him. If he is the officer upon whom I called at the Hotel, and who went with me to the scene of the violence, then I owe him a great many thanks for his assistance, instead of an accusation of guilt...The mistake was a very natural one owing to the confusion and darkness."

Unsuccessful in their attempt to halt the rioters, Vance telegraphed President Davis and demanded that no more troops be routed through Raleigh. This left only the Wilmington route open and placed an even greater strain on its meager resources.

The roots of the destruction of the *Standard* office might be traced back to the ongoing feud between Holden and the editor of the *Raleigh Register*, as well as Holden's peace platform. The two editors had long been at odds and North Carolina soldiers had been writing letters home suggesting that the time had come for "something more effective...than resolutions[.]" At a meeting called on 17 August at Camp Sparrow, near Wilmington, members of the 1ˢᵗ N.C. Battalion (Heavy Artillery) resolved that due to "our...late reverses...patriots are rejected, and tories exultant, chief among whom is W.W. Holden...[And] that we are driven...to regard W.W. Holden...the certain ally of Abraham Lincoln[.]"

It was Holden, however, who raised the specter of mob rule when he editorialized: "Physical force mean mob rule...We [oppose] mob rule...We have thousands of friends...who would avenge any injury inflicted on us or our printing establishment...if they...dare lift a finger against us, their bodies will soon adorn the trees and lamp posts of Raleigh."[8]

The troop movement that September, with all its setbacks, was successful, albeit just barely. Not all the troops arrived in time but enough did to turn the battle into an immediate Confederate victory. Due to Bragg's hesitation, the opportunity to more completely thrash the Federals was lost. Two weeks after the battle, the railroads to Chickamauga had more freight to transport: fifty-five ambulance wagons, loaded in eleven freight cars, meant for the 18,000 Southern casualties.

The movement of Longstreet's Corps caused a massive pileup of goods and supplies at Wilmington. In October, General Whiting wrote to Richmond about his men being stretched thin guarding public property. Another unforeseen result of the heavy demand of transportation by the military, in addition to the delays to private citizens who were ordered off the trains, was the delay in sending laborers to Whiting. The Wilmington railroads did yeoman duty throughout the war (and made huge profits as well), but were not able to stand up to the heavy traffic now so necessary to maintain a war.

Accidents became more frequent, the loss of life more incidental. In the fire of April 1864, the terminal of the Wilmington and Manchester railroad was destroyed. The shops were saved, but the president, treasurer and superintendent had to find new office space. The fire, it was strongly suspected, was the work of an arsonist or alien enemy. The familiar refrain of "not enough men" was heard again when the force of firefighters dwindled down to only a few exempts to man the hose.

Arson was not always the cause of fires. On one occasion, a conductor, running an A&NC train from Tarboro to Wilson, on the W&W tracks, reported to his superior, Major Whitford: "In accordance with your orders, I proceeded with the State cotton train...as per general orders on our Rail Road when loading cotton I placed the two box cars next to the locomotive to shorten and protect the cotton cars as well as possible from the sparks when running[.]"

When he approached Goldsboro, he noticed smoke coming from the third boxcar and "immediately give the signal to stop the train[,] it was answered at once by the engineer who blew on brakes[.]" The fire was not large and could possibly be put out quickly, but as he wrote, "Unfortunately we were running down grade...the wind blowing fresh...directly up the Road therefore by the time we could stop...the cotton was blazing on the third car[.]"

Things quickly got worse as the fourth and fifth cars were now also aflame. As the train came to a stop near a bridge (Black Creek), the crew, along with the bridge guards and train hands, fought the fire and saved the bulk of the freight by throwing off the burning cotton. About forty bales were destroyed with several more damaged. The conductor finished his letter by reminding the major that Whitford himself had made up the train and therefore knew that the best engine (the one throwing the least sparks) had been used.

He also stated: "as this is the first cotton that has been lost by me on any train since I have been in the service of the company which has been several years[,] I am satisfied that it was one of those accidents that...will sometimes happen on any Rail road however careful we may be."

The conductor probably kept his job.[9]

Endnotes

1. *ORA*, I:51, 270-276. Perhaps Wadley was a bit too outspoken, for his commission as Colonel would not be confirmed by the Confederate Congress and he was replaced by Major Frederick Sims. *Daily Journal*, 2 January 1864. Also on the company's risk list were wagons, furniture and crockery.
2. Fonvielle, *The Wilmington Campaign*, 129.
3. *Vance Papers*, 18:458, letter dated 2 July 1863, 19:294, letter dated 23 August 1863, 19:413, letter dated 30 August 1863. See also the Fremont Collection,

N.C.S.A. file titled "Business Papers, Nassau, 1863-1865." Fremont took it upon himself to secure permission from the government for the A&NC to send out cotton. *Vance Papers*, 20:501, letter dated 28 October 1863.

4. *Vance Papers*, letter dated 22 July 1864. Fremont may well have imported T-rails through the blockade from a manufacturer in Massachusetts, see the Fremont Collection, "Blockade Running" file. The superintendent was not above using his status to import personal items from abroad; from pie plates and hairpins to buttons and beef. It all came into southern ports. In July 1864, Fremont received notice that axes, shovels and spades would soon be delivered to his Road.

5. National Archives, Citizen's Papers, Wilmington and Weldon Railroad, letter dated 24 April 1864; Vance Papers, 24:289, letter dated 16 August 1864, 26:813, n.d. In a letter to the Governor, Fremont changed his report somewhat, writing that he had "consented to spare McQuestion from the service of this company some time ago when he was in bad health to go on the state steamer," *Vance Papers*, 24:200, letter dated 6 August 1864. National Archives, Citizen's Papers, Wilmington and Weldon Railroad, letter dated 9 June 1864. Concurring in Engineer Ramsey's report was John M. Brooke, the designer of the ironclad *Merrimack*. Sifakis, *Who Was Who in the Civil War*, 75.

6. *Daily Journal*, 23 June 1863.

7. Whiting Papers, II:346, Endorsements, entries dated 26 and 28 November 1863.

8. NCSA, Whitford Papers, box 89-4, "Circular" dated 11 October 1862. This notice also listed the rates to be charged when the government loaned rolling stock to a road: when run over 50 miles, .04 per car and .20 per engine per mile. Powell, *North Carolina Biography*, 6:187-188; NCSA, Whitford Papers, box 89-4, 12 September through 31 October 1863; *Daily Journal*, 11 September, 2 and 3 October 1863. General Benning was absolved by virtue of being asleep on a crosstie at the station. Shepherd's letter is in the *Vance Papers*, 20:156, dated 8 October 1863 and Vance's reply is in Zebulon Baird Vance, 1830-1894, Copies of Letters and Telegrams Sent and Received, 878:360-361, entry dated 13 October 1863, microfilm collection of Randall Library, UNCW. The *Raleigh Register*, 17 and 19 August 1863.

9. Bradley, *North Carolina Confederate Militia and Home Guard Records*, I:98, entry no. 1274, dated 10 October 1863. Whiting Papers, II:336, dated 4 October 1863. Whiting "impressed" a company of the 66th NCT to assist him, ibid., 3 November 1863. Whitford Papers, box 89-4, letter dated 29 November 1864; the conductor was John P. Thomas.

10

Mr. Bronze John Comes Calling

Yellow fever, some believed, was a "Yankee trick." The fever may have been introduced to town via the blockade runner *Kate*. The captain of the vessel, carrying candles as part of its cargo, avowed that his ship could not have brought the fever. They were so hotly pursued that when they put into Wilmington they only had empty boxes, because "the great heat generated on the ship had melted [the candles] and only the wicks remained in the boxes." He maintained that the heat would have killed the germ.

Perhaps the Captain was right, for there had been several deaths from the disease prior to the *Kate*'s arrival. It had rained heavily in July and August, with many pools of water collecting around town in which mosquitoes could breed. Since most of the "scavengers," those who collected and sorted through the town's garbage, were hard at work on the area's fortifications, the piles of garbage increased throughout the city. That refuse collected and clogged the drains along Market Street, below Front, and flooded basements with stagnant water.[1]

"Mr. Bronze John's" first recorded victim was Louis Swarzman. He was, with his partner, Jacob Loeb, a dealer of wood and coal and had supplied the *Kate*. Yellow fever was identified in the fall of 1862 and once discovered there was an exodus from town. Businesses closed, families packed up and left, mail and railroad service was halted.

The telegraph office shut down. The chief operator, Joseph Durnin, a native of Maine, who had remained in the South upon the outbreak of hostilities, was ordered out of the city by his employers. Durnin chose to remain, contracted the fever and died. This effectively shut down the system, at least in

Wilmington, and the telegraphic instruments were taken to Goldsboro. The telegraph was constantly subject to the vagaries of the weather. Wires were knocked down by wind and ice, or cut by Yankee raiders. Now, however, even disease conspired against the town. There were calls for anyone who had immunity from the disease to come to the office and although several soldiers volunteered for the job, they were never released for the work. It wouldn't be until year's end that service was restored.

As the fever raged, the military took action. They moved troops away from the city and closed down most military offices, including the hospitals and the provost marshal's office. For a time, the detested passport system was abolished.[2]

The surrounding towns established a strict quarantine for anyone coming from Wilmington. Fayetteville set up a station outside town, while Lumberton levied the heavy fine of $500 for anyone caught trying to get into that town. This was a normal procedure, meant to protect the citizens of those towns.

In the past, Wilmington had done the same when contagious disease struck their neighbors. Some refugees, able to get out of town, could find nowhere to stay and were forced to sleep outdoors. Farmers stopped bringing produce to market, which caused an immediate need for food as well as medicine. Charleston quickly became the port of call for runners and those that dared to come to the Cape Fear ventured no further than Smithville.

Realizing they must act during the crisis, the mayor and town commissioners turned to one of the few druggists left on his feet. Calling upon their municipal powers, they ordered William Lippitt to keep his drug store open, or "steps will be taken to have it kept open by the authorities."

There were several pharmacists in town, but virtually all of them had been hit by the fever. Louis Erambert died in September; Henry McLin was ill and his chief assistant, William Pratt had died. A local paper reported that Pratt "died...at his post as did ever a soldier in battle. He contracted the disease... while making up prescriptions...for the sick."

Ironically, that summer Pratt had obtained "some government office and went away from here to escape conscription." He was called upon to return and did so. The Pratts had difficulty finding a place to stay when they returned and were told the only house available would have to be vacated by October. William died on 27 September and upon his death left a wife and child to get by as best they could. Later that year, a collection was taken up for the unfortunate family and enough money was donated to allow them to leave the port and get to the Islands. Unfortunately, there the money ran out, but through the good graces of a blockade running captain, Mrs. Pratt was soon on her way to join relatives in Canada.[3]

Mr. Willis, said to be the town's most experienced druggist, was stricken, while another, John Lewis, succumbed to the disease. When William

Lippitt became ill, the sole remaining apothecary was Walker Meares. A letter written at that time said of him: "He has been exerting himself nobly for the sick putting up as many as 150 prescriptions a [day,] if he is sick there are no apothecaries in Wil. He says no one can form an idea of the desolation and gloom of our poor town."[4]

The writer had seen Meares at the funeral of a young victim and added, "Walker Meares has been taken with a chill. Your mother is in great fear for him." Meares did indeed fall sick, and although he recovered, he lost his one-year old son to the epidemic. It would appear that for a time at least, Wilmington was without the assistance of any druggists. Within a short time, pharmacists, as well as doctors and nurses from Charleston, answered the call and filled the void. R.M. Lain's grocery store was set up as a centralized warehouse for food, to be distributed to those needy citizens who couldn't get away. Lain soon asked for help, since at this point, he may well have been sick himself. He died shortly after.[5]

Near General Hospital No. 4, a soup kitchen was set up "under the supervision of Captain Jonas P. Levy." Captain Levy was a likely choice to stay in town and administer to the sick as he had been in Norfolk in 1855 when the disease struck that city. Back then the Norfolk *Herald* reported that "he had hundreds of cases of yellow fever under treatment" during his naval career and he offered the following cure: "Dissolve in a wine glass of water, a table-spoon of common salt, and pour the same into a tumbler, adding the juice of a whole lemon, and two wine glasses of castor oil."

Also to be applied were several mustard plasters and "forty grains of quinines" given three times a day. With this treatment, Levy guaranteed recovery.

As soon as it opened, the soup kitchen fed about 75 people and within a day or two, some 200 people were eating soup, meat and bread. The kitchen remained open throughout the contagion.[6]

Army Quartermaster Christopher Styron remained in town and tried his best to have corn brought in. He wrote to William Harvey of the A&NC: "I have been to the railroad men at this end of the line, and have been promised, day in and day out, that corn would be brought down – Forebearance ceases to be a virtue, after a very long time."[7]

The Sanitary Committee, established during the emergency, gave out rosin, used for fumigating, and copperas, used to purify water. They requested the railroads and steamboats not to carry any soldiers's family members into town.

About the only thing not in short supply was turpentine. Barrels were set up at various locations and set afire. The smoke, it was thought, would purify the air. Wood, necessary for fires to ward off the approaching chill of winter, was nowhere to be found. Food was so scarce that several concerned citizens went along the line of railroad and purchased livestock and other supplies. This time there were no restrictions or compunctions about leaving town. Indeed, the authorities provided transportation and asked others to stay away. Less people, less food required; less people, less food for yellow fever, went the thinking.

Another who remained in town was Dr. Thomas B. Carr. As secession had approached, Carr, originally from New York, joined the "Cape Fear Minute Men," a group of rabid secessionists. One day Carr, who also supplied the town with milk from his nearby dairy, was seen wearing his badge by a pro-Union citizen. The man asked Carr what the letters "CFMM" stood for. He proudly informed his questioner, whereupon the man replied, "Oh, I thought it stood for Cape Fear Milk Man!"

When the epidemic struck and many fled Wilmington, Dr. Carr volunteered to remain, taking over the duties of apothecary in General Hospital No. 4. The quartermaster, Major John Cameron, donated the use of the army's two ambulance wagons to convey patients to the hospital. There, it was reported, they would "find Dr. Carr...at all hours, ready to attend to them." While he persevered at the hospital, a thief struck his home and made off with a shotgun and a buggy.

Another who surprised many by staying in town was the Reverend Alphonse Repiton. Repiton, the Baptist minister,

Rev. Alphonse A. Repiton (NHCPL)

proved them wrong when he stayed. It was thought by some that he would be among the first to leave town. "Mr. Repiton is there [in Wilmington], he has always had the reputation of beinng so timid, I was astonished at his remaining – George Davis says it must be a great triumph of the spirit over the flesh with Mr. R." Others, whose flesh triumphed their spirit, also stayed in town. Dr. William Wragg, one of the physicians sent from Charleston, reported: "I was called to see a girl, boarding at Mrs. McLin's; her name was Georgia Morning...[she] lived in Water Street in a house called 'Hole in the Wall'."

There appeared to be no end in sight as the epidemic spread. As late as the 20th of October, the *Journal* reported: "The demand this morning for coffins, hearses and other adjuncts of internment seemed to equal if it did not exceed any morning yet." Several hundred citizens would die from the disease.

Barrels of tar and turpentine were burned during 1862's yellow fever epidemic in Wilmington, in hopes of scouring the air of the disease. (Aubrey J. Acuna)

Yet another view of the prostrated town was offered by a courier from Fort Fisher. As the rider walked his horse through town, he saw a: "blowsy, unkempt head and a neck [that] craned from an alleyway; an ill-dressed, cadaverous man stared at me in a stupid, dull manner. Hailing this only sign of life that I had seen...I asked boldly, 'Where's everybody?' 'Dead or dying' he replied and with those few foreboding words, the staggering man gulped, emitted the dreaded black vomit, fell dead in the head of the alley, a yellow fever victim."

After delivering the dispatches he carried, the rider headed out of town, but paused when he saw yet another person, "a well-dressed man in black...He hailed me from his position at 5th and Market, just across from the site of the Bellamy mansion. He came out on the street...[and] asked me my name, my command and my business...I did not see what right he had to question me so closely; but I was a mere boy in age compared to him, a dignified, imposing man and as I started away from him he called me back and said: 'Son, my name is John Dawson and I'm the Mayor of this death-ridden town.' He than invited me to breakfast."[8]

Looking back some years later, one newspaper remembered: "The streets were empty...The dogs howled from hunger, and the very birds of the air had deserted the city. Death and pestilence had possession of every place. Want and misery was everywhere[.]"[9]

The free black and slave population suffered greatly also. In writing to his mistress, who had left town, William Henry Strumber noted that: "I hav Bin Laid up all mos five weeks[,] but the Lord has spar my lif in [midst] of death... [I] send you this letter to let you know that Wellington is at the pint [point]of death...Daniel is Better to day and Setting up[.] Beller [Bella, another slave] is still bad off...all the res is Better."

William also told his owner that Doctor Greenhowe, who visited the house, "puts me in mine of my old marster [how] kind he was to us when we was Sick[.]" Many would agree with Strumber's words that: "I beeleves that wee hav Sinned Agans the Lord and the Lord...Whippin us forret [for it.]" William's missive included this description of town: "I never saw the like bee for of our town[.] If you walk in the street it look like a lungful time All Days long the hurt it going." While William's letter may be difficult to read, it must be remembered that he was one of the few who could read and write and while yellow fever was killing those all around him, he too stayed at his post.[10]

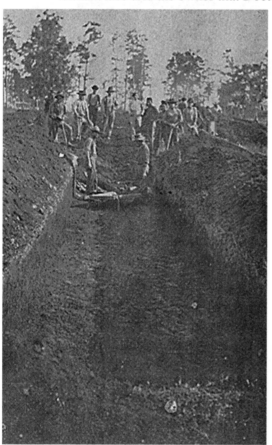

During Wilmington's yellow fever epidemic mass graves became necessary.

The official death toll of about 650, that is, 650 white victims. An inaccurate count of deaths to the black population estimated 150 lives lost. It must be recalled that, in a purely economic move, most slave holders removed their chattels from town. The fever finally abated with the coming of cooler weather, whereupon most businesses called their scattered workers back. Those that did not report back were warned that their names would be turned over to the Enrolling Officer and they would soon find themselves in the army. Wilmington had changed and would never be the same.

After the fever lessened, a strong rumor swept the area that the city was the target of the next Union attack. Many long-time citizens simply stayed away

The section of Wilmington's Oakdale Cemetery holding the mass graves of yellow fever victims.

for the remainder of the war, perhaps making an occasional trip back to check on their property.

Many of those citizens that remained in town were taken aback when the town physicians presented them with a bill for services rendered during the epidemic. They were somewhat irritated with the doctors because, as one patient recounted: "You know...that a number of Physicians were detailed by General Beauregard...to come to the aid of our suffering community...They did yeoman's service – pay as I know was in some cases tendered them by those who were able to pay. They refused any compensation. These are facts. Now I wish to know what right certain resident Physicians have to charge for the services of those very Doctors who refused pay themselves?"

Appealing to those doctors who had traveled from other states to tend patients, the town doctors received a letter in reply. It stated that: "While scrupulously abstaining from receiving any compensation for our professional services among the inhabitants...we were equally careful to hand over to the resident Physicians who were temporarily incapacitated from visiting their patients...and who requested us to do so for them, a memoranda of our services."

In a follow-up letter, sent to Doctor Edwin A. Anderson, the Charleston doctors clarified the facts by stating that they had been sent to Wilmington to attend to those "who had no attending Physician." In other words, any patients who came to see the doctors were not charged and there was no record kept of their visit. From time to time, however, the town doctors distributed a list of their patients to the visiting physicians and it was of these visits that a strict record was kept. These were the patients being charged. Doctor Anderson ended his letter to the local paper by saying: "After the above explanation, if any one who may have paid us money is still dissatisfied," he offered to return their money.

The fear of another epidemic rose in the fall of 1864 when Doctor William J. Love reported he had lost a patient from the disease and another "has the black vomit." The letter to the mayor was published in the newspaper as a warning, but the fever never got a grip on the town as it had two years earlier. Once again the weather, "cool, dry and bracing," did away with the disease.

Endnotes

1. *LCFHS Bulletin*, "The Prevailing Epidemic," compiled by Leora H. McEachern and Isabel M. Williams, XI:1 (November 1967) 6. See also [*Wilmington Morning Star*, n.d.] "U.D.C. Historian Urges Marking of Fort Fisher," Fort Fisher newspaper articles, copy at Fort Fisher State Historic Site.
2. *Daily Journal*, 1 October, 1862. As an indication of how bad the telegraph system became, in the summer of 1866, an ad was run by the American Telegraph Company. They sought "500 telegraph poles, 28 feet long, not less than 6 inches at the small end." The poles, when planted, stood no more than twenty feet above the ground; see the *Daily Journal*, 18 July 1866.
3. Wilmington *Weekly Journal*, 22 January 1863, 29 July 1863; *LCFHS*, "Calder-Lazarus Collection, " copied by Ida B. Kellum, 1959, from "KTC" letter dated 7/19/62.
4. *Southern Women and Their Families in the Nineteenth Century*, hereafter cited as *Southern Women*, deRosset Family Papers, 15:874, letter to "My Dear Kate," (Catherine deRosset Kennedy) from Eliza deRosset, dated 15 October 1862.
5. McLin's drug store was on the northwest corner of front and market Streets. It remained a drug store (Tom's Drug Store) until closing in 2007.
6. *Daily Journal*, 29 October, 1862; *The New York Times*, 17 August, 1855.
7. *LCFHS Bulletin*, November 1967, 16. NCSA, *John D. Whitford Papers*, box 89-4, letter dated 8 December 1862.
8. *The Wilmington Light Infantry Memorial*, by Henry Hayden, privately published, copy in the New Hanover County Public Library. Southern Women, 15:890, 28 October 1862. Wragg, W.T. "Report on the Epidemic of Yellow Fever Which Prevailed at Wilmington, N.C. in the Fall of 1862," New York Medical Journal, 9:478-496 (1869).
9. *Wood*, n.d., n.p., 1862. *Morning Star*, 14 October 1870. Interred in Oakdale Cemetery were 654 souls, including 399 in the Public Ground.
10 *Southern Women*, 15:887, 882, letters dated 23 and 28 October 1862; 15:892, letter dated 4 November 1862. See also 15:859, letter dated 3 October 1862. Another writer commented on the disparity between male and female victims, "Does it strike you – how few women comparatively have died?"

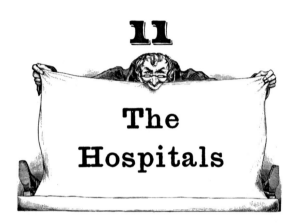

11

The Hospitals

There were several hospitals for both military and civilians in Wilmington during the war. The U.S. Marine Hospital, constructed in the late 1850s, became the Confederacy's General Hospital No. 5, but locals always referred to it as the Marine Hospital. Located "on a well drained sandy elevation at Eighth and Nun Streets," the site encompassed the area from 8th and Nun to 13th and Ann Streets. In the beginning of the war, it was used as an encampment for troops passing through Wilmington and had a capacity, probably with additional hospital tents, for about 250 patients.

In the spring of 1862, Confederate authorities called for "wayside" hospitals to be set up. These were located in larger towns along the line of railroads from Virginia and spread throughout the Confederacy. In North Carolina, such hospitals were established at Weldon, Raleigh, Goldsboro, Tarboro, Salisbury, Salem and Wilmington. As mentioned above, the Wayside Hospital in Wilmington was located in the W&W depot near the river. A fairly large building, it contained bathing and kitchen facilities. Usually alerted by telegraph, the town doctors made their way to the depot, examined and redressed wounds. Also on hand to assist were members of the Soldier's Aid Society, an outgrowth of the prewar Ladies' Aid Society. Exactly how many soldiers were treated at this hospital is unknown, but a glimpse might be obtained by examining the roster of another such, albeit smaller facility, the Salem Wayside Hospital. At that site, during a one-month period seventy-one soldiers were fed 215 meals.[1]

Confederate General Hospital No. 5. (Fales Collection, NHCPL)

By March 1864, there was a call for a Wayside Home for soldiers as well. This home, it was felt, was necessary to house and feed any soldiers in town. The *Journal* reported that it would be used for men "going home on furlough or returning to the army, or for other traveling on duty." It would eliminate, the paper hoped, the unpleasant scene of hungry soldiers wandering around town. The idea of a Wayside Home was never pushed and soon fell by the wayside itself.

Mrs. deRosset (NHCPL)

Mrs. Armand deRosset, president of the Ladies' (or Soldiers) Aid Society, was often seen at the railroad depot. In September, 1862, she wrote about a visit to the site: "I have been up all morning at the wayside hospital[,] some poor fellows wounded ever since June, others sick for three or four months, it is delightful to see the pleasure they express and many of them so grateful for every act of kindness – Their wounds are dressed, their faces washed and fed with little delicacies to those who cannot eat substantially.[2]

Mrs. deRosset also noted that "it cost our society about $25 a day[,] a great deal too much." The women of the Aid Society, organized in the

1840s to assist the indigent, met the soldiers at the depot with hot food and coffee. Since troop trains generally traveled at night, bypassing other towns in the early hours of the morning, the burden of care was thus thrust upon the citizens of Wilmington.

Wilmington was also where the troops had to change trains because the tracks of the Wilmington and Manchester had a different gauge. As the Cape Fear River was as yet unbridged, it was also necessary to ferry across the river. It was a good spot for a "Way" hospital. Due to the difference in gauges, even when the bridge was built later, in 1867, a change of trucks (car wheels) was needed.

After a pause of nearly two hours, the wounded boarded the ferry *Harlee*, crossed the river and continued their journey southward. There was also a Naval Hospital, located at the foot of Chestnut Street. This was likely a private residence taken over by the navy for their use.

Before the war there were about eighteen medical practitioners in Wilmington. It is likely that several physicians left for the north before the outbreak of war, but most of them remained to minister to the needs of the population. Several joined the army and at least three of them, Doctors E.A. Anderson, James H. Dickson and William G. Thomas traveled to Virginia to attend to the wounded during the Seven Days Battle.[3]

Dr. James Dickson
(NHCPL)

Dr. Dickson was a long-time practitioner. Born in 1806, educated at UNC, he was only thirteen years old when he entered college and later studied under Doctor Armand deRosset II, and was later schooled at Columbia University in N.Y. He began practicing in the Cape Fear area in 1827. Dr. Dickson performed an operation on his brother in 1835; he corrected his sibling's abnormality of clubfoot in a procedure said to be the first tenotomy in the United States. In 1853, well ahead of his time, he performed a blood transfusion from one sister to another, saving her life.

He served as president of the N.C. State Medical Society and influenced the formation of a State Board of Medical Examiners. Active in community affairs, he served on various committees, ranging from "managing a ball in honor of Henry Clay's visit" in 1847 to being a founder of the Wilmington Library Association. A former Whig and Unionist at heart, it was he who cautioned Wilmingtonians against moving too quickly to secession, but when his State seceded, he too, went with it, heart and soul.

Doctor Dickson was probably the leading physician of the town by the time of the war. He would sometimes open his home to sick or wounded soldiers and it is presumed he would also treat those unfortunates. He, like several of the town's doctors, stayed at his post when yellow fever struck and after contracting the disease, ordered his family away, so they would not be contaminated. He died "eleven days after the epidemic began." At least one chronicler of his life termed him the "Stonewall" of the medical profession, "undaunted, unmoved, determined to do his duty even if death were the penalty."

Another whose life was claimed by the pestilence was Doctor Peter B. Custis. Born in New Bern, where he lived until joining the 31st N.C. Regiment, he was, by April 1862, in charge of the Marine Hospital (General Hospital No. 5). Due to his earlier bouts of illness, caused in large part by his confinement upon being captured at the fall of Fort Hatteras, and the effects of yellow fever, he succumbed in March 1863.

Another town physician was James Schonwald. Born near Budapest, Hungary in 1801, Janos (or Johann, or later, James) was formerly a surgeon in the Austrian army, and was quite educated. He spoke not only Hungarian and English, but German, Italian and French. A nasty rumor followed the young man when he migrated to America. It was said that Schonwald and a fellow officer, after having imbibed quite freely, had gone to the theater in Milan, Italy. While seated in a box, he noticed "an attractive lady" across the way. He stared at her, even after being told by the other officer that not only was it rude, but the lady was a friend of his. Schonwald continued to gaze at her and words were passed between the two men. A fight was the outcome, "in which he was stabbed in the

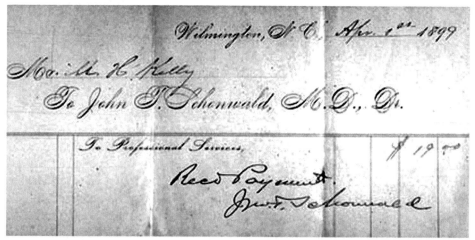

This receipt for payment for services rendered bears the signature of perhaps Dr. James Schonwald's son. (Fales Collection, NHCPL)

throat." Schonwald in turn killed his assailant and was forced to flee the country in disgrace. Forever after, he would wear a "speaking tube" in his throat and it was said that he spoke with a high pitched voice.

Another version of his leaving Europe was that his siblings had cheated him out of his inheritance and he "thereupon deserted the family and took the name Schonwald." A granddaughter once wrote that his given name was Johann Tossy. Whatever the circumstances that caused him to come to the United States, after stopping in New York for a time, by 1844 he settled in Baltimore, Maryland. It was in New York that he met and married a young lady named Fanny Frolick (or Froelich) and had at least one child by her. When he heard that a ship had come to Wilmington with a crew of Hungarians that could speak no English, he came south and not only translated for them, but treated them as well.

Schonwald was in a failing marriage. Though he sent for his wife, they were soon separated. She returned to New York and he stayed in Wilmington. Not bothering to obtain a divorce, he married a local girl in 1857. He practiced medicine in town and did quite well, acquiring a plantation of nearly six hundred acres on the Sound and siring a number of children. His special field of endeavor seems to have been working with children. He wrote a well-received paper entitled "The Child: A Treatise on the Diagnosis and Treatment of the Diseases of Children According to the Laws of Nature, 1851."

In 1860, his wife Fanny traveled to North Carolina and sued him for alimony. She came to Wilmington to press charges against him but lost the case. One cannot help but feel that as Schonwald had by this time become a pillar of the community, and because he married Catherine Joyner, daughter of a well respected citizen, Fanny's loss was a foregone conclusion.

Although James Schonwald never joined the Confederate service, it was said that he "furnished Medical supplies for the Confederate army. Much of what he obtained came in on blockade runners and was paid for out of his own pocket." In October 1863, Schonwald offered to sell 200 ounces of quinine at his "drug store on Princess Street." Always an enthusiastic Confederate, even to the point of naming three of his boys after Confederate leaders, (Robert Lee, Jackson and Jeff Davis), after the war his woes increased. He lost two of his three boys. One (Jeff Davis) died during the war, another (Robert Lee) in 1869. In 1868, Fanny returned to Wilmington to again present her case. This time she won. With Unionists now on the court, it was yet another foregone conclusion and he was forced to pay her alimony. Schonwald soon declared bankruptcy, but by 1880, he was again practicing medicine and also ran a drug store almost up to the time of his death in 1882.

One of the most well-known doctors in town was William George Thomas. An early member of the State Medical Society, Thomas was also the brother-in-law of Governor Henry T. Clark and "at a time when specialties were rare…he had established himself as an outstanding obstetrician." When war came, he volunteered to administer to the wounded soldiers in Virginia in 1862. He, like many of the town's outstanding denizens, was active in the community. Thomas was not only a founding member of the Library Association, but also a fire warden and for a time, the Port Physician. In this latter capacity he would board incoming blockade runners, examine their crews and make the determination as to whether or not they were healthy enough to dock at a town wharf. For this service he was paid twenty-five dollars per visit.

For all their combined knowledge of the healing profession, doctors were still unable to cure all the ills which might strike the town. They also felt the effects of inflation and by July 1862, most of his associates signed an ad which ran in the local paper. It read in part: "Payment in Cash. In conformity with and as a necessary result of the new universal usage in all other branches of business, the Medical Faculty of this place will hereafter require settlement in cash for their services as soon as rendered. Visits in the country cash in all instances." The ad also informed the public that the "poor and soldiers' families [would be] attended gratuitously as before. Salaried officers, clerks, mechanics and laborers charged in proportion to their ability to pay." By this point of the war, most of the town's merchants were also on a "cash only" basis. By the

Photo: NHCPL

The Seaman's Friend Hospital as it looked in the early 1900s....

latter stages of the war, the barter system was in effect; physicians would accept payment in cash or produce or even merchandise.[4]

During the yellow fever epidemic, the military evacuated all patients from General Hospital No. 4 and turned the premises over to the civilian authorities. It remained underutilized, for only 18 people were being treated when the facilities were visited by the *Journal*'s editor. The hospital, a four-story brick structure, was taken over as early as June 1861 for the use of the military and had a capacity of nearly two hundred beds. Doctor James A. Miller was initially placed in charge, but he soon left for more active service. The

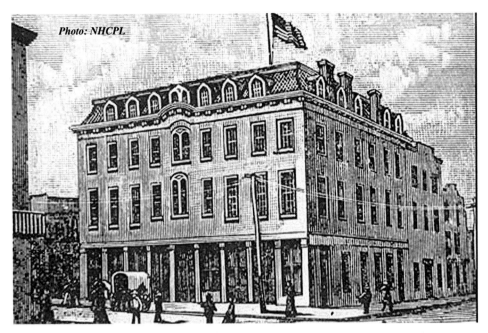

Photo: NHCPL

...and as it looked shortly after the Civil War.

hospital, located on the southwest corner of Front and Dock Streets, was the former Seaman's Home.

Some years earlier, the Seaman's Friend Society had purchased property and built a small home about two miles south of town. Known as Mount Tirza, the building soon fell into disrepair and was virtually abandoned. During the war, a Confederate gun battery was erected on the site.

Seeking quarters in town, the Society incorporated in 1853 for the "social and moral improvement of seamen [and built] a Boarding house of good character, where they should be protected in their money and morals." To help insure that the sailors' morals were kept high, a "Bethel" or chapel, together with a library and reading room, adjoined the building.

On the ground floor of the building were two stores, the larger one known as the "corner store," the other as the "south" store. Before and during the war, one of the stores was occupied by Scottish-born Robert Thorburn's "Eagle Bakery," where one could buy not only rolls and pilot bread, but crackers and "all kinds of cakes...[which could be] furnished for weddings and other parties." The other store was occupied by James H. Mitchell's "Gas and Steam Fitting" establishment.

The hospital itself was gas-lighted and supplied by the town's water works. It contained a "dispensary, store...baggage room [and] dining rooms" for both patients and staff. In February 1862, an advertisement was run seeking "two tin bathing tubs" for the facility. The Home, rented to the Confederate

Wilmington's Reel Cafe sits on the site of the old Seaman's Friend Hospital at Dock and Front Streets.

government for $35 per month, could house two hundred patients while the house across the street, which had been a private home, contained eighteen rooms with a capacity of over forty patients. This last had been Mrs. Quince's boarding house. It was well known, even in 1861, as the house in which George Washington stayed when passing through Wilmington in 1791.

As the need arose, two additional homes adjacent to the Quince house were available for use. Visiting hours for the hospitals stretched from eight in the morning to ten at night and members of the Ladies Aid Society brought not only foodstuffs, but bandages, lint and other items needed by the men.[5]

For a time in 1862, Doctor Adam Empie Wright had been in charge at the hospital, but he soon relinquished control to Dr. Thomas Atkinson. George Williams, the Society's prewar "Keeper" (or agent) was prevailed upon to remain as hospital steward, while his wife stayed on as matron. He soon had a run-in with Dr. Atkinson. Apparently Williams had purchased supplies for the hospitals, something stewards were not to do. Shortly afterwards, a directive was issued from the Surgeon General advising stewards not to spend any monies unless so directed by the Surgeon-in-Charge. Money was indeed being spent to stock the hospital. Dr. Wright had purchased over $1,000 worth of drugs from a local pharmacy. Included in the purchase were the standard medicines of the day: syringes, oils of cloves, cinnamon, peppermint, olive and cod liver; surgical and dental instruments, bedpans and bandages. In short, everything a large-sized hospital would require.

The unfortunate Dr. Atkinson died soon after reporting for duty and Surgeon Wright again took the helm for the remainder of 1862.

Thomas M. Ritenour, who reported to the hospital in early 1863, was placed in charge. Some soldiers were not happy with Ritenour's tenure. In June, a private wrote to Governor Vance asking why "the Surgeon of this hospital don't grant furlows and discharges a cordin to the Laws of the Confederate Congress[;] it appears that he maks his [own] laws[.]" The man also complained that since being in the hospital for two months, Doctor Ritenour hadn't "so much as bin to my room to see me[.]"

The following month, Sergeant William Buie wrote to the Governor about his brother who, he claimed, had been mistreated by both Ritenour and the city commandant, Lieutenant Colonel Charles E. Thorborn.

"I have the honor to appeal to you in behalf of one of my Brothers who has been treated very wrongfully by some petty Virginians…[H]e was wounded in the battle of Cedar Run and sent to Staunton Hospital from whence he was furloughed…On the 25th of June he came to Wilmington and asked Dr. Ritnor [sic] to detail him in the Hospital as he was unable for active service. Whereupon Dr. Ritanor [sic] demanded of him his papers…which he showed[.] Ritenor immediately ordered him to the Guard House after taking away his paper[.] He took his furlough…which was signed by the lamented T.J. Jackson[.]"

After discovering the plight of his brother, Sergeant Buie proceeded to Wilmington and had his brother released. At this point, Lieutenant Colonel Thorburn ordered the wounded soldier back to his regiment, giving him twenty-four hours to leave town. Ritenour had taken the soldier's railroad ticket as well and since he had neither clothing nor money, he remained in Wilmington. Sergeant Buie requested the governor to send his brother a pass, a request to which the governor acceded.

The patients, who referred to themselves as "hospital rats," often looked for sources of humor. In April 1863, several convalescing soldiers observed one of their numbers return to the hospital dressed in the most stylish clothes. When asked what the occasion had been, he replied that he had been wooing and won the hand of one of the "fair damsels" who worked at the hospital as a laundress.

"From a conversation with him…one of the 'rats' learned that this was his third wife, and he boasted that he would have seven more before the war ended. This 'rat' thinking seven too many for one man, while some had none, concluded to give him a ride on the wooden hoss, which intention he communicated to the other 'rats.'"

Everything was made ready and the unsuspecting soldier, who had been confined to quarters, was "very gently mounted" on his "hoss" and "with a band, consisting of a bell and a tin pan," the man was paraded around the hospital. As the procession moved out onto Front Street, Dr. Ritenour suddenly appeared and "Old Tom" put an end to the festivities.[6]

While battles raged in Pennsylvania and Virginia, action of a different sort was going on in Wilmington. In June, Doctor Ritenour found himself in difficulty with higher military authorities when a blockade runner (the *Arabia* or

Arabian) docked in Wilmington. It was not uncommon for blockade runners to donate foodstuffs to the various hospitals. Indeed, Ms. Mary Ann Buie, known as the "Soldier's Friend," actively sought donations from the masters and owners of the steamers. The purser of the *Arabian* offered gifts of fruit to Hospital No. 4, but Major General Whiting suspected the vessel was actually owned by northerners. Whiting placed a guard on it and even arrested several of the crew who were from New York and sent them to Richmond for further questioning.

As early as April of that year, Whiting had written to President Davis: "I hope you take notice of the extraordinary fact that almost every vessel carrying arms on private account is captured while those containing Yankee goods go with impunity." He also pointed out, "The people engaged in this business [blockade running] here, are men who have done nothing else during the war, many of them Yankee by birth & sympathy and all...if not openly union, then at least of doubtful faith to our cause." As far as the gifts from the *Arabian* were concerned, Whiting's standing orders were to have the goods delivered to the medical purveyor, who would then distribute them equally among the hospitals.[7]

Ritenour saw things differently. As the gifts were offered to his hospital, he went to the wharf where the runner lay docked. Pushing aside the sentry, he brought the fruits to the hospital. When Whiting found out he was incensed. Dr. Ritenour's actions came at the very time Whiting was drawing up charges against the vessel and he ordered the gifts back to the medical purveyor's warehouse. Ritenour complied, but took the additional step of writing his version of things to the newspaper. For his actions and for airing the army's dirty laundry in public, Whiting had Ritenour placed under arrest. The Confederate Medical Department then became involved, with Richmond's Surgeon General Moore stating that Whiting had no authority over Dr. Ritenour. Whiting then wrote to General Samuel Cooper: "I request that you will...define the limits assigned to Department Commanders in the matter of General Hospitals...I cannot understand...that Medical Officers assigned to General Hospitals are entirely and altogether independent of the Military Commandant." After giving Cooper a synopsis of what occurred, Whiting advised him that he "shall order a Court Martial upon Dr. Ritenour's case."

It was only after Ritenour wrote to Whiting, a letter that Whiting considered somewhat insubordinate, that the charges were dropped. The medical purveyor, Doctor Thomas J. Boykin, became embroiled in the controversy, being questioned by Surgeon General Moore. A letter from Dr. Moore to Whiting questioned whether or not medical supplies from abroad were being opened and pilfered at Wilmington.

Whiting was quick to defend Boykin by stating that the doctor was merely following the general's orders, but a shake-up was in the wind. Moore ordered Boykin to Petersburg, while Ritenour was replaced by Doctor Thomas Micks. Ritenour was given a proper send off by the hospital staff, complete with a testimonial delivered by his steward, Richard Paddison. From this, it would appear that Ritenour was well liked by his staff, but even the testimonial was controversial and stirred up bitter feelings.

In Ritenour's defense, it might be said that he was trying to make a point. Although there was a medical purveyor's office in Wilmington, the hospitals were required to make their requisitions to Raleigh and then draw upon the purveyor's office in Charlotte. This resulted in unnecessary delays and would not be corrected until Dr. Micks took charge of the hospital.

Letters to the newspaper revealed that not all at the hospital favored Ritenour. Some were glad to see him go. This resentment to Ritenour might have stemmed from the fact that he was a Virginian and the feeling, which was becoming widespread, that North Carolina was not receiving recognition for its contributions to the war. On the state level, this was exemplified by Governor Vance's request to have a reporter attached to North Carolina units serving in the Army of Northern Virginia. This request was denied by General Lee and many North Carolinians felt that President Jeff Davis disliked the state because of its reluctance to leave the Union. On a more local level, this feeling was manifested in Wilmington by Virginians treating citizens of the Old North State in a high-handed manner. This feeling would reach fever pitch in July, when Virginian Colonel Thorburn treated Governor Vance in a disrespectful manner.

After reporting to Virginia, Dr. Boykin wrote to his old friend, Governor Vance. Boykin had served as surgeon of Vance's 26th Regiment and had kept up a correspondence with Vance during and after the war. In October, from his new post at Petersburg, he penned his resignation and submitted it first to the governor for his perusal and then sent it to Richmond.

Moore, a former U.S. Army surgeon, was a stickler for military protocol and according to one who knew him, "the Emperor of the Russians was not more autocratic. Moore commanded and it was done[.]" Boykin received a "very ascetic business letter" from the surgeon general, which showed plainly that he was on the wrong side of Surgeon General Moore.

By the end of November, his resignation had still not been acted on, so Boykin wrote again to Governor Vance: "It has been some ten or twelve days, since I sent in my resignation, and not a word…yet. As I am…convinced that Dr. Moore intends giving me all the trouble he can, has heretofore treated me with great injustice & seems determined to treat me badly."

Boykin requested that Vance write to the War Department to move things along and soon enough the good doctor was out of the army. It is likely he asked the governor for a place aboard the state's blockade runner, the *SS Advance*. In consultation with the former purser and Joseph Flanner, the state's agent in town, the governor was informed that the position of surgeon aboard the vessel was no longer required. However, the position of purser was available, so

Boykin went aboard in that capacity. He made several trips on the steamer and as Vance's man on board the ship, he reported on what he saw and made recommendations for improvements.

He was at Bermuda when a fire destroyed some of the state's cotton and was often the go-between for Vance and cotton brokers Power, Low and Company. He resigned his position in April 1864 and that fall, he and auctioneer Wilkes Morris were selected to go abroad with North Carolina's purchasing agent, John White.

In August and September, after several failed attempts to leave the port aboard the *Advance*, they finally got out aboard the *SS Virginia*. As yellow fever was rampant in Bermuda, White remained aboard and started for Halifax the next day. While there, he came down with the illness and was delayed in getting to England. The only word his family heard was from Wilkes Morris, who assured them that White was recovering. White stayed abroad until late in 1865 when he returned to his home in Warrenton, N.C.

In late 1864, blockade running from Wilmington was becoming much more dangerous as U.S. forces were concentrating in and around the Cape Fear area in preparation for an all-out attack on Fort Fisher. After a failed attempt in December, the Yankees returned the following month and this time, took the bastion. Only a few weeks later, in February 1865, Wilmington was taken by the Federals.

Boykin found himself stranded in Halifax, Nova Scotia. After war's end, he remained in Canada until assured he would not be arrested on his return. He came back that fall. Tragedy followed him when his wife, who had been sent away to the safety of her parents' home in New Jersey, passed away in November 1865. He later remarried and moved to Baltimore. It was there that he began supplying hospitals with medicines, even calling upon his old friend, once again Governor of North Carolina, Zeb Vance.

In 1877 Boykin quite bluntly wrote: "I don't want office…But there is your penitentiary, your Deaf and Dumb Asylum, your Insane Asylum, all buy medl. supplies. I will sell them as low as any one else…This is what I want[.]"

He and a partner bagan marketing "worm-candy." Worm candy, or vermifuge, used to eliminate worms from the intestines, was made from the lowly Jimson weed. Boykin paid children throughout the south to gather the weed and send it to Baltimore where the medicine was manufactured. He became quite wealthy in his adopted city, but in 1863, both his and Dr. Ritenour's future was clouded.[8]

Dr. Micks, Ritenour's replacement, reported for duty in September 1863. He was a no-nonsense disciplinarian, a good doctor and an able administrator. Upon assuming command, he issued a directive to his staff warning that all rules and regulations must be adhered to.

Born in Sampson County, N.C., Micks was an experienced doctor, having been twice examined by Army Medical Boards in Florida and Tupelo, Mississippi. He would be taking charge of a medium-sized facility. Known also as the "surgical hospital," General Hospital No. 4 was said to be the best in the state, even supplying mosquito netting in the summer months.

An inventory taken on 1 January 1864 showed the hospital well equipped with everything from bunks, bed sacks and blankets to stools, quilts, candlesticks, washtubs and coffee pots. There was a washing machine as well as foot tubs and even one writing desk. Micks reorganized the hospital by assigning the doctors to specific wards and reassigned the steward in charge of the dispensary, warning the new man that it was also "his duty to see that loungers are not permitted in the dispensary." Being located "in the central part of the city, it was," as Dr. Micks reported, "difficult to keep the convalescents from straggling." The location was also noisy, being in the business district and surrounded on all sides by buildings. It was "very close and confined in Summer." There was no space for a garden to provide fresh vegetables. Dr. Micks wanted a garden, not only for the fresh vegetables, but because it would provide work to occupy men recovering from their wounds.

Morning reports from the assigned officer of the day were logged in every day. The hospital was not always in tip-top shape, as the following report, entered by Surgeon Sterling Eve on 16 October 1863, shows: "I have the honor to report the Hospital only in a tolerably fair condition, in consequence of the weather. Ward Master Sims is reported for dereliction of duty. Two intoxicated sailors were placed in the Guard House last night."

Other surgeons agreed with Eve's assessment, noting that a stronger guard was needed: "The hospital yesterday was in a very dirty condition, the stairs leading to Ward 5 & the nurses room...particularly so. For the last few weeks there has been no night guard, the hospital being unwatched. I had a guard detailed & think that it should be continued."

Later that month, another officer recorded that some of the patients were griping about short rations. Upon investigation, the officer found a portion of bacon missing and wrote: "The convalescents had nothing for breakfast except rice and bread. There was a small quantity of bacon...issued to the working hands. The Commissary said that he issued the usual rations. The only solution ...that has been offered, is that the meat shrank away. It is somewhat remarkable that this property of extreme contraction in bacon, has lain dormant for so long a period, only to be developed in these latter times."

Another entry written by Dr. Eve suggested reducing the number of officers fed, because the matron complained that it was nearly impossible to cook for so many men in so small a kitchen.[9]

Surgeon Micks, as the senior officer in charge of a General Hospital, was paid about two hundred dollars per month. His assistants received anywhere from one hundred to one hundred fifty dollars, depending on their length of service. They were granted extra money for "fuel and quarters," something the doctors would need when inflation raised prices in Wilmington. His uniform, as set forth in army regulations, was "of gray cloth, known as cadet gray [it] was to have black facings with a stand up collar. His 'trowsers' were to be made of dark blue cloth and [they] were to have a 'black velvet stripe…with a gold cord on each edge of the stripe.' A black cravat, ankle or Jefferson boots, white gloves, a star on the tunic collar, a sash of 'green silk net' and a cap on which the letters M.S. were embroidered in gold, completed the medical officer's prescribed dress."

As the head of a Confederate hospital, Dr. Micks was to visit every patient at least once a day, but Micks was a busy man. He was wrapped up in the paperwork and administrative details necessary to handle a hospital of that size. Indeed, one writer has said: "The medical officer in charge of each general hospital was responsible for the efficient administration of his institution. He was to receive patients, distribute them to the proper wards, visit them as often as necessary each day, and 'enforce the proper hospital regulations to promote health and prevent contagion.'"

Prior to the establishment of General Hospitals, states funded aid for men from that state alone, but it was determined that a general hospital system, one that accepted patients from the units of all Confederate states, was much more efficient. A surgeon could be inundated with paperwork. There was the register of patients to keep up, a "prescription and diet book, a case book, copies of all requisitions, annual returns, returns of property and an order and letter book that were required to be kept. There were monthly and quarterly reports to be filed and statements of how much money was in the hospital fund as well as how it had been expended. Most important of the myriad of reports was the monthly report to the Surgeon General concerning the hospital fund."

At the beginning of the war, hospitals were allowed a commutation ration for each patient. Costs rose from one dollar per day to $1.25 in May 1863 and then doubled by February 1864. If two hundred patients were in the hospital, this amounted to $3,500 per week. This money was to be expended in purchasing "such perishables as fruit, eggs, butter, chickens, milk and vegetables."

Dr. Micks kept a copy of the "Regulations for the Medical Department of the C.S. Army" to refer to if needed. It laid out what was expected of the medical personnel in treating their patients. Proper hospital regulations to promote health and prevent contagion were to be strictly followed: rooms were to be well "ventilated and not crowded," bedding and linens were to be changed frequently with fresh straw added to the "bed sacks and pillow ticks." The book laid out the ratio of attendants: one steward, one nurse as ward master, one nurse for every ten patients, one laundress for every twenty patients and one cook for every thirty sick or wounded men. Doctors were cautioned about granting "certificates of disability" to soldiers exhibiting symptoms of epilepsy, chronic rheumatism, convulsions, ulcers "or any obscure disease, liable to be feigned." They were to make certain the man being discharged had not received any head injury that "may impair his facilities" and to make sure he was not a drunkard. When a soldier was furloughed, discharged or transferred, an attendant went with him to the railroad station to ensure the man got a seat on the train.

Micks had the assistance of four assistant surgeons: Doctors Joshua C. Walker, Adam E. Wright, Sterling C. Eve and Javon Bryant. Walker and Wright were native sons of the town. Walker was Major General Whiting's brother-in-law. Whiting had tried, unsuccessfully, to obtain the position of Surgeon-in-Charge at Hospital No. 4 for him.

Walker had served with the Third N.C. Regiment, Wright with the 30th. Eve, whose father Paul was a well-known and respected physician, had served with both the First Georgia and Jackson's Corps while Bryant, a South Carolinian, had been in the field with the 13th S.C. All had done their share of hazardous duty, had performed their share of amputations and all had seen disease ravage their regiments.

Delegating part of his arduous duties, Micks made sure there was at least one doctor on duty at all times and made sure his surgeons visited the wards assigned to them twice daily, at 9 a.m. and 6 p.m., and "as often in the interim, as the condition of the sick may render necessary."[10] Divided among the physicians were the mundane but necessary duties of ordering medicines, instruments, furniture, record-keeping (case books of the patients and operations performed, records of deaths and personal effects of the deceased) and the hospital fund – something that had been depleted under Dr. Ritenour's tenure. Although there was no chaplain assigned to the hospital, the Reverends Edwin Geer and Alphonse Repiton frequently visited the wards, praying with the men and distributing religious tracts.

The hospitals in town had to be prepared when a regiment encamped nearby was ordered to the front. As the regimental doctors left with their unit, the sick were moved from their campsites to the hospitals. The hospital records indicate that on moving day as many as fifty or sixty men were admitted to G.H. No. 4, with many more coming the next day. Such movements quickly filled up the wards. Negroes were admitted, although many of them, not unlike many Confederate soldiers, were simply given their dosage of medicine and sent on their way. There are, however, several instances of black men who were assigned a bed in a common ward.

As it was originally a refuge for seamen, the hospital continued to accept mariners and Confederate sailors as patients. At least one woman was admitted while the hospital was under military control. When Private James Jones was admitted in late July 1862 with fever, his wife was also given a bed. Apparently she had come to nurse her husband and contracted an illness. After spending a week in the hospital, they were both discharged.

When Luther Toon came to the hospital suffering from congestion, he remained less then a week and was discharged on 1 August 1862. Just s few days later, he was aboard the steamer *Petteway*, returning to town from Fort Caswell. Dozing, he awoke with a start, jumped up and walked off the deck of the boat. Toon drowned in the Cape Fear River.

When Private W.G. Fox of the 79th Virginia Militia was captured by Federals on 23 March 1862 in Greenbriar County, Virginia, his captors described him as a "Bushwacker." Sent to Camp Chase, "4 miles from Columbus, Oh.," the hospital register told the rest of Private Fox's story: "He remained there from 3 April until 6 Sept., then to Lake Erie, there until 22 Nov., then to Cairo, then to Camp of Exchange at Vicksburg, Miss. To Mobile, sick three weeks. Left there Jan. 8[th][,] landed at Wilmington Jan. 12[th][.]" Still ill when he arrived, he was given a bed in General Hospital No. 4. Disease and exposure had taken a terrible toll on his body and doctors were unable to stem the course. Less than two weeks later, on 23 January, Private Fox died.

More men died from disease than from anything else during the conflict. This fact is reflected by the hospital records. Many recruits that came from the rural areas were more susceptible to disease than were those from the cities. One surgeon wrote that "one town regiment was more efficient than two or even three from the country."

Contagions of course outnumbered gunshot wounds throughout the war. Fevers, diarrhea, erysipelas, dysentery, pneumonia, even a few cases of anthrax and at least one case of "Malingeria" were recorded in the record books. Upon being admitted, men were examined by a doctor and assigned to a ward based "on their complaints." They were given a hospital uniform, shirt, pants and drawers. Any personal effects brought with them were registered and labeled with the man's name, rank and unit. Particular care had to be taken when patients reported a disease that could be faked. Soldiers were told not to bring firearms into the hospital with them, but they often did. Under no circumstances was ammunition to be stored in the hospital. Patients were sometimes put on "half" or "low" rations, a procedure many soldiers complained of. It was thought that the body needed to concentrate on healing, instead of consuming food. One soldier said of the diminished rations, I "would just as soon lie on my back and let the moon shine in my mouth."

As for food in general, there seemed to be enough and was quite varied. A report in the summer of 1863 showed veal, beef, chicken and fish, blackberries, strawberries, and whortleberries, potatoes, peas, beans, bread and butter. Two beverages highly sought were coffee and brandy. When the coffee "boiler" broke down, the hospital paid $4 to have it quickly repaired. Coffee was, by far, the cheaper beverage. Seven gallons of brandy cost two hundred eighty dollars.

Rank bestowed little privilege at the site. Lieutenants, captains and colonels were bedded next to each other and enlisted men. In quite a few instances, though, a home in town was opened for sick soldiers, especially officers.[11] At various times, a newspaper ad would alert all those in "Private Quarters" to report to the hospital. There they would be re-examined and either allowed to return home or were given passes and sent to their unit.

If a soldier was furloughed, he was expected to return to duty upon recovery. Those that passed away in the hospital had their relatives notified. If no one came to claim the body, they were buried in Oakdale, the town cemetery. Their name, date and cause of death, along with any belongings they may have had, were logged in and Richmond was notified of the man's death. Personal items were held for the family. If no one came, the effects and any money they may have had, were turned over to Quartermaster Christopher Styron. Usually listed in the book were such things as socks, shoes, bedclothes, blankets and jackets. Most poignant of the entries is the notation that a soldier died and his effects were valueless, his last possessions consigned to the trash heap.

Dr. Micks was able to change the procedure for ordering supplies. Doctor Hugh Stockdell, the new medical purveyor, had the supplies delivered to his warehouse, rather than having them sent from Charlotte. Shortly after assuming his duties in November 1863, Stockdell had difficulty obtaining urgently needed brandy and was required to buy it locally at a much higher price. Doctor Stockdell was supposed to have on hand a rather large supply of items besides medicine. He also kept "bed sacks, pillow ticks, sheets, boxes, canisters, bottles, jugs, paper envelopes, wrapping paper, brandy, wine, whiskey, tea, mosquito nets, pencils, pill boxes, trusses, forceps, operating tables, amputating instruments, candles and dishes.

It is no wonder that in August 1864, Dr. Stockdell's budget reached $400,000, "for the purchase of supplies arriving [at Wilmington] through the blockade."[12]

Endnotes

1. *Vance Papers*, 26:882.
2. *Daily Journal*, 16 March 1864; *Southern Women*, 15:822, letter dated September 1862.

3. *Wilmington City Directory*, 1860, 100. Copy in the New Hanover County Public Library. *Daily Journal*, 15 April 1862

4. Powell, *North Carolina Biography*, I:66 and 5:297-298; *Proceedings of the Fiftieth Annual Convention of the M.E. Grand Royal Arch Chapter of North Carolina* (Durham: The Educator Co., 1898) 107. *Transcripts of the 15th Annual Meeting of the Medical Society of the State of North Carolina* (Wilmington: Englehard and Price, 1868) 23. This work encompasses the years 1868-1870, and is hereinafter cited as *Transcripts*. The quote about Dr. Dickson was dated 1870. Cashman, *The Lonely Road*, 22-23, 189. New Hanover County, *Minutes of the Superior Court, 1856-1871*, spring term, No. 18. Bill Reaves Collection, *Family Files*, New Hanover County Public Library. *Morning Star*, 30 August 1882; *Daily Journal*, 19 April and 8 July 1862, 12 December 1864. Clark, 4:368

5. *Daily Journal*, 10 March 1854, 16 March 1864. National Archives, Record Group 109, Medical Department Records, *Letters Sent, General Hospital No. 4, 1863-1865*, 18 November 1863, Dr. Thomas Micks to Dr. P.E. Hines, hereinafter cited as *Letters Sent*. See *also Book of Vouchers, of Articles Bought By General Hospital, Wilmington, No. Carolina, June 25th 1863*, hereinafter cited as *Market Supplies*. *Daily Journal*, 20 October 1862. The total capacity for the hospital was just over 200. Sprunt, *Chronicles*, 208. *Daily Journal*, 10 February and 15 July 1862. The hospital could handle closer to three hundred patients spread throughout eight wards, when necessary. See also LCFHS, *Seaman's [sic] Friend Society Minutes*, hereinafter cited as *Seaman's Minutes*. Gas fitter James Mitchell's warehouse was located next to the Bethel, see the *1860 Wilmington City Directory*, 59, 77. Mitchell's brother William, was the superintendent of the Gas Works and died in the yellow fever epidemic.

6. *Vance Papers*, 18:487-488. *Daily Journal*, 25 April 1863.

7. *Whiting Papers*, II:335, letter dated 29 April, 20 and 22 June 1863. The *Arabian* left Wilmington but was chased ashore by the U.S. Navy and "has gone to pieces near Fort Fisher," *Daily Journal*, 24 September 1863.

8. *Vance Papers*, 18:359-360, dated 25 June 1863, 18:487-488, dated 3 July 1863. *Daily Journal*, 18 February 1863; *Whiting Papers*, II:336, letter dated 14 August, 17 August 1863. *Daily Journal*, 15 August 1863. Boykin's involvement can also be found in the *Whiting Papers*, 1 September 1863. Other information on Boykin is found in *The Heritage of Sampson County, N.C.* (Winston-Salem: Hunter Publishing Co., 1983) edited by Oscar M. Bizzell, 37, 198. See also the *Vance Papers*, 3:337, letter dated 3 October 1863; 4:532, letter dated 15 July 1865, 29:301, letter dated 2 February 1877. See also Dr. Jeanette L. Jerger, *A Medical Miscellany for Genealogists* (Westminster, Md.: Heritage Books, 1995) 74-75. Jimson weed was the main ingredient in atropine, "a drug frequently used in the practice of medicine."

9. National Archives, RG 109, Chapter VI, vol. 404, *Reports of the Officer of the Day, General Hospital No. 4, Wilmington, North Carolina, 1863-1864*, 80, 7-10.

Surgeon William Considine wrote about the dirty condition of the hospital on 22 October 1863; Assistant Surgeon Javon Bryant authored the missing bacon report the previous day.

10. *Daily Journal*, 31 March 1862. H.H. Cunningham, "Organization of the Confederate Medical Department," *North Carolina Historical Review*, volume 31, number 3, July 1954, 385-409. In this work Cunningham listed the number of principal hospitals in the Confederacy by state: Virginia- 30, N.C.- 21, Georgia- 50, Alabama- 23, Mississippi- 3, Florida- 4, Tennessee- 2. See also H.H. Cunningham, *Doctors in Gray: The Confederate Medical Service* (Baton Rouge: Louisiana State University Press, 1993) 74, 80-81. *Regulations for the Medical Department of the C.S. Army* (Richmond; Ritchie & Dunnavant, 1863) 10-11, 56. General Hospital No. 4, "Letters Sent," 16 November 1863. Dr. Eve was reassigned in early 1864 to the hospital at Augusta, Georgia, where his father Paul was Surgeon-in-Charge. Still extant in the National Archives, in RG109, are the *Records of General Hospital No. 4: Case Books*, 1863-64, Records of Transfers, 1865, Register of Deaths and Effects, 1864-65, Register of Patients, 1862-65, Reports of the Officer of the Day, 1863-64, Letters Sent and Received, 1863-65, Accounts and Morning Reports, 1862-64 and the Reports of the Examining Boards. In all, a pretty extensive record of the operations at the hospital can be reconstructed. See also *C.S. Army Regulations*, hereinafter cited as *Army Regulations*, page 8, copy in the North Carolina Room, New Hanover County Library.

11. National Archives, RG109, Medical Department, General Hospital No. 4, Register of Patients, 1862-1863, chapter VI, vol. 282, 54, entry number 1578; roll M324, reel 1049, "William G. Fox, Company F, 79th Virginia Militia." Duncan Dudley, "Coloured" was admitted in June 1863. In place of a regiment, "Cav. Services" was written. "Market Supplies," several dates. Hospital Steward Richard Paddison's name appears quite often in the voucher book, he went into the countryside to make purchases. Cunningham, *Doctors in Gray*, 86, 166. *Army Regulations*, 9, 11.

12. For four dozen bottles of brandy, stockdell paid J.P. Levy $840, Citizen's Papers, Reel 584, 7 and 11 Novermber 1863.

Richard P. Paddison after the war. (Confederate Veteran)

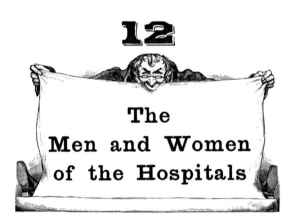

The Men and Women of the Hospitals

In 1864, General Lee issued an order directing all men to report back to their commands. This order weakened the hospital staff as Medical Boards convened and traveled around the state examining patients and sending back those men thought fit for field duty. To many army officers, men detailed as nurses were considered "shirkers," or malingerers, and many times company commanders demanded the men be sent back to duty. As the local labor pool shrank, many saw the hospital as an available source of laborers from which they could draw needed bodies. This did not always work, however. After seeing the requested men sent from the hospital to guard his warehouse, Purveyor Stockdale asked to have them removed, as they "were more trouble than profit[.]" One of the convalescents put on guard duty caught pneumonia and died upon being returned to the hospital. Purveyor Stockdale got his sentries from the city garrison instead.

At G.H. No. 4, Dr. Micks still wanted to get a garden started, but there was no place nearby, so he looked at the grounds around General Hospital No. 5. That site contained more than enough space for gardens and Micks desired to hire a gardener to help tend it. The garden was allowed, but there would be no money for a gardener. When he attempted to transfer a patient to the hospital at Wilson, he was told by his superiors: "It would not be in [the] spirit of the orders of the Surgeon General concerning patients with gonorrhea and Syphilis… because such patients are not entitled to any privilieges[.]"[1]

If there was a constant lack of money, there was also a dearth of laborers. In addition to the physicians, there were wardmasters, two hospital stewards, nurses, both "detailed" and "hired," laundresses, cooks, a baggage master to secure the patient's belongings and one chief hospital steward.

"Detailed" nurses were simply wounded or sick convalescents who were assigned to the hospital for as few as ten days, or for as long as several months. Most of the detailed men would do anything to remain where they were, rather than go back to the battlefield.

In July 1864, with 130 patients, the hospital was staffed as follows: 1 surgeon, 1 acting assistant surgeon, two stewards, 13 detailed and 9 hired nurses, 4 cooks, 10 laundresses (paid about $8 per month), 1 chief matron (at about $50 per month), 1 assistant matron ($30 per month), 2 ward matrons ($25 per month) and six guards. In addition, there were 21 detailed and 27 hired attendants.

Female matrons worked at the site. A law passed in September 1862 ensured that two matrons, plus two assistant matrons, were allowed for each ward. Mrs. McCauslin was the chief matron at G.H. No. 4 and she was there at least as early as January 1864.

Considered essential to the hospital was Private S.D. Owens, the baker. When it looked as though he might be sent back to his regiment, Dr. Micks wrote to General Whiting that the man's services "were invaluable to this hospital." Since the soldier's commanding officer agreed, Owens stayed, at least for a bit longer. By December 1864, he was returned to his unit, Company B, 17th N.C.[2]

Although the baker was important, the chief hospital steward would have to be considered the number one enlisted man at the hospital. It was he who really ran things. He was the senior enlisted man and at General Hospital No. 4. That man, for several years, was Richard P. Paddison.

Paddison was the epitome of what a Chief Steward should be. Stewards were to be "skilled in pharmacy and to possess such qualities as honesty, reliability, intelligence and temperance." In addition, Paddison was compassionate, knowledgeable and amiable.

He was born in Virginia in 1837 and "at the age of 12 was apprenticed to an apothecary in Harper's Ferry. When only 17, he went to Alexandria and then to Boston." When war threatened, he returned to North Carolina and enlisted early in the war as a private in the 51st Regiment, serving at Fort Johnston until being appointed hospital steward in 1862. After the yellow fever and smallpox epidemics, he was assigned to Hospital No. 4.

As an indication of the trust which Dr. Micks placed in Paddison, in March 1864, when Micks was sent to examine the operation of General Hospital No. 2 (located in the former Female Seminary at Wilson), he brought Steward Paddison along. In charge of that institution was Dr. Solomon Sampson Satchwell. Said to be an excellent orator, he had obtained his M.D. from New York University in 1850 and practiced in the Cape Fear area. In 1860 Satchwell traveled abroad to France, where he studied at the Sorbonne in Paris, where "he spent time mainly…in the hospitals and dissecting rooms, adding to his store of

professional knowledge[.]" Still in France when the war broke out, he had a
difficult time making his way South. He had to travel to the west, "after a hard
scruff to get through at all," reported the *Daily Journal.*

After passing through New York City, the paper continued, "Neither
Massachusetts in general, or Boston in particular can hold a candle to New York
in rancorous bitterness. Such appears to be the result of the Doctor's
observations...We understand that the history of the Doctor's meanderings
would form quite a narrative. Any Southern man coming home from New York
now has to go on a 'winding way.' "

Upon reaching his native state, Satchwell joined the army and was
commissioned a major in the Medical Department and assigned to the 25th
Regiment. It was while with this regiment that the following took place: "The
regiment became infested with malaria, and Dr. Satchel, [sic]...recommended a
little whiskey, which he had issued from the hospital tent in the mornings. It
wasn't long before the malady became chronic. The Doctor soon cured this,
however, for he gave them something with the whiskey [and] 'They had the
pleasure of tasting their licker twice – going and coming.' "

In 1862, he was appointed head surgeon at General Hospital No. 2.
Satchwell was "a pioneer in 'hygienic therapy' – fresh air, sunshine, diet and a
minimum of drugs – and in public health." His hospital reflected his views on
cleanliness. Doctor Micks commented that there was "a place for everything
and everything in its place." Micks gave the hospital high marks for everything,
ranging from the discipline at the site, to the "hot and cold" baths available for
patients. The following year virtually the same comments were uttered by one
who "spent a few days within its walls...Cleanliness and discipline are strictly
observed and enforced." In his report, Dr. Micks described the hospital, with its
outbuildings consisting of "Blacksmith, carpenter, Turner, Wheelwright, Cooper
and Shoe Maker shops," which were manned by convalescent and detailed men.

On the grounds, but separate from the main building, was a smaller
building in which those infected with contagious diseases were housed. Micks
also was impressed with the large garden on the premises, which all agreed
would provide "an abundant supply of vegetables" to the hospital. Perhaps
Micks was a bit envious of the hospital; he must certainly have thought how
much good a garden would do for his hospital.

Hospital Steward Paddsion would remain in the Cape Fear region for
most of the war. As a steward, he was "the machine of a hospital...All matters,
all requisitions, orders, etc." came to him "for approval or disapproval." It was
he who often notified the relatives of the death of their brothers, fathers, and
sons. On at least one occasion the brother of a soldier who died in the hospital
wrote to him, thanking him for his "attentions to [his brother] in his last

sickness. I witnessed your attachment to him, and know you did whatever you could for him."

Included in Paddison's letters to the bereaved was an inventory of the dead soldier's effects. Property of deceased soldiers was always carefully guarded and on at least one occasion, a Confederate surgeon was arrested for the misuse of this property. Paddison's personality and work ethics endeared him to a large group of friends, both soldiers and surgeons alike.

In the summer of 1863 he sent a package to friends in Raleigh. It contained several bottles of liquor, which by then was becoming difficult to obtain. On of the recipients wrote back: "Dr. Covey and myself have received the magnificent treat sent by Dr. Ritenour and yourself. I swear we will enjoy it. It is decidedly the best thing I've had since the war began. Kill Dr. Hughes for smashing the brandy bottle. I don't know yet what the examinations for Hospital Stewards will be, but I presume moral character will be rigidly inquired into. Reform immediately. Again I thank you from the bottom of my heart – and stomach."[3]

The following year, a friend returned the favor: "Dick, there is a trunk… with something for nearly everybody in the Confederacy, and I mean to trouble you with the disposal of them…Four bbls. of alcohol…to Tom J. Johnson. Six cases of liquor to Street…one case and cask to W. Norris[.]"

When, in February 1865, Wilmington fell to Federal forces, Paddison stayed at the hospital with those who were too ill to be moved. He was ordered out by the Federal authorities and removed to a vacant home in town. With the Federal occupation, food conditions improved and Paddison was able to keep his hospital well stocked, in large part due to the U.S. Sanitary Commission agent, Flaval W. Foster and the chief U.S. surgeon, Dr. Shipman.

Paddison later wrote: "I wish to state that we had courteous treatment from the authorities, but of course we were very short of supplies. The first genuine treat we had was by Mr. F.W. Foster, who was acting as sanitary agent. He drove up one morning and inquired about the sick, and asked if I would like to have some milk punch for the men. I said 'Yes,' as it had been a long time since we had any such luxury. He went out and soon returned with two large pails and a dipper, and personally served to each all they could stand. This he continued to do for several weeks. On one of his visits he asked me if I would like to have some canned goods for the hospital. I replied, 'Yes,' and he said, 'The steamer *General Lyon* is unloading a cargo of hospital supplies. If you will go down there you can get what you want.'…The vessel was unloading…We backed up and I began to select what I wanted. I was not at all modest…I loaded to the limit. Strange to say, no questions were asked."

Staying at the improvised hospital until the last soldier left in June, he was finally released from duty: "I came out of the army as I had entered it –

without one dollar, but with a clear conscience...From April 20, 1861 to June 5, 1865 I never had a furlough or a day's absence from duty."[4]

Paddison retired to Point Caswell where he died 23 November 1915 at the age of 77. Shortly before his death he made two requests: the first, that when the time came, he be buried in his Confederate uniform. As he was a Master Mason, his second wish was that his funeral services be conducted with the honors of that society. Both requests were fulfilled.[5]

General Hospital No. 4 was well prepared to receive patients who had been wounded or became ill from disease, but it was not ready to receive Private Archibald McCormick. Forty-four years old when he enlisted in August 1863, McCormick had been born in Robeson County and was assigned to the 36th N.C. Regiment. A heavy artillery unit, the regiment was stationed at Fort Fisher. It didn't take long for everyone to realize that something was wrong with McCormick. Before long, the fort's surgeon, Singleton Spiers, examined the man. He reported to his superiors and McCormick was eventually discharged "by reason of insanity of a hereditary origin." One year later, yet another, diagnosed with the same ailment, was sent to General Hospital No. 4. Dr. Micks, unsure of what to do with the man, as there were 'no cells or other places of security" in the hospital, turned him over to Major James Reilly, commander of the city garrison.

Major James Reilly, CSA

Reilly lodged him in the military prison while General Whiting made his decision as to whether he should be discharged. The man's brother-in-law came to town and verified that insanity was hereditary in the family and he was soon out of the army. There was at least one more "lunatic" in the ranks at Fort Fisher, but just how real was their malady, one may never know.[6]

In 1862, when Dr. Ritenour was in charge of G.H. No. 4, he planned to establish a fishery in the region. It was thought that mackerel, menhaden, herring, shad and sturgeon could not only supply the hospitals in Wilmington, but could be sent to the other hospitals throughout the state. Fish oil could be used for machinery, for tanning leather, and was a substitute for linseed oil, necessary to waterproof blankets and coats. It was not an idle proposition. In the years before the war, North Carolina fisheries provided much of the seafood caught in the South.[7] The business would be set up at the mouth of the Cape Fear River, at Fort Caswell. Although Ritenour applied for permission to fish, he left shortly before the idea came to fruition.

After Dr. Micks assumed charge, Dr. E.N. Covey, Medical Director of the State, wrote to him inquiring about the status of the fishery. Micks pointed out that he could find no information about the fishery among Dr. Ritenour's papers; indeed, Ritenour had left very few records to go by. They had apparently been misplaced or lost when "the hospital was broken up and removed during the summer of 1862." What was readily apparent was that the hospital fund had been exhausted in setting up the fishery.

Micks also informed Covey that the commissary had "very few of the articles necessary for the sick" and thought the fishery a good way to raise funds. He suggested that Dick Paddison be placed in charge of the operation, "to insure its success." He went on: "I have [had] what tents &c. he wishes invoiced to you. Please give him as many men as he may need. I have asked that you may be allowed [to] purchase salt from the government."

As early as July 1863, Paddison was supplying G.H. No. 4 with seafood, so it is quite possible that the idea of a fishery originated with him. Any fish caught were to be sold at cost to the other hospitals "at such rates as will pay the expense of catching, packaging &c." Before anything could be done, permission was needed from General Whiting to allow fishermen to go out in small boats at the mouth of the river. All boats along the river and sounds had been collected and put under guard because deserters were using them to slip away to the U.S. Navy blockading fleet just offshore. Even the men who earned a living fishing were barred from practicing their trade.

One letter to the paper asked: "How is it that soldiers of certain artillery companies...are allowed to catch fish, and bring them to market in Government wagons with Government horses and artillery harnesses, and sell them at one dollar for two and three fish, when our regular fishermen are deprived of the privilege of fishing. We all like fish in Wilmington, having been accustomed to them all our lives. Is this right?"

Micks did obtain permission. Empty barrels were sent down from storage from the Mount Olive depot, salt was purchased and a fishery was finally established under Paddison's control. This was a fairly large undertaking for the hospital. At Fort Caswell, salting-houses and coopering sheds were needed, as well as quarters for the men, who probably lived in tents. Paddison made the necessary purchases including barrels, salt, coopering tools and even oyster tongs. The most expensive item was the net, for which he paid $500 (for the seine) and $100 for twine.[8]

In 1861 there were several fisheries being worked for the Union in the recently captured Albemarle Sound. The seines used at these fisheries measured anywhere from 2,200 to 2,700 yards in length and were from eighteen to twenty-four feet wide. One Federal observer of the operation noted: "This enormous length of netting is packed upon the stern platforms of two ten-oared boats, which are rowed out together to a point opposite the landing, about a mile distant. Here the boats separate, moving in different directions, and the seine is played out as they row toward their destined points."

One boat would continue downstream while the other turned into the shore. In this manner the fish were "corralled" within the net. The net had corks on top and was weighted down with lead sinks. In one of the Albemarle Sound fisheries, heavy ropes, "made fast to the staves securing either end, are carried in to the...four mule windlasses at the extremities of the beach." As the windlasses reeled in the net, the circle tightened and the fish would begin to swarm, leaping up into the air, trying to escape the huge trap. When the time was right, the workers would wade into the mass. Shad were especially prized, but everything caught was put in baskets, taken to the packinghouse, cleaned, salted and placed in barrels. The Union fishery employed anywhere from eighty to one hundred men, but the Confederate fishery at Fort Caswell, although similar, was most likely a smaller-scale operation.[9] When Dr. Covey was unable to visit Wilmington, Dr. Micks informed him that he had been unable to visit the fishery, since it was "situated at Fort Caswell, some thirty (30) miles distant by water[.]" Paddison, he wrote, was in charge and had expended about $1,100 and had caught only about twenty barrels of fish. By November, the results were still not promising. Micks surmised that the very hot weather and warm water and also the constant cannonading off the coast had prevented "the fish from coming in." Only about 35 or 40 barrels were packed at a cost of about $30 each. These could then be sold from $100 to $150 per barrel.

Paddison was left with about three or four hundred dollars, which was to be used to buy salt, in the event a large catch was secured. Ending his letter on an upbeat note, Micks wrote: "we ought with ordinary success soon to have a sufficient quantity of fish to supply all the Hospitals in the State." For the present, Micks was ready to divide only nine barrels among the hospitals in Fayetteville, Raleigh and Wilmington.[10]

The idea was a good one and another attempt was made the following year. Micks had chosen the Sounds to start fishing, even though it was thought to be dangerous. Union blockaders were apt to raid the fishery, much as they had the salt works in the same area. There was another problem: a labor shortage. He initially applied to General Whiting for slave and free black laborers, but Whiting was not about to release any of his workmen. Micks was informed that none were available.

Turning to the Medical Department, he canvassed the hospitals in the State, asking for men who had fishing experience. While Micks needed only about sixteen workers, some fifty men were sent, but many of them were not up to the job. Micks complained "at least four-fifths [of them] know nothing at all about fishing and are otherwise worthless." He pointed out that one soldier sent from Raleigh had been wounded only one week earlier and was now lodged in the hospital.

Micks selected the best of the men, hoping to be able to teach them the trade. Since they were convalescents, soon to be returned to duty, he hoped to keep them for fishing. Although Dr. Micks wrote he needed only a few workers, it is not known how many men Paddison already had. Seines over 2,000 yards required at least ten men per boat and at least two men on shore to tend the horses and watch the rope as it was pulled in.

At least most of the men selected to work at the fishery had seen fish before. Earlier in the war, a company from Henderson County encamped near Masonboro Sound. A fisherman appeared at their camp one morning, selling his catch. When the men asked about an odd-colored fish, they were told it was a flounder. Whereupon, one fellow asked "where in the world [the fish] had been floundering to get himself in such a shape as that."

Doctor Micks thought that if he could again get a permit from the military he hoped to "commence fishing" within a week. He sought permission from General Whiting but "as there seems to be some apprehension that this place will be attacked soon, I fear it will be withheld." The general finally relented and allowed men to go out in the Sounds but they were to be Dr. Micks' responsibility. Micks reported that Doctor Abram Newkirk, a local practitioner, had offered help: "& has promised us his assistance in its management & as I design having an effective guard over our boats, I apprehend no danger from the enemy."[11]

Newkirk, who had served as a captain in the 41st N.C. Cavalry and had recently been discharged, offered his home on the Sound as a likely spot to operate from. It was hoped that the catch this year would be a big one. Many relished the thought of a seafood dinner, even some who were not able to join in the repast.

A former visitor to Wilmington wrote Paddison: "I know you are enjoying the mullets, oysters & c. by this time. As you were getting ready to cast your nets into the waters when I left Wilmington, I expect to enjoy very few of either fish or oysters this winter."[12]

The idea of fishing dimmed after June 1864. On the 23rd of that month, U.S. Navy Lieutenant Commander William B. Cushing entered the river on yet another of his forays and captured a party that was out fishing.[13]

Very few in the region enjoyed the winter of 1864. Wilmington had been selected as the Union's next target. As warships gathered at the inlets, fishing opportunities were severely curtailed. The next large haul of fish would

Fort Holmes, on Bald Head Island.

have to wait until after the war ended. Perhaps it was the cannon fire that kept the big ones away.

In the latter part of 1864, it was deemed necessary to activate both the Senior and Junior Reserves. In addition to many of them needing shoes, blankets and clothing, many of the younger troops contracted rubeola (measles), while many of the older men suffered from a variety of illnesses, including rheumatism.

The complaints to Governor Vance from the men were many, but one letter from the officers of a Senior Reserve Company was typical: "We the undersigned...Have been called out, for a few days, as we supposed, on a great emergency, and have left our familys [sic] in a most deplorable condition. There are 401 of us, of which number 367 are farmers...This month & the next are important to farmers to secure the next years [sic] crop...Our families are exposed and frequent instances of depredations have occurred...We...therefore ask your clemency in our relief, by sending the Home Guard to take our places, seeing...that they are effecting considerable destruction to 'new dip' & but little good in catching deserters."

The writer also noted, "for the past few days, from 6 to 13 are conveyed to the hospital daily." If the big killer (at least in the summer months) was typhoid fever, a close second in the winter was pneumonia. Yet another hospital was found necessary when, in late 1863, smallpox struck the area.

Surgeon Stephen Doar was placed in charge and ordered to construct a smallpox hospital. It is likely that this hospital was established on Bald Head Island and ministered to the black laborers constructing Fort Holmes. A cow was kept at General Hospital No. 4 in order to obtain vaccine for small pox, but in April, the animal wandered off. Chief Steward Paddison ran the following ad in the papers: "Strayed from General Hospital No. 4, a dark brindle COW, with large body, short legs and crumpled horns, one of which…has been broken." A reward of $25 was offered for the return of the cow, but it is likely it was never returned.

Forage for the cow had come from the army. One of the few remaining mills in the area was operated by Captain Charles McKinney's Commissary Department. The bran produced, he reported, was "unfit for issue to troops" but was instead given to animals. By the end of 1864, Doctor Micks reported that he had vaccinated 35 people, but none were successful, as he was still "unable to procure any good virus." Ever mindful of his reputation, when serious casualties began to come in from Fort Fisher in the winter of 1864, Micks felt compelled to write: "In justice to the Hospital I would state that the great mortality appearing in this monthly report is due the class of patients admitted; many of them coming from Hoke's Division…[and] were retained until in a moribund condition before being sent [here]…two of them died within six hours after admission, and others we found impossible to rally." The day after the fall of Fort Fisher, Micks was ordered to begin evacuating patients to other hospitals.

Many of those doctors and nurses struggled to treat the ill consigned to their care. During the four years of war, there were nearly 10,000 patients treated at General Hospital No. 4. All in all, the doctors and hospitals throughout the Confederacy performed miracles with the limited means available to them.[14]

ENDNOTES

1. National Archives, RG 109, Medical Department, Chapter VI, Vol. 284, "Register of Deaths and Effects, Gen. Hosp. No. 4, Wilmington, N.C., 1864-65." *Whiting Papers*, "Letters Sent," 8 August 1864; Cunningham, *Doctors in Gray*, 135, 153. *Citizen's Papers*, Reel No. 584, J.P. Levy file. The brandy was sold by Levy. *Whiting Papers*, "Letters Received," 6 March 1864.
2. General Hospital No. 4, "Letters Sent," Chapter VI, Vol. 399, 23 March 1863; "Morning Report," Vol. 404, 28 July 1864, 5 November 1864; *Whiting Papers*, Chapter II, Vol. 247, entry dated 9 August 1864. Pvt. Owens was listed as a guard in a letter inquiring into his physical condition. Owen's commanding officer was also named Owens and was possibly a relative, Manarin 6:221.
3. General Hospital No. 4, "Letters Sent," Chapter VI, Vol. 399, letter dated 3 March 1864; Powell, *North Carolina Biography*, 5:284-285; *Daily Journal*, 4 December 1862; *Confederate Veteran*, 16:161-162 (1908). After the war Satchwell settled in Rocky Point and as a leading member of the N.C. Medical Society would help create the State Board of Health and from 1879 to 1881, served as its president. Satchwell was also quite influential in the creation of Pender County, then a part of New Hanover County. He died of typhoid fever in

November 1892 and is buried in Wilmington's Oakdale Cemetery. LCFHS Bulletin, "The Richard P. Paddison Papers," XI:2, March 1968. LCFHS archives, Paddison file, letters dated 13 October 1862, 20 July 1864, 14 August 1863.

4. Sprunt, *Chronicles*, 356-358.

5. Paddison was originally buried in Point Caswell, but was later removed to Oakdale Cemetery. See the *Morning Star*, 24 November 1915, Daily Dispatch, 24 March 1915. For a time "Captain" Paddison operated a steamer between Wilmington and Point Caswell, - "Fares $1, meals extra." See the *Morning Star*, 7 December 1870.

6. General Hospital No. 4, "Letters Sent," Chapter VI, Vol. 399, 11 and 17 August 1864.

7. *Wilmington Star-News*, undated article in the "Sword Factory" file, Bill Reaves Collection, New Hanover County Public Library. Lefler and Newsome, *The History of a Southern State*, 373.

8. General Hospital No. 4, "Market Supplies," Chapter VI, Vol. 283, voucher no. 8, dated 8 July 1863. Paddison bought three bushels of clams to the hospital and also supplied berries, beef, fish and tomatoes. *Daily Journal*, 23 September 1863. Eighty-nine empty barrels were sent to town via the W&W. General Hospital No. 4, "Letters Sent," Chapter VI, Vol. 399, 15 September 1863, from E.N. Covey to T.R. Micks. Paddison Papers, "Expenses of fishery from Sept. 1st to Dec. 31st 1863[.]" Collection of Joel Cook Pretlow, courtesy of Dr. Chris E. Fonvielle, Jr.

9. The State, "The Fisheries of North Carolina," Vol. 30, no. 6, 18 August 1962, 13-16; see also Edmund Ruffin, "The Great Fisheries of the Albemarle," Vol. 25, no. 20, February 1958, 13-14. General Hospital No. 4, "Letters Sent," chapter VI, Vol. 399, 5 September 1863.

10. General Hospital No. 4, "Letters Received," Chapter VI, Vol. 401, 15 September 1863; Chapter VI, Vol. 399, 16 November, 20 October 1863. By the end of the year the hospital had spent $1,230 for a seine, twine, barrels, boat, rope, salt, compass as well as boarding for the workers. In addition, Paddison spent $1,136 on repairs and tools, LCFHS, Paddison Papers. After the war the Navassa Guano Company would operate a fishery (catching "fatbacks") and oil works at Fort Fisher, see the *Morning Star*, 5 October 1871.

11. *Whiting Papers*, II:336, letters dated 1 September and 9 August 1864. *Confederate Veteran*, 16:161, 1908.

12. *Whiting Papers*, II:336, letters dated 1,5 and 6 September 1864. LCFHS, Paddsion Papers, 13 September 1864. The writer, Dr. R.F. Lewis, stationed in Richmond, had worked with Paddison at Fort Caswell.

13. Admiral David D. Porter, *The Naval History of the War* (Secaucus, N.J.: Castle Books, 1984) 478.

14. *Whiting Papers*, II:338; General Hospital No. 4, "Register of Deaths," VI:279. On 13 January 1865, between one and two hundred patients were sent from Fort Fisher and about forty more were wounded the next day. *Daily Journal*, 5 April 1864. *Whiting Papers*, II:347 dated 30 March 1864: "Capt. McKinney will issue bran for the two cows belonging to the hospital."

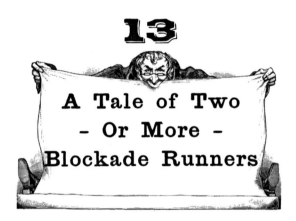

13

A Tale of Two
- Or More -
Blockade Runners

In August 1861, United States Consul Samuel Whiting was so incensed that he penned a protest to Nassau's Governor General Nesbitt. A "low black schooner, of 40 tons burden," had dropped anchor near his office at the wharf. He wrote to the British Governor: "On the 7th day of Augt. The Schr. *Wm. H. Northrup* of Wilmington, N.C., Joseph A. Silliman, Master, arrived at this port with the secession flag flying at her peak and she now lies at the wharf in front of the U.S. Consulate with an ensign displayed which is only recognized by the rebels against the U.S. Government."

The schooner, with a rounded stern and "raking masts" had been built in Wilmington in 1859, while her master, Joseph Silliman, had come to town sometime prior to 1860. In the Federal census for that year, he was enumerated as a seaman, 55 years old, born in Ireland. Consul Whiting protested "the liberty accorded to a vessel bearing an unacknowledged flag" and claimed it was an insult to the United States. He further wrote that Silliman had "also neglected to deposit his papers at this Consulate."

Governor Nesbitt had heard this before and had his secretary answer: "It does not appear to His Honor that he has any power to interfere in the matters mentioned by you. Occurrences of a similar character…were brought under the notice of His Honor…by your predecessor."

The Governor General declined to take any course which "might be considered a departure from that line of strict neutrality which Her Majesty the Queen is desirous of preserving[.]" The correspondence between the two men passed along official channels and eventually reached Lord Russell in England, who approved Nesbitt's actions.

As for Consul Whiting, he sent a notice to the State Department. Secretary of State Seward's son, Frederick, passed along the information to the Navy Department: "Mr. Whiting…has reported…that a schooner named the *Wm. H. Northrup*, commanded by Joseph H. Silliman, belonging to Wilmington, N.C., has repeatedly entered Nassau with the flag flying of the insurgent States."

The Union authorities even knew what her cargo consisted of: lumber, bran and peanuts. As brazen as Silliman was, he was snared on Christmas Day, 1861, by the U.S. bark *Ferdnandina*. He tried to talk his way out of trouble by stating that he was an "old coaster," bound for New York and had merely run in close to shore to escape rough weather, but Lieutenant George Browne did not believe a word of it. Found on board was a copy of her clearance from Wilmington plus "an abundance of evidence among her papers to condemn her."

The vessel had gone to Havana, unloaded rice and taken on coffee, drugs, sugar and salt. In his report, Browne wrote that she had already run the blockade twice and was "attempting it a third time. In fact she is a regular trader." Silliman tripped himself up when he pleaded not to be sent to New York, as his sails were in such a bad condition, they wouldn't make it. Browne then reminded the "old coaster" that he had originally stated that he was bound for New York to begin with!

Silliman was soon set at liberty and once more went back to his trade. In May 1862, the U.S. gunboat *Unadilla*, patrolling off Charleston, captured the schooner *Mary Teresa*, with Captain Silliman once again at the helm. When stopped by the *Unadilla*, he was flying, as he had done on previous occasions, the British ensign. Naval officers reported that her cargo of salt and assorted merchandise had been loaded at Nassau and although her papers had her bound for Halifax, in reality she was attempting to run into Charleston. They went on:

USS Unadilla

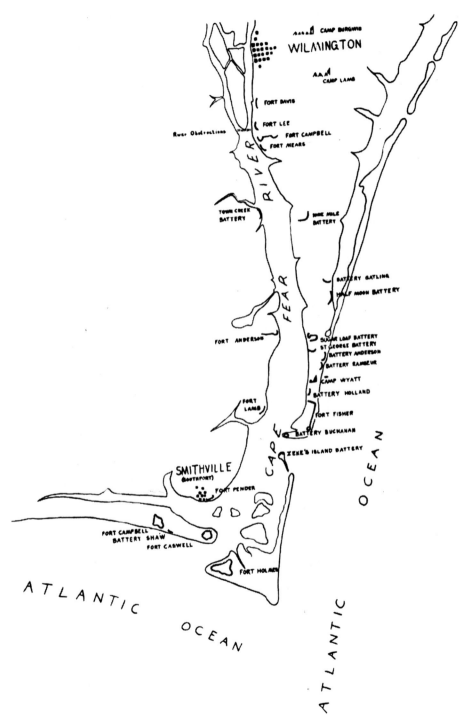

The Cape Fear River defenses.

"She [the *Mary Teresa*] was formerly the pilot boat No. 10, of Charleston, and was built in 1852 at Wilmington, N.C."

Set free once again, Silliman was again caught by the U.S. Navy when, in September 1862, he was aboard the schooner *Agnes*, when it was taken off the Georgia coast. Also aboard was a Savannah pilot, so it would appear that Silliman was more than just a passenger; his services might have been required if the *Agnes* had been forced instead to run into Wilmington.[1]

Wilmington was ideal for blockade running. The port city was 28 miles upriver, far enough to be protected from an offshore bombardment. It was well fortified by several large, strategically placed strongholds, along with smaller gun batteries emplaced on the banks of the river. As the Union grip tightened about Charleston and other ports, Wilmington became the favored anchorage, especially for runners from the Bahamas.

Taking about two days to cover the 570 miles to Nassau, runners tried to follow the cycles of the moon. Dark, moonless nights were much preferred. Storms, although sometimes helpful by dispersing the blockaders, could destroy the runner. Early in the war, some town merchants were quick to see opportunity in running the blockade and invested in the trade.

Born in Swansboro, Onslow County, Oscar G. Parsley came to Wilmington as a young man, back in 1830. He soon found work with the firm of Dudley and Dickinson and after a few years controlled the company. He became quite wealthy and was at one time president of the Commercial Bank and a Director of the Wilmington and Weldon Railroad, as well as several other corporations. In 1856 he

Oscar G. Parsley, from an image on a four dollar note from the Commercial Bank of Wilmington.

was elected mayor and by the time of the war was a commission merchant and owner of an importing firm. Described as "Active, energetic and enterprising, thoroughly honest and self-reliant," Parsley was one of the first to capitalize on the blockade.[2]

On 6 August 1861, the schooner *Adelso* left Wilmington headed for Halifax, Nova Scotia, with a cargo of turpentine and rosin. Aboard as supernumerary (or agent) for Parsley was Louis de Bebian, a Frenchman from Guadaloupe. Later that month the vessel ran into rough weather and lost some of her sails as she hugged the coastline. Forced to seek shelter at Newport, Rhode Island, it was later reported that the schooner was boarded by the commander of a small cutter, the *Henrietta*.

"When the...schooner on board which M. de Bebian sailed as a passenger ...foolishly run into Newport...she was boarded by young [James Gordon] Bennett in martial panoply, with drawn sword and several revolvers."

Bennett was the son of James Gordon Bennett of the *New York Herald*. He had offered his yacht to the Government and had been cruising near Newport when the *Adelso* anchored there. The Frenchman's troubles mounted when the collector of the port became suspicious about their papers and passengers. When questioned, de Bebian freely admitted sailing from Wilmington but claimed French citizenship. Upon

James Gordon Bennett, Jr.

further examination, it was discovered that the cargo was consigned to a Boston, Massachusetts firm and that de Bebian had been instructed by Parsley to purchase "5,000 to 10,000 army blankets, 1,000 bags of coffee, blank tons of iron of various sizes" as well as clothing "on private account."

Also uncovered during the search was a letter from Parsley to a British company in which he expressed surprise that the firm's New York office would not forward $6,500 owed Parsley's company. He ended his missive with the admonition: "Old Abe hasn't whipped us yet, and we hardly think he will."

The money, it was suggested to the U.S. State Department, might "be attached for the benefit of the United States." Telegraph wires between Newport and Washington began to heat up as messages flew back and forth about what should be done with de Bebian.

Answering the port collector's inquiries, Secretary Seward ordered de Bebian arrested and sent to Fort Lafayette. The Frenchman's demeanor changed at once and: "He commenced abusing both the government and the people of the United States...He also stated that he should go to France and return with fifty ships of war and have full redress."

His anger only hastened the inevitable. He was taken to New York and lodged in a prison cell. Allowed to write to the French Consul, he stated in his letter: "We anchored in the bay of Newport...The schooner was very soon taken possession of by a gang of men armed to the teeth...After four or five days of the worst treatment [they] removed the seals from my trunk...I am going to

Europe…to learn the decision of the two great powers on the question of blockades[.]"

The return cargo, he swore, was merely "negro blankets" commonly referred to as army blankets and his trip was "purely and entirely commercial." By the end of August, de Bebian's family was writing Secretary Seward on his behalf, but he remained incarcerated until mid-September when he claimed ill health and was allowed, by giving his word to return at a certain time, a "leave of absence" to join his family, then in New York.

Early in October, de Bebian was set free, but without any papers or a passport, he could not leave the city. Stuck there, he contended that since the U.S. Government had "rendered his voyage abortive, and would not let him return to his place of residence and business, thus depriving him of supporting himself, they must support him."

The U.S. Government finally allowed him to leave the country. He boarded the *City of New York*, headed for Liverpool, but before leaving sued the United States for damages. Aboard the steamer, he struck up a friendship with a fellow passenger and informed him that he intended to "expose in the French press the villanies and tyrannies of the Lincoln Government." His new friend, who was actually the U.S. Consul to France, managed to gain de Bebian's confidence and calmed him down so that he promised to "go about his business in France."

After a visit to England, de Bebian went on to France and discovered that the French Government had no intention or desire to become involved in American affairs. He returned to Wilmington without the fifty French warships he had threatened to bring with him. Louis de Bebian would, at war's end, return to New York where his wife died. He eventually remarried and became quite wealthy as the agent for a line of French steamers plying from that city to LeHavre.

Some twenty years after the war, de Bebian associated with the elite of New York. He was invited to a party thrown by actress Sarah Bernhart. Shortly before his death, he was on a Committee of Three Hundred, looking into the feasibility of holding a World's Fair in New York City. Among the other members of the committee were Charles A. Dana, Grover Cleveland, Levi P. Morton, William Astor, Joseph Pulitzer and J. Pierpont Morgan. Another committeeman was James Gordon Bennett, father of the man who had arrested him twenty-three years earlier.

As for Oscar Parsley, he managed to get coffee from Cuba. He was selling it by the time de Bebian returned to Wilmington. Around that same time, Parsley was buying up all the iron produced by a works in Savannah. He attracted the attention of the officer in charge of the area's defenses, a general by the name of Robert E. Lee.

Lee wrote to the chief of ordnance in Richmond: "Captain Culyer, ordnance officer at this post, has just stated to me that O.G. Parsley & Co. of Wilmington, N.C. have bought the whole stock of iron in Weed, Connel & Co. … at the market price at which it has been sold to the Government. He has left the iron here, with directions that it be sold at double the former price…I have directed that all the iron…should be taken and paid for at the original price."

General Lee considered the purchase by Parsley "a palpable act of speculation" and should be stopped at once.[3] Parsley continued to do business, even with the Confederate government. Later in the war, he sold over three-quarters of a million feet of lumber used in the Wilmington defenses. Most of it went for the construction of magazines and gun batteries, but some was used for river obstructions (cribs) and also to bolster Fort Fisher. Some wood even went for repairs of the steamers and lighters used by the Engineer Department at Wilmington.[4]

Although some blockade running ventures were unsuccessful, other Wilmingtonians were willing to gamble in their pursuit for profit. When the new runner *Phantom* arrived in mid-July 1863, merchant James McCormick was quick to purchase some of her cargo and within a few days offered combs for sale, "dressing…pocket and fine tooth." Also for sale was a lot of C.S.N. buttons at his store at 41 Market Street. McCormick ran a dry goods and tailoring shop and in the fall of 1862 advertised for four or five coat makers and "three or four neat girls" to work in his employ. He was one of the few who had remained in town during the yellow fever epidemic but paid a stiff price for it. He lost three children to the fever.

Commenting on the state of affairs in Wilmington at this time, as she passed through town, was Rose O'Neal Greenhow. She said: "I think I should

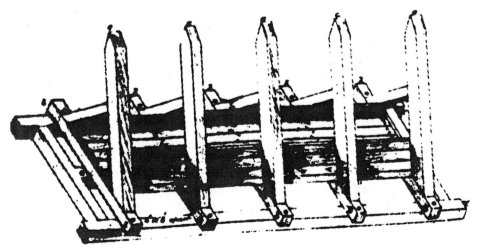

An example of the type of obstructions sowed in the Cape Fear River.

Rose O'Neal Greenhowe

brave any fate rather than remain here two days longer. It is the hottest and most disagreeable place in the world, and the very atmosphere seems laden with disease. The better class of inhabitants have left the city."

The firm of Jacob Loeb & Co. was able to provide "Regiments and Companies…with caps, haverlocks and enameled cloth coats of the best quality." James McCormick offered knapsacks, pistols and bowie knife cases, twine, powder, shot, whips, saddles and bridles. He needed extra workers: harness makers, "to work on military trappings."

James Wilson, who had a shop on Market Street, sold leather goods. He ran into some difficulty when he was publicly called a speculator because he seemed to be charging a lot more for leather goods than he paid for

them. He explained the difference by saying that the price marked on the leather was the price he bought them at. Left to stand for a while, the leather dried out and was likely to weigh less when sold. It was also noted that Wilson was "a native of the North," an allegation that he denied and stated that he was "a good Southern man."[5]

A few more good Southern men were the Kahnweiler brothers, Jacob, Daniel and David, all of whom had been born in Bavaria. They ran a dry goods store at the intersection of Market and Front Streets. Yet another brother, Simon, ran a store adjacent to that of his brothers. The stores, it was said, were easy to find if one simply looked for the "sign of the Golden Eagle," or asked where "Kahnweiler's corner" was. When war came, they soon depended on the uncertain flow of goods through the blockade.

Shortly after the firing on Fort Sumter, the editor of the *Daily Journal* wrote: "We have floating on our flagstaff a beautiful flag of the Confederate States, ordered by us from Charleston, through Messrs. Kahnweiler & Brother… There are seven stars there now, but there is room for more, *and they are coming*."

In addition to flags, one could purchase ladies millinery, shoes for the entire family (when in stock, that is), thread, suspenders and as the war progressed, "mourning bonnets." It is likely they sold the "cork jacket life preserver," as did their competitor O.S. Baldwin at 38 Market Street. The jacket was said to have been invented by David Kahnweiler.

Sometime in 1862, after forming a partnership with Mayor Parsley, Simon left the country for Europe.[6] It was, as one writer said, a mixture of profit and patriotism that motivated many Southerners to try their hand at running the blockade. Kahnweiler would become the European end of the partnership, buying up much-needed goods, chartering a vessel and sending it off through the blockade. In England, he found a British agent, a Mr. Dobson, who procured the steamer for the trip. Their agreement allowed Kahnweiler to load 75 tons of supplies aboard the *Latona* (or *Ladona*), an iron-hulled, single screw steamer which would be making its first such voyage to a southern port. By June, preparations were finished and the ship set off with 50 tons of general merchandise and 25 tons of saltpeter.

Saltpeter, declared contraband by the United States, was to be used in the making of gunpowder and was desperately needed by the Confederacy. Saltpeter was added to the cargo to insure government cooperation in obtaining cotton for the return trip. It was agreed by both parties (Kahnweiler and Dobson) that if the vessel failed to get through the blockade, she would go to Nassau or Bermuda and dispose of the cargo there. The vessel was then to continue its journey to an "open Southern port." This meant a port in Union hands, perhaps New Orleans, Beaufort, North Carolina or Port Royal, South Carolina. After all, there was no more illegal freight aboard.

Arriving in Bermuda, the 25 tons of saltpeter was discharged and quickly bought by the firm of "Smith and Jones." That company, as it turned out, was a New York company. The *Latona* then weighed anchor and attempted a run into Savannah, where she was fired upon and captured by the *USS Unadilla*. Illegal cargo or not, she was now in Federal hands.[7]

When Kahnweiler was informed of the loss of the *Latona*, he said "it struck me like a thunderbolt, but it was no use crying after spilt milk." When he found out the saltpeter had been sold to a Yankee company, he declared, "he had rather that it had been thrown overboard than it should get into the hands of the Federal Government."[8]

Kahweiler had already been working to load yet another runner. He secured the *Peterhoff*, loaded her with goods bought in Germany and wrote to Dobson: "I must confess the more I hear the more I am convinced we cannot get any cargo at any of the ports proclaimed open. How can it be possible, when they don't allow goods to go out of the city? Mr. Parsley will think us crazy to send a steamer to an 'open port.' If no cargo can be obtained, send the vessel to Havannah [sic] or St. Thomas."

Kahnweiler left no doubt as to his feelings when he again wrote: "The war will last until both parties are broken down. The South will not give up until they have established their independence, and the North must break down before they make peace, which I hope will be before long. My advice is to sell the *Peterhoff* cargo at Nassau or Havannah."

USS Peterhoff, *a former blockade runner.*

Kahnweiler's instructions were not always clear. At one point, he told Dobson not to go to Nassau, but to try a run into Wilmington. Later, he wanted his cargo taken off the *Peterhoff* because he had heard from Parsley that it was useless to attempt to get into a port in Federal hands, as there was no cotton or naval stores to be had there.

As for the *Peterhoff*, she arrived safely in the islands. The cargo, which consisted of brandy, whiskey, claret, madeira and champagne, as well as raisins, soap, tea, cotton shirts, "Men's Ready made suits," matches, Epsom salts, socks, and blankets were unloaded. The *Peterhoff* was back in England by October.

When Kahnweiler discovered that the cargo remained unsold at Nassau, he began to question Dobson, stating that his orders were not followed. Dobson put him off and Kahnweiler sued him in a British court. The case attracted a lot of interest as it involved steamers running the blockade, but was not settled until 1864. Kahnweiler was awarded the proceeds from the sale of the saltpeter, but he did not make the immense profits he had hoped for.

What attracted even more attention was the seizure of the *Peterhoff* by the U.S. Navy. Ostensibly bound for Matamoras, Mexico, she had indeed intended to run the blockade, but near St. Thomas the *USS Vanderbilt* overhauled and boarded her. Discovering irregularities in her papers, she was sent on to New York where the vessel was condemned and sold to the U.S. Navy. To the British, this was yet another high-handed action on the part of the United States. The seizure put more strain on an already delicate situation, reminiscent of the "*Trent* Affair." Interestingly, Charles Wilkes, Captain of the *San Jacinto* when it stopped the *Trent*, was also the officer who ordered the seizure of the *Peterhoff*.

Now in the service of the U.S., the *Peterhoff* was equipped with seven guns and sent to the blockading fleet off Wilmington in February 1864. She was accidentally sunk the following month by the *USS Monticello*. After the war, the owners of the *Peterhoff* sued and the case went to the U.S. Supreme Court. It was decided that the U.S. had no right to stop shipping to "a neutral port no matter what its ultimate destination."

In August 1863, the public was notified that the Kahnweiler Brothers were selling out their entire stock of goods. An auction was held in mid-August, but they continued to sell merchandise of "direct importation" until the very end of the war. Simon, who contracted to supply the State of Georgia with uniform cloth, remained abroad for most of the war. It was said that he made and lost a fortune, finally returning to the U.S. in 1866. He settled in New York where he opened a "Fancy Goods" store. His brothers eventually followed him there and it was in that city that he died in 1876.[9]

Simon's brother Daniel also wanted to leave the country. He had tried several times to obtain permission from the authorities. Daniel wrote several letters and sent telegrams to Governor Vance and to George Davis, a fellow Wilmingtonian who had recently been appointed Secretary of State. General Whiting pointed out, "This man is a citizen of Wilmington liable to militia duty. I twice refused to let him leave." All seemed to be for naught until, as James Sprunt recorded: "A day or two after the landing of the Arabian horse [a gift from Egypt, the animal came in on the *Banshee*]…a well-known dry goods merchant, who had prospered on Confederate contracts, and who had often tried unsuccessfully to obtain General Whiting's permission to visit Nassau, sauntered into Mr. John Dawson's store…and obtained permission to search the loft above the store for anything worthwhile which might be put to good use…He found nothing but a soiled and greasy horse blanket which had been used upon Mr. Dawson's well-known race horse, and afterward thrown aside…It was originally of fine blue padded silk, with Mr. Dawson's monogram, 'J.D.' in large letters tastefully embroidered on it."

Dawson freely gave the old horse blanket to Daniel. He brought it home and "with the assistance of his accomplished wife" made it as good as new. He then made his way to Richmond and got an audience with Mrs. Davis. While asking her if she desired anything from Nassau, the president entered the room. It was at this point that Kahnweiler presented Jefferson Davis with the beautiful blanket, adorned with the president's initials, "J.D." Daniel's pass to Nassau was signed "by the highest authority…and a few days afterward a favored son of the Scattered Nation was a very seasick man on a voyage…through the Cape Fear blockade" aboard the *City of Petersburg*. Once safely abroad, he sent Governor Vance "a bundle of Boys shoes" from Halifax.[10]

Blockade running continued unabated throughout 1863 and 1864, although more and more captures were made by the U.S. Navy. Outbound steamers, laden with cotton, had to notify the military that they were leaving port. In the fall of 1863 Major W.H. Gibbs was put in charge of "all business relating to vessels running the blockade and military passports."[11] After seeing Gibbs, outbound and inbound steamers were required to pay the Harbor Master's fee of five dollars, after which they could apply for a pilot.

River pilots were needed to navigate through the man-made obstructions. In 1864, their charge was set at $200 each way. Range lights, used to guide runners in across the bar, were placed on the small islands near the mouth of the river. These lights were set so enemy ships could not see them and

Capt. John Wilkinson

were turned on upon demand. For this service, there was a charge of $300. The pilots who guided the runners out to the safety of the Atlantic were charging much more, sometimes demanding payment in gold.

General Whiting, displeased with what he perceived as greed on the part of the pilots, had them conscripted and set their rates at what he considered quite liberal, $300 per month in gold. Forced to back down by the Conscription Office, who claimed that he had overstepped his bounds, Whiting attempted an end run around using pilots by reestablishing several of the lighthouses at the river's mouth.

Lieutenant John Wilkinson was placed in charge of getting the houses operational again. The lenses from the lighthouses had been removed early in the war and stored out of harm's reach. Wilkinson was also given the task of assigning pilots to outbound vessels.

Wilkinson, a Virginian, was well known in town. He was born into a naval family and entered the U.S. Navy in 1837. He, like the famous blockade running skipper, John Newland Maffitt, had spent time charting the coast and was quite familiar with its dangers. By the time of the war, Wilkinson commanded a vessel and had risen to the rank of lieutenant in the Confederate Navy. Sent to New Orleans, he was assigned to the ironclad, *Louisiana*. Captured and exchanged in 1862, he made a favorable impression with all he came in contact with and was one of the more successful blockade runners throughout 1863.

When Wilkinson was assigned to command the *CSS Chickamauga*, in September 1864, the responsibility of the lights devolved on Captain Patrick McCarrick, another veteran of the U.S. Navy. After obtaining the services of a knowledgeable pilot, who signed an agreement pertaining to pay and service, permission was granted "to vessels of known loyalty" to leave port.

A list of the ship's crew and passengers was telegraphed by the military to the forts downriver. The steamers then cast off from the wharf and were "hauled" to mid-stream where they fired up their engines. They were not allowed to start their engines while at the wharf due to the danger of fire. There were always bales of cotton on the docks and sparks from the smoke pipes had been responsible for several fires. Even a fifty dollar fine for leaving such combustibles as turpentine, tar, pitch, lumber and staves, failed to gain the hoped for results. Those items were to be removed within forty-eight hours, but many times the freight remained unclaimed for as long as two weeks.

When an outbound runner approached the forts, Lieutenant Zach Ellis and a contingent of his "River Guards" boarded the vessel. The crew and passengers were mustered on the deck and the manifests checked. Ellis, an officer of the 1st Battalion N.C. Heavy Artillery, was in command of the men who searched for runaway slaves, deserters or escaping prisoners. Runners were also required by law to have their ship fumigated. This is where Theodore McKeithan came aboard. At Smithville, or perhaps at Fort Anderson, McKeithan brought his equipment aboard the vessel.

McKeithan charged a fee of $15, later raised to $25, per ship to fumigate, or "smoke," the vessel. One of three fumigators that worked on the river, McKeithan would direct clouds of sulphur into the hold. Soon, unable to breathe, stowaways clambered out only to be arrested by the River Guards still on the ship. These unfortunates would usually wind up working at Fort Holmes on Bald Head Island, which in 1864 was not the idyllic location it is today. Being sent there was virtually a death sentence, due to the severity of the work and exposure to the unrelenting elements.

On occasion, a stowaway might slip through by pulling a silk net over his head, and down to his waist. The fugitive, hoping that with his mouth covered by a wet towel and the silk net tightened by a draw string, could withstand the fumes and remain in hiding. Despite the precautions taken by the officers, there were still desperate men and women who slipped through Whiting's web.

Inbound pre-war shipping went upriver to town and anchored at the "Visiting Station" just south of town. Upon hoisting the signal for the Port Physician, they would be examined and cleared to dock. The town's

Commission of Navigation, chaired by Phineas Wines Fanning, regulated much of the port's activity.

By law, the commissioners were, among other duties, to fix "[T]he number of pilots, licensed pilots, set pilotage fees…established quarantine procedures, settled disputes between shipmasters and pilots, and decided where ballast might be deposited."

The commissioners also selected who would be harbor master, port physician and fumigator. After the yellow fever epidemic in 1862, they took a stronger role in regulating the blockade runners. The year following the epidemic, during the "sickly season" between June and November, all vessels arriving from ports south of Wilmington were to be questioned as to sickness aboard. If there was, they were required to anchor at Deep Water Point, on the western side of the river. There was, in addition to a gun battery, a hospital at that site. After being assured steamers were disease-free, they were allowed to proceed to town, dock and unload their cargoes.[12]

Later the regulations became even more stringent. Vessels were required to lay at quarantine for up to thirty days at Fort Anderson, north of Deep Water Point. The military authorities cooperated with the board as far as possible, but the commanding officer of the Department reported that quarantine delays were affecting the supplies required by the army. General Whiting bristled at being hamstrung by Fanning and his Board and complained in several letters to Secretary of War Seddon. Forced to unload cargoes at Fort Anderson, Whiting had wagons or lighters bring the supplies up to town, a process he found very time-consuming. The blockade runners fumed over the quarantine rules, which many times caused them to "lose a moon" and money. Even Governor Vance noted, "the port of Wilmington is more effectually blockaded from within than from without." Relations between Fanning and the general, cordial at first, strained as the war progressed.

Both military and private cargo was warehoused at the fort, guarded by the garrison. When it was imperative that dispatches or desperately needed munitions, or even occasional ice and fruits, be brought directly to town, Whiting notified Fanning that the ship would be coming in.

When Major John Cameron, the chief quartermaster in town, requested permission to bring in a cargo of blankets, he was told he could not do so, as: "Blankets are considered the most dangerous articles of importation – most liable to risk infection." Fanning did allow "other articles not liable to infection…to come up."

Fanning, a native of Nantucket, Massachusetts, was born in 1800 and came to Wilmington as a youth. In 1833, he was the co-editor of the *People's Press*, but within four months, after realizing the difficulties of publishing a newspaper, "laid down the pen after an article in which the honesty and frankness characteristic of him explained his disgust with the profession."

Fanning was active in community affairs since his arrival as a youth, even to the point of performing on stage with Wilmington's Thalian Society. It was said that he played the part of an old man so well, that for years afterward he was remembered by many as "that 'good old man.'" He was instrumental in establishing one of the first public schools in town and by the time of the Civil War, was listed as a house painter. Elected to the Board of Navigation, he took his job seriously. In late summer, 1862, when a runner anchored at the mouth of the river, Fanning, as a member of the Board, went aboard to observe the "sanitary inspection" but was quickly removed "with indignity." This vessel may well have been the *Kate*, which was thought to have brought yellow fever to the Cape Fear.[13]

Another maritime problem, according to General Whiting, was that when vessels lay at anchor for a while, they were required to be hauled out of the water to have their bottoms scraped. This work could be done at Cassidey's already overworked marine railway in town.

Relations were also deteriorating between General Whiting and Governor Vance. In late June 1863, when the Governor came to Wilmington to meet the state's new blockade runner, the *SS Advance*, he was taken downriver to where the vessel lay at quarantine. There he boarded the vessel as it slowly made its way to town, docking just as evening fell. The problem was that its time in quarantine had not yet expired. When it docked, Lieutenant Colonel Charles E. Thorburn was there to meet it. As the governor and his party attempted to leave the steamer, the colonel stopped them. Thorburn declared that to allow Vance to debark would violate the quarantine. He ordered the vessel back downriver.

The governor, his temper near the breaking point, answered Thorburn, "Do you dare say, sir, that the Governor of the State shall not leave the deck of his own ship?"

Words escalated, tempers flared and at one point Thorburn, who by now had lost his temper, shouted that he "did not care for Gov. Vance nor Gov. Jesus Christ!" The colonel was not allowing anyone off the ship for fifteen days.

Cooler heads prevailed when Chairman Fanning was notified and allowed the party to debark. As he left the steamer, Vance turned to Fanning and declared, "No man is more prompt to obey the civil authority than myself, but I will not be ridden over by epaulets or bayonets." The crowd, which had gathered, cheered the Chief Executive as he walked away from the wharves.

Upon his return, General Whiting, who had been out of town when the incident occurred, immediately telegraphed the governor: "I have just learned the highly improper interference with your movements on Sunday...Be assured

as far as my authority extends I shall vindicate the respect due to the Governor –
I will write you on the subject as soon as the blame is fixed."

Writing later to Vance, Whiting admitted that Thorburn, "under the
excitement of opposition to the execution of his orders, [had been] disrespectful
in language," but technically he had been carrying out his orders. Orders, which
came, Whiting added, from the civilian authorities, the Board of Navigation, and
over which he had little control. Regretting "exceedingly…any disrespect to the
Governor" he informed Vance that he had removed Thorburn as commander of
the city. In reality, it was Whiting's fault. He had allowed Vance and his party to
go downriver in the first place.

Lieutenant Colonel Charles Edmunston Thorburn was born in Norfolk.
He was one of those rare men who served in both the Navy and Army. He
entered the Navy in 1847 as a midshipman and served aboard ship during the
Mexican War and graduated from the Naval Academy in 1853. He attained the
rank of Lieutenant in the U.S. Navy and in 1857 was loaned to the Army's
Topographical Corps. That year he joined Army Lieutenant Edward Beales
expedition to "trace a cross-country wagon trail to California." It would appear
that this expedition was equipped with camels as well as horses.

Returning to sea duty in 1858, he was sent with Captain John M. Brooke
to sound the depths of the Pacific "from San Francisco to Honolulu." Then it
was off to the Far East, Guam, China and Japan. In Yokohama their vessel was
wrecked and Thorburn remained in that country for a few more months,
returning to the States in 1860. Seeking a more bucolic life, he purchased a
sheep ranch in Texas and intended to remain there, until the war came.

He reported for duty in Virginia and was soon appointed a lieutenant in
the Virginia Navy. Sent to the Chesapeake Bay area, he participated in the
capture of several vessels and was commissioned a major in the 50th Virginia
Infantry. Wounded at Fort Donelson, he was promoted to lieutenant colonel and
became Major General W.W. Loring's chief of ordnance, as well as his Inspector
General. When Loring was sent to North Carolina, Thorburn went with him,
was then transferred to General Whiting's staff and given command of the city.

Several citizens, outraged at the manner in which the Chief Magistrate
of the State had been treated, wrote to President Davis: "The undersigned, loyal
citizens…beg leave…to request…the removal of Lt. Col. Thorburn…He has
offered a most gratuitous indignity to the Governor of North Carolina and thus
insulted and outraged the whole state."

General Whiting was in a fix. He respected and liked Thorburn.
Possibly to show that he needed him, when Yankee raiders struck Kenansville
and the W&W rail line the following week, Thorburn was sent after them. In an
attempt to rescue Thorburn's career, Whiting telegraphed Vance, "…Thorburn is
in pursuit" and another message saying, "Enemy are in retreat before Thorburn."

It was to no avail. The very day Whiting sent the telegraphs, Vance was penning a letter about the incident to President Davis. Demanding that Thorburn be removed, he added, "If it be deemed indispensable that North Carolina Soldiers should be commanded by Virginians, I should regret to see the Old Dominion retain all her gentlemen for her own use and furnish us only her blackguards."

By the end of July, Thorburn was gone. Many in town felt that one more Virginian who had insulted North Carolina had been rightly chastised. Indeed, there were many battle-weary Carolinians who felt that F.F.V. really stood for "Fleet Footed Virginians."

Richmond eventually promoted Thorburn to colonel and sent him to London and Paris to buy steamers for the blockade running trade. Upon his return to Wilmington, he was "fired on, and in order to escape…he swam ashore, wading the swamps to the mainland."

In 1865 he was given the task of planning an escape route for the Richmond Government and "decided the only safe route led through Florida[.]" He joined in the flight and "was with President Davis up to a few hours of his capture." On 10 May, while making his way through Georgia, he suddenly encountered a squad of Union cavalrymen. He drew his pistol and fired at the closest pursuer, knocking him out of the saddle. Riding at breakneck speed, he continued on to Florida and met up with Captain Louis M. Coxetter, a renowned blockade runner. Thorburn had arranged for a small vessel to be secreted on the Indian River and the pair made their escape.

After the war, Thorburn relocated to New York City, was quite active in the Confederate Camp in that city and died there on 27 October 1909.[14]

Handling and shipping cotton was a complicated process. William Oliver and others bought cotton for the state. Major John Devereaux, state quartermaster, found rail or river transportation for the cotton going to Wilmington. At the port, it was turned over to the state's agent, Joseph Hudson Flanner, who ensured it was properly compressed by the state's cotton press, located on Eagles Island. After it was secured with bailing wire and, if necessary, the bagging repaired, the cotton bales were placed on board the *Advance*.

It was also Flanner's duty to make sure that only those authorized to ship cotton did so. Governor Vance many times gave permission for private citizens to send their cotton out on the steamer. Flanner made sure they did not send out more than was allowed.

Flanner was well known in town. In May 1856 he and Doctor William C. Wilkings, a former friend, were engaged in a duel to the death. Flanner killed

Wilkings over their differing political leanings. Flanner was an ardent "Know-Nothing," the political organization founded "on American opposition to foreign immigration and Roman Catholicism." This group remained strongest in the years just prior to the war, but eventually many of its members, former Whigs, shifted to the Democratic Party. Flanner's opponent was a Democrat.

The *Wilmington Herald* called the affair, which was said to be the last duel fought in the South, a "great calamity" and further reported: "Our community was painfully startled…by the reception of a telegraphic dispatch from Marion, S.C. to the effect that a hostile meeting had taken place near Fair Bluff…They fought with pistols at ten paces, Dr. Wilkings being the challenger."

June 1861 found Flanner still in Wilmington, actively seeking to have a side-wheeled tugboat armed and sent to sea to "give us warning of any approaches from sea." In a letter to Warren Winslow, chairman of the state's Military and Naval Board, he wrote: "The Wilmington Steam Tug Comp'y., of which I am Pres't. is desirous of fitting out one of its steamers, the *Mariner*, 138 tons for sea service…Can't we borrow the Rifled Cannon here at the Depot, and thirty muskets, here at the Clarendon Foundry[?]"

Flanner was having trouble getting cannon and muskets. In several letters to Raleigh, he insisted "The Tugs properly armed will be of greater service to our people than one Hundred Companies at the Forts" and pointed out that the cannon had already been at the depot "for six to eight weeks."

Thwarted in his attempt to get armaments for his tug, in the latter part of June, he sent Captain J.A.S. Price to Raleigh to further plead his case. Finally equipped with several cannon, "one 6-lb. rifle cannon, two 12.lb. cannon, 25 muskets[,] 8 side arms for the crew," the steamer was converted from "a seagoing tug into a gunship" at the shipyard of Benjamin and William Beery.

After receiving their "Letter of Marque and Reprisal" in mid-July and "with a crew made up of 'Patriots and adventurers' and experienced 'gunmen' drawn from the ranks of the military, Benjamin Beery was given command of the *Mariner* with orders to 'prey upon enemy shipping, capture merchantmen and bring them into port to be dealt with as contraband and prizes of war.' "

With their new gunboat the crew of nearly forty men sailed to the Sounds. On 25 July, they espied a sail off Ocracoke Inlet and made after her. The vessel, a schooner named the *Nathaniel Chase*, was soon captured by the *Mariner*. With a prize crew aboard, she was taken to Hatteras. Prizes from raiding along the Sounds were brought back to Beaufort, New Bern or Wilmington.

The *Gordon, York* and *Coffee* were among the several privateers operating in the area. After a few vessels were taken, northern marine insurance companies began to raise the alarm about their losses.

Toward the end of 1861, the *Mariner* was successfully returned to Wilmington. Under the command of Captain Joseph Price and renamed the *Lizzie*, she was being prepared to enter the blockade running business. After a successful run to Nassau in the fall of 1862, with a cargo of cotton, tobacco and turpentine, she remained in the Islands for some time, probably to avoid fever-stricken Wilmington.

Upon her return in January 1863, General Whiting eyed the vessel for military use. When he called for more and better river transportation, he specifically mentioned the *Mariner* as the type needed. It was armed and could go over the bar to assist stranded or grounded runners. Whiting brought out that as a runner she couldn't carry much cotton, 100 bales at most, and "[her] engines, boiler and hull are too valuable to permit them to be sacrificed in order that a party of speculators should make money."

Whiting ordered the *Lizzie* to remain in port while Richmond worked out the details of her purchase. As late as May there was still no decision as to her fate and in a reply to a letter, Whiting informed Flanner that the matter "is entirely in the hands of the War Department[.]" Whiting felt that she should be bought at a fair price, but when the War Department and the owners could not agree on what that should be, Whiting refused to submit to arbitration and looked elsewhere. The *Lizzie*, or *Mariner*, was eventually turned over to the C.S.N.[15]

Capt. Joseph Price

As for Flanner, now out of a job, he sought the position of purser aboard the state's runner, the *Advance*. Brought to Wilmington in the latter part of June (1863) the steamer proved to be one of the best in the trade. Authorized by the state legislature to "run the vessel where and how" he thought best, Vance also maintained control over who had access to the ship. In addition to providing all those necessary supplies to the war effort, the *Advance* was a political plum for the governor. It was he who placed the purser, surgeon, mechanics, carpenters and Signal Officer aboard.[16]

Just as important was the power to permit certain people and companies to send cotton abroad. An example of this occurred in July 1863 when the Governor's friend, Dr. Boykin, requested permission to "send out a bale of cotton or box of tobacco to enable me to get 'some things' that" he needed.

Vance gave his okay, but advised his aide to remind Boykin to "mention it to no body at all. I have had to refuse a number of such applications."

Vance was indeed besieged by those who sought to send out cotton and those who wanted a job. From booksellers like Sterling, Campbell and Albright, who needed books "for the common schools" which were "suffering for books" to Mr. Basset French, who desired to send out cotton to raise money for the T.J. Jackson fund, all implored the Chief Executive to grant space on his vessel. One such plea came from A.H. Van Bokkelen of Wilmington.

Mr. Van Bokkelen wrote Vance that he wanted to ship "out a few bales" to be able to buy supplies for General Hospital No. 4 in Richmond. He added, "it is under the very best management, as many can testify whose knowledge has been gained under circumstances equally as painful as my own, my only son Capt. Van Bokkelen 3d No. Ca...having died there 22 June '63." Vance likely allowed the cotton to go out as he seldom denied such heartfelt requests.

John H. Wheeler

In September 1863, John Wheeler, author of a history of North Carolina, and father of Captain Woodbury Wheeler of the 10th N.C. Battalion (and also father of Union naval officer Charles S. Wheeler), requested the governor to allow him to go abroad along with twenty bales of cotton to enable him to continue on to England and "procure...documents which no historian has ever copied." He received an affirmative reply although it is doubtful Vance allowed him to take that many bales. Alerted by fellow passengers that the ship was getting up steam, Wheeler was forced to board the steamer "on the run" because Captain Thomas Crossan, the ship's commander, intended to leave port without any civilian passengers.

Crossan was "[a]n enthusiastic admirer of Shakespeare, [and] he stimulated discussions, gave lectures...and was able to keep...a lively conversation going about this author. There was music when the topic was concluded, or the well-known historiographer...[John] Wheeler...would read a treatise about the politics of this frequently controversial state." Surely Crossan enjoyed having Wheeler, who was not just another passenger, on board.

Captain Julius Schiebert, who wrote about Crossan and Wheeler, was so taken with the man that he wrote "a humorous illustrated work...Wheeleriana, which was dedicated to and later presented to the Governor[.]"[17]

When former purveyor Dr. Thomas Boykin, needed a job, he asked a favor of his friend, Zeb Vance. He wanted to be assigned aboard as the ship's surgeon, as the first such medical officer, Dr. John Swann, had resigned. Another town physician, Dr. William J. Love, sought the sinecure when he wrote the governor, "I have been told by a friend…that [Swann] will not make more than one or two trips…I merely write to ask you, to give me the place when a vacancy occurs."

Boykin tattled on Swann when he told Vance: "Common talk says, Swann is a confirmed sot, and that there is much dissapation [sic] on board. I am not an informer, for I know nothing." Boykin went aboard, not as a physician, but as purser. Later, when Mrs. Swann asked to have her husband reinstated, for his health, she was told the position had been eliminated.

As for signal officer aboard the state's runner, there was never a question as to who should fill that job. John Baptist Smith, a young enlistee from Caswell County, had devised a method of signaling between ships and land. While stationed at Fort Fisher, he saw firsthand the problems involved as a runner attempted to enter the river. Flags by day and torches by night were the norm for signaling, but this proved difficult, especially at night.

In 1863, Smith wrote: "While in the ordnance department of the fort, I chanced to spy a pair of ship starboard and port lanterns, the thought flashed in my

John Baptist Smith later in life.

mind, 'why not by the arrangement of a sliding door to each of these lanterns, one being a white, the other a red, substitute flashes of red and white lights for the wave of torches to the right and left, to form a signal alphabet[.]' "

Thus was born the present-day system of signaling at sea. As a reward to Smith, Secretary of War Seddon allowed him to pick his duty station. As signal officers would now be required on all runners, Smith opted to board the *Advance* for that duty and remained aboard until 1864.

For the most part, being assigned as signal officer to a runner was good duty. One young Virginian who volunteered for the duty had passed through the most horrific engagements of the war, having been wounded at Bull Run and Chancellorsville. Virginian J.M. Royal had earned such duty. In July 1864, the runner *Old Dominion* ran towards the safety of the guns at Fort Fisher. As she approached the breakers one of the enemy's shells struck its target. Sitting in the steward's pantry below decks was young Royal. He had just settled in for a cup of tea when the shell passed through the pantry and exploded. The man's head was taken "off as clean as a whistle." The signalman was only twenty-two years of age.

One of the strangest requests to Vance had to be the one from the naval commander in Wilmington, Flag Officer William Lynch. In November 1863, that officer had an idea to turn the *Advance* into something more than just another runner. He wanted to attach a spar torpedo to her stern and "put a gun, officers and crew on board, and endeavor to inflict some injury upon her foe."

Flag Officer William F. Lynch

Vance's reply has not been recorded, but the vessel was never so armed.

The state's steamer continued to be utilized to export cotton. Once credit was established by selling cotton bonds in England, the state's agent, John White, purchased cotton and wool cards, cloth, arms and ammunition, medical supplies, shoes and leather.

The agent in Wilmington met the ship at the wharf, checked the invoice and secured the freight until it could be shipped to Raleigh. Guards were placed on the train as it made its way to the capitol to ensure that everything got there intact. All in all, it was a very successful venture.

Joe Flanner ran the blockade and succeeded in getting to England, where he assisted N.C. Commissioner John White. It was later written that "he survived the four years' war, died some years later…unhappy and under a cloud in a foreign land."

As for the state's runner, the *Advance*, she was snared by the U.S. Navy in September 1864. Renamed the *USS Frolic*, she took part on the bombardment of Fort Fisher later that year. The taking of anthracite or "English" coal by the C.S. Navy raiders, *Tallahassee* and *Chickamauga* had forced the *Advance* to burn coal from the Egypt coal mines. This coal was of a poorer quality, containing a high quantity of shale which gave off a telltale plume of black smoke, more easily seen on the high seas. On former runs, the captain and crew of the vessel had been allowed to bring aboard a few bales for their own profit. Even Vance's partner, Power, Low and Company, were wary of halting the practice. Vance was determined and once stopped, the crew expressed displeasure with what they perceived as money taken from their pockets. This was suggested as another reason why the steamer had been captured.

The coal from the mines was carried to Fayetteville by the Western railroad for a distance of about fifty miles. Once at Fayetteville, it was loaded on flatboats and towed downriver to Wilmington. It was this coal, it has long been said, that led to the capture of the *Advance*, but it may be that the runner used this type of coal before. A year prior to her capture, letters to Vance indicated that a "Flat Boat…in tow of the steamer *Chatham* with a cargo of fifty three tons of coal…left [Fayetteville] this morning for Wilmington." Vance was quite interested in that shipment because he feared the War Department might appropriate it for their own use.

Upon writing to James Seixas, the War Department's agent in town, Vance learned that although Seixas had: "Every disposition to oblige you and the State…The necessities of one of the government steamers may require the coal alluded to, but if in any way practicable it will afford me pleasure to transfer it to the *Advance*." After consulting with General Whiting, the coal, it would appear, was not needed and was sent to the *Advance*.[18]

In mid-January, General Whiting seized, for government use, the steamer *Kate Mclaurin*, owned by Fayetteville businessman Robert Orrell.

James Madison Seixas

One of three steamboats that ran between Fayetteville and Wilmington, Orrell was rightly incensed because not only was his other boat, the *Sun*, taken, but his flatboats as well. The seemingly arbitrary seizure left the two opposition lines, Lutterloh and Worth's, still plying the river.

News of the takeover spread quickly around Fayetteville, with one rumor having it that "[s]ome of the officials at Wilmington, some of the highest, have their families residing here, at Fayetteville & many of the officials at the Arsenal here are appointees from Wilmington, having their residences there – it would be a very snug thing for them to have a free transit up & down the River on a government Boat, instead of having to pay for themselves and families… like common passengers."

Orrell had been told, in no uncertain terms, that "until further notice, his line of boats must be run exclusively on government account carrying neither passengers nor freight[.]" Whiting hoped to use the steamer to bring a larger quantity of coal to town to "prevent stoppage [sic] of work in any of the Departments." As the need for coal increased, the Navy asked the Army for the "loan of 20 tons." Whiting responded by telling Flag Officer Lynch that when additional coal came in, he would give them some.[19]

Another runner, the *SS Merrimac* (formerly the *Nangis*), had earlier been purchased by the Confederate's man in England, Caleb Huse, for the use of Colonel Josiah Gorgas' Ordnance Bureau. The steamer, "an extremely fast" iron-hulled side-wheeler, was reported to have made 18 knots on a trial run. Controlled by British interests, she was at St. George in Bermuda in early September 1862.

Some two hundred and thirty feet long, the *Merrimac* had a draft of only eight and a half feet. She could easily slip across the bar at New Inlet at high tide. While docked in Bermuda, the steamer was seized by the British authorities and tied up in litigation. Huse solved the problem by purchasing the vessel. Soon after, the *Merrimac*, originally built for the opium trade in China, made the run for Wilmington and although fired at, safely entered the river. When docked in town, it was found that not only had her engines fouled, but other repairs were needed also. She had laid so long at St. George, her bottom needed to be cleaned, so she was sent to Cassidey's Marine Railway, the only one able to haul her out of the river.

General Whiting was quite pleased and relieved when, in April 1863, the *Merrimac*, skippered by Captain S.G. Porter, brought him "3 splendid Blakely guns[,] 8-inch rifled 130 pdrs." Whiting got to keep two of the guns; one was emplaced in Fort Fisher, another at Fort Caswell. The third was sent on to Vicksburg.

Also aboard the ship were well over one hundred mechanics, destined for the factories of the South. When the general examined the ship, however, he remarked in a letter to Colonel Gorgas: "I do not think it advisable to send the *Merrimac* out in her present condition – She ought to go into dock, on account of barnacles on her bottom – Staying at Bermuda so long has affected her very much – Her guards are too low…& seriously interfere with her speed…To send her to sea as she is would expose her to certain capture. I am very much disappointed in the Steamer."

Captain Porter, the ship's commander, wanted to alter the vessel somewhat, so Whiting suggested to the naval commander that a military board, composed of both Army and Naval officers, as well as Porter, be convened to "consider certain alterations" proposed by the skipper. It was felt that the changes would make the steamer not only more seaworthy, but faster. About the middle of May, Whiting ordered the iron-founders, Hart and Bailey, to perform the repairs, thus placing the owners of the foundry in a quandary. Their company had been building ironclads for the C.S. Navy and that work was deemed highly important. Whiting's directive made it clear that he wanted his work done as well.

They responded: "There is required for the work on the C.S. steamer *Merrimac*…forty eight lineal feet of 7x1 in. iron – The Navy Dept. have such iron – Com. Lynch refuses to let us have the iron and he has positively forbid us doing the work as it will conflict with his work and retard the completion of the iron clad gun boat N.C."

Whiting and Lynch were once again at odds. After reading a letter sent to him by Lynch, he answered the Commodore by stating that he had "carefully ascertained that the work in question would not interfere with yours[.]" He took exception to Lynch's assertion that the machinists at Hart and Bailey worked exclusively for the Navy. The firm, said Whiting, "are iron founders in general business" and as such, anyone can contract with them.

Problems encountered in obtaining the needed items to repair the *Merrimac* convinced the authorities to sell the steamer. Stock options were offered in Wilmington and she was sold to private interests in town. Among those purchasing an interest in the vessel were Joseph Reid Anderson, the owner of Richmond's Tredegar Iron Works, and Wilmingtonians Edward Kidder and Thomas Roberts. Once in private hands, the repairs went forward and although her departure was delayed for a time due to a collision with the runner *Venus,* she was soon ready for sea. Loaded with cotton, tobacco and turpentine, she received permission to depart and headed downriver. She crossed the bar in the company of two other runners, the *Eugenie* and the *Emily*. On 24 July, they slipped through the blockade.

Joseph Reid Anderson

When only one day at sea, she encountered two blockaders. James Sprunt later wrote: "This fine, large steamer, which had been successfully run into Wilmington…was laden with a very valuable cargo…and put to sea for Nassau. On the second day out she was chased, as they thought by a cruiser which steadily gained on her, and when the stranger fired a small gun, the Captain of the *Merrimac* ignominiously surrendered to an unarmed passenger steamer, whose little popgun, containing a blank cartridge used for signaling … would not have harmed a fly."

The monitor **USS Merrimac.** *(U.S. Navy)*

Sprunt went on to note that the capture "caused much merriment on board" the Union ship. The naval records tell a different story, however. The six-gun steam sloop *USS Iroquois*, cruising at the mouth of the Cape Fear, was alerted by signal rockets that a runner was slipping away. She gave chase and some forty miles east of Masonboro Inlet, she was snared. The *Iroquois* was aided in her capture by an unknown vessel that cut off the *Merrimac's* only avenue of escape. It is likely this was the *USS Magnolia*, a small steamer mounting three guns.

When news of the capture got back to town, it caused much consternation. *Journal* editor James Fulton noted that although no "man...likes to lose money...it is a comfort to know that those who have lost money most heavily, are those upon whom the loss will...fall most lightly."

Several Wilmington citizens were captured on board the *Merrimac*, including Thomas E. Roberts, the proprietor of the Clarendon Iron Works. Roberts was from Rhode Island and had been employed at one time as Master of Machinery for the North Carolina Railroad. He spoke freely to the officers aboard ship.

U.S. Navy Captain A. Ludlow Case warned his superior, Admiral Lee, that "one of [the *Merrimac's*] late owners, Mr. Roberts, told some of the officers of this ship that...he was very desirous of going to New York in her, and is largely (from his own account) engaged in blockade running. I thought it might possibly be with a view to get some of his friends to purchase and start her for Bermuda...to load again."

Roberts was not allowed to go to New York, but was instead sent to Fort Lafayette, thence to Fort Warren, where he was to be imprisoned. Due to the influence of some of his Northern friends, he was released and soon turned up again in Wilmington.

Another who was aboard the vessel was the pilot, T.E. Burris (spelled Burroughs by U.S. officials). To avoid being jailed, he volunteered to aid the Navy as a pilot. His services were accepted. He was placed on board the *USS*

Minnesota, flagship of the blockading fleet. Throughout that summer, Burris remained aboard and in July 1863, took the Oath of Allegiance.

Yet another captive was engineer John Niemeyer. Niemeyer was born in 1831 in Hamburg, Germany. He migrated to Wilmington at the age of twelve and by 1851, had learned the steam engine trade by working as an engineer on the Wilmington and Weldon Railroad. After working for a short while for the Wilmington and Manchester Road (where he "pulled the train that brought Ben Butler and the Yankee delegates back from the memorable Charleston convention"), he plied his trade aboard Cape Fear steamers. In 1863, he became the engineer on the *Merrimac*. With its capture, he was sent north on the *USS Penobscot*. He was treated rather harshly by the *Penobscot's* crew, which he related were "...a gang of hogs compared to the jolly clever tars of the *Iroquois*."

If Niemeyer's career aboard blockade runners is indicative of others in the trade, it was an active one. After being paroled in 1863, he served aboard the *Eugenie, Bendigo, Coquette, Mary Ann* and *Cyrene* (or *Siren*). On the *Cyrene*, he made at least fifteen runs between Wilmington and Nassau. After the war, Niemeyer returned to railroading, finishing up his days as one of the oldest active locomotive engineers on the W&W.

In October, 1863, Thomas Burris (Burroughs), son of U.S. pilot T.E. Burris, a Confederate sailor stationed on the *CSS North Carolina*, deserted to the U.S. fleet along with two of his shipmates. In a message to his superiors, Captain B.F. Sands wrote that he "had not much faith in them," and thought they may have been sent out as spies. He recalled the "case of a man taken in the *Merrimac*, having been taken into the squadron as pilot, and subsequently escaped and returned to the rebels by way of New Berne."

The pilot he spoke of was likely T.E. Burris. Burris was almost captured again when the runner *Fannie and Jennie* grounded in February 1864. It was reported that "its pilot was named Burrows [Burris] and from the description I imagined him the same man we took on a previous occasion, was appointed a pilot and deserted from the *Shekokan*...he escaped and got on shore safe." Had Burris been taken, he would have faced the hangman's noose.

As for the *Merrimac*, she was sent to New York for condemnation and was purchased by the U.S. Navy. Commissioned the following year, she was armed with a 30 pdr. Parrot, four 24 pdrs., and two heavy 12 pdrs. The effects of the capture rippled across the Atlantic. The *Journal* reported, "A Gigantic Bankruptcy – In the London Court of Bankruptcy...Zachariah Charles Pearson...came up...This was one of the largest failures which ever came into the Court...The bankrupt's speculations were various [including] the sale of the celebrated vessel the *Merrimac*."

The vessel's former owners had invested in several ventures, one of which was the *Merrimac*. The combined losses led to the firm's demise. The only ones that made money from the runner was the crew of the *Iroquois*.

Proceeds from the sale brought them over $190,000. Perhaps that would account for them being "jolly!" Once in the U.S. Navy, the *Merrimac* was sent to sea as a cruiser, but was lost in a gale in February 1865.[20]

Confederate blockade runner and former skipper of the *Merrimac,* Captain Seth Grosvenor Porter, was given command of the Ordnance Department's runner, the *SS Phantom* and made several trips to and from the Islands. In July 1863, that vessel carried as a passenger Confederate spy Rose O'Neal Greenhow, who was on her way to Europe.

As another indication of the real meaning of Civil War, Captain Porter's siblings may be examined. Seth Porter had four brothers who fought for the Union. Brother Stanley was killed at Bull Run, Henry died in 1861 and Frederick was killed in 1864. Captain Porter's youngest brother, Union Lieutenant Benjamin Porter, commanded the *USS Malvern*, flagship of the Union fleet that devastated Fort Fisher. Described by one who knew him as "the bravest of the brave," Benjamin was killed in the dunes before the fort as he struggled to plant his vessel's standard upon the ramparts.

Clement Vallandigham

When he commanded the *Phantom*, Captain Porter's luck ran out. His steamer was forced to beach near New Inlet in September 1863, and was set afire. Seth Porter survived the war and stayed on the high seas. He commanded the *Morro Castle* for the Atlantic Mail Steamship Company on her runs from New York to Havana and later in life was often seen cruising in his thirty-foot yacht, the *Circes*, in the waters around New York. In 1888 he went to Germany and remained there until his death in 1910.[21]

Although General Whiting insisted on all runners leaving the port to be filled with government cargoes, this was not always possible. In June 1863, Whiting allowed the *Cornubia* to depart Wilmington with only a partial cargo. This was due in large part because a well-known passenger, Clement Vallandigham, the "Man without a Country," was being sent "beyond the lines" of the Confederacy after having also been expelled from the United States.

Another reason for allowing the vessel to leave without its government quota was that cotton belonging to the government was not forthcoming. Private goods, it seemed to many, took precedence on the limited means of transportation; more money was flowing into private hands as well as the hands of the railroads.

By the beginning of 1864, virtually all runners were steamers. Sailing vessels just couldn't escape the ever-tightening net of blockaders. In the fall of that year, editor Fulton was so taken with a reminder of "Old Times," that he wrote about the "fore and aft schooner" that had come upriver. Indeed, it had been a long while since a sailing vessel called on Wilmington. Fulton lamented, "The 'smokers' as the old 'salts' call the steamers, will never have the picturesque beauty that belongs to the sailers."

Problems continued to surface as the war years went on. It was not only with Whiting that Flag Officer Lynch was at odds. The chief of the Wilmington squadron wrote to the governor that he had been "unable to purchase provisions here for those under my command except at exorbitant prices[.] I authorized a paymaster to procure a supply in the vicinity of Tarboro[.]"

The naval agent, William H. Peters, was prevented from buying anything due to Vance's order that only the army could purchase supplies. The constant bickering between Lynch and Whiting reached a boiling point in early 1864. By law, runners were required to carry some government cotton on their outbound trip and needed war materiel on their return voyage. When the War Department did not have enough cotton, the Navy was allocated space. "Such situations often occurred, and in February 1864, [there was not] enough cotton available for the *Hansa* and the *Alice*."

When Lynch attempted to put Naval cotton on board, the owners refused to take it. He allowed them to leave port on condition that they take the Navy's cotton on their next trip. When the *Alice* returned and again tried to leave without the cotton, Lynch ordered the ship detained. When Peters complained to Whiting, the general informed the naval agent that Whiting alone had the authority to detain vessels. The War Department, however, acceded to the request of the Secretary of the Navy.

When the second steamer, the *Hansa*, appeared to be getting ready to depart without the Navy's cotton, Lynch stopped her as well, by seizing and anchoring her next to the *CSS North Carolina*. "Whiting was outraged by the seizure...The next morning March 9, he sent the *Cape Fear*...with a battalion of soldiers to the *Hansa*...ejecting Lynch's Marine guard."

He then towed the vessel back to her wharf and placed a guard around her. It was now Lynch's turn to be outraged. He boarded his flagship, the *Yadkin*, and towed the gunboat *North Carolina* opposite the *Hansa* "in a threatening position." Both services were now ready to do battle with each other. The affair caused both officers to be called to Richmond where President Jefferson Davis, with his Secretaries of both the Army and Navy, worked out the problem.

*The Confederate
ironclad
North Carolina,
moored at Smithville
(modern Southport).*

Photo: NHCPL

When Navy Lieutenant John Wilkinson was sent to the Cape Fear, one of his duties was "to do all in his power to secure harmony of action" between the services. As for Lynch, he was eventually sent to a different command where he was given the mundane task of penning a history of the Confederate Navy.[22]

There was another industry which blossomed along with the blockade running trade. When a U.S. cruiser "heavily pursued" a runner, the Captain would often intentionally beach his steamer. This served a dual purpose. First, the cargo stood a better chance of being salvaged; secondly, the ship would not be taken as a prize and be used against other swift runners.

To unload the ship's cargo required a bit of finesse on the part of the consignees, as well as the help of the military. To begin with, if the beached vessel was within range of the big guns of Fort Fisher, the blockaders usually stood well out to sea. A grounded vessel outside the range of those guns was considered fair prey for the U.S. Navy. If all went well for the lucky blockader, they would first board her, attach hawser lines and pull her off the beach. If successful, they now had a pretty well intact prize. Taken to a Court of Arbitration at Boston or New York, the ship and cargo were condemned at auction and sold. The Navy was the primary purchaser of the former runners and soon, armed with cannon and crew, another fast steamer was ready to take her station with the blockading fleet.

Sometimes things did not go smoothly for those sailors eyeing a potential captive. If the steamer was somewhere up or down the coast, Colonel William Lamb, commanding at Fort Fisher, would dispatch a company of artillerists with his "pets," the famed and feared Whitworth guns. The guns were imported from England by the Confederates from Sir Joseph Whitworth of

Manchester. In 1864, these guns were cutting-edge technology. They could fire a twelve-pound solid shot (or explosive shell) with deadly accuracy out to five miles. They could be hauled up and down the beach by horses or mules. Once emplaced, they could open up on an unsuspecting blockaders. Two or three of these guns would nearly always drive off the U.S. ship.

Once the U.S. Navy was out of the way, the *Yadkin*, or some other steam tugboat, would cross the bar and assist the runner off the beach, or pull her to safety if she had grounded. Armed with cannon, she could at least offer a modicum of resistance to any enemy vessel that might approach. If the vessel was stuck fast, she could be "lightered." The cargo was unloaded onto barges or flat boats and taken to port. This is where the "wreckers" came into play.

In Wilmington, there had always been a Commissioner of Wrecks. His job was to declare a vessel a wreck for insurance purposes and then remove whatever could be salvaged. This included not only the cargo, but the ropes, anchors, lifeboats, even the furniture of the boat. In short, anything of value, however insignificant, was removed.

When the remains of the wrecked steamer were taken to town, ads notified the public that an auction was to take place. Advertisements warned "all persons" who may have found things on the beach, that the items were to be turned in to the commissioner.

They were also told that "When any person shall find any stranded property on or near the seashore, and no owner appears to claim the same, he shall…give information to the nearest commissioner of wrecks, and…shall be entitled to his reasonable salvage."

When some soldiers discovered lengths of rope along the beach, they dutifully turned them in. It was discerned that the rope had come from a Federal blockader that lost it during a recent storm. The rope was sold and the men were quite happy to divide the spoils of their find.

The alternative could be harsh. When Captain Daniel Bennett of the 36th Regiment stationed at Fort Fisher was found to have stolen leather from the wreck of the *Kate* in November 1862, he was court-martialed, found guilty and dismissed from the army. He was later drafted into an infantry regiment as a private.

Finders had ten days to turn in the goods, after which time they were considered thieves and if discovered, would be fined ten times the value of the items. "Wreckers," those men who toiled to salvage cargoes, many times came from people living on and near the sounds. Quite often it was the troops from the nearby forts that struggled through the surf and manhandled the cargoes ashore. These men too, were not allowed to keep any of the rescued goods. Somehow, if there was any liquor on the vessel, that portion of the cargo seemed to disappear with the troops.

General Whiting was adamant that all salvaged property be returned. He sent out patrols to visit homes near the wrecks to recover any goods taken surreptitiously "whether by troops or citizens." Wrecking was hard work, in all kinds of weather and was oftentimes dangerous, especially if a U.S. cruiser decided to take a few shots to disrupt the operation.[23]

Blockade running had certainly changed the face of Wilmington. In many minds, it was not for the better. State's agents, military officials, "speculators," Confederate soldiers and sailors, foreigners, thieves, cardsharps, pickpockets, and those simply trying to exist in the midst of it all, packed Wilmington. By the fall of 1864, crime was rampant in town. The local paper advised many to carry a pistol and to be prepared to use it. J.P. Levy, living in town, wrote to the governor that "Our town is infested with Robbers & Burglars, our Mayor says he has no authority to Linch [sic]...our military authorities have no power...as General Whiting informs me." The writer implored the governor to turn the town over to the military, to remove the citizens from the clutches of "an unscrupulous set of villains who are a prowling about the town to treat us worse than the Enemy."

Vance's reply was certainly not very encouraging: "I can give no other protection than the laws which are still in existence." It would seem that the townspeople had just as much to fear from their own countrymen as from the "Yankee hordes."

Endnotes

1. Letters Received from the Colonial Office, file in the Bahamas Archives, Nassau, Bahamas, 23:166. *ORN*, I:6, 165-166, 487-489; I:12, 809-810; I:13, 346-347.
2. *Morning Star*, 5 June 1885.
3. *ORA*, 2:2, 432-457. *Daily Journal*, 10 February 1862. de Bebian returned to Wilmington in early February 1862. *ORA*, I:6, 375-376; The *New York Times*, 14 November 1880. The Frenchman was instrumental in getting the Statue of Liberty to this country and in 1889, was invited to join the Committee of Three Hundred, see The *New York Times*, 18 July 1889. He died in December 1891, The *New York Times*, 12 December 1891.
4. National Archives, "Citizen's Papers," reel no. 612, Oscar G. Parsley.
5. Wise, 235. *Daily Journal*, 31 July 1863, 20 November and 15 December 1862; *Marriages and Death Notices in Wilmington, North Carolina Newspapers, 1860-1865*, compiled and indexed by Helen Moore Sammons, privately published, Wilmington, North Carolina, 1987, 137. *Confederate Veteran*, 50:187, 1932. The *New York Times*, 14 April, 19 March, 30 April and 3 May 1862.

6. *Daily Journal*, 17 April 1861; The *New York Times*, 8 November 1898, *Daily Journal*, 5 January 1860. Confederate Papers, 15 November 1861. Simon Kahnweiler was, for a time, (14 February 1859 to 1 January 1862) in business with Morris M. Katz, another Wilmington merchant. Simon provided the capital, Katz, the business acumen.

7. The Kahnweilers also had an agent (B. Kahnweiler, likely their father, Benedict) in Philadelphia. *ORN*, I:13, 237-238; The *London Times*, 18 August 1863. O.G. Parsley would declare bankruptcy in 1879, see Bennett, 62.

8. The *London Times*, 18 August 1863.

9. New Hanover County Public Library, Bill Reaves Collection, "Kahnweiler Family file." Simon was married in Aix-la-Chappelle, Germany, to Miss Alwine Levi on 5 June 1855, Sammons, *Marriage and Death Notices, 1851-1859*; The *New York Times*, 13 January 1870. The 1870 Federal Census listed a Simon Kahnweiler living in Trenton, N.J. A son, Robert, had been born in Frankfort in 1863.

10. *Vance Papers*, 26:706, dated 2 September 1863, 3:464, dated 18 January 1864; *Whiting Papers*, II:347, dated 20 February 1864. Whiting indicated that Kahnweiler had left on the 13th. Sprunt, Chronicles, 448-449; Vance Papers, 23:864, dated 7 June 1864.

11. *Daily Journal*, 16 September 1863.

12. *Daily Journal*, 21 and 6 June 1863. Whiting Papers, II:346, November 1863. Deep Water Point was in Brunswick County, about a half-mile south of the present-day Wilmington to Southport ferry landing

13. Sprunt, *Chronicles*, 177, 252, 659; Dr. Walter Gilman Curtis, *Reminiscences of Wilmington and Smithville-Southport, 1848-1900*, 31. Manuscript copy at Fort Fisher State Historic Site. After the war Fanning would work for a time as cashier for the Wilmington Savings Bank.

14. *Wilmington Weekly Journal*, 24 June 1864. Sometimes as many as ten vessels lay at Deep Water Point, where, according to General Whiting, they were in full view of the blocking fleet and offered a tempting target for a boat raid. *Whiting Papers*, 1 July 1863, 16 August 1864. *Vance Papers*, 188:407, 490, 13:291, 21:945. Whiting assumed the governor would return by the steamer *Flora*. Sprunt, *Chronicles*, 454-455; Clark, V:360-361. Sprunt erroneously names the officer as Major Strong; writing to the Secretary of War, Whiting admitted "though I regret to lose the services of that energetic officer [Thorburn] he had him removed from command. *Whiting Papers*, II:336, "Letters Sent," 31 July 1863; *Confederate Military History*, edited by Robert S. Bridgers, 3:64, 352-354; Robert K. Krick, *Lee's Colonels, A Biographical Register of the Field Officers of the Army of Northern Virginia* (Dayton: Morningside Bookshop, 1979) 347. "Confederate War Department," Copies of Letters and Telegrams Sent and Received," reel no. 878, 291, microfilm copy at Randall Library, UNC-Wilmington. Thorburn is buried in Norfolk, Va. The F.F.V. quote comes from

Captain William A. Graham, who lamented the lack of N.C. brigadiers, in a letter to Governor Vance, *Vance Papers*, 18:1076. Before splitting up, President Davis gave Thorburn $1,510 of treasury money, see A.J. Hanna, *Flight Into Oblivion* (Richmond: William Byrd Press, 1938) 92, 96.

15. North Carolina State Archives, Military Collection, box 36, file 11; *ORN*, I:6, 68, 96; II:1, 259, 371. James Sprunt, *Tales of the Cape Fear Blockade, 1862-1865* (Winnabow, N.C.: Clarendon Imprints, 1960) 1-2. Wise, in *Lifeline of the Confederacy* indicates that the *Mariner* was captured in March 1863, "while attempting to return to Wilmington" but General Whiting wrote that "The steam tug *Mariner*...has come in from Nassau...she is absolutely necessary here, for the Navy first, and then for us." Flag Officer Lynch concurred with Whiting, probably the only time they ever agreed on anything. See *ORN*, I:8, 861-862, 874.

16. *Vance Papers*, 18:617, dated 10 July 1863; 26:721, n.d.; 18:670, dated 13 July 1863.

17. *Vance Papers*, 18:588, dated 9 July 1863; 19:825, dated 25 September 1863; 19:721, dated 15 September 1863; 19:549, dated 5 September 1863. Powell, *North Carolina Biography*, 6:168. Scheibert, *Seven Months in the Rebel States*, 147-149.

18. Johnson, *Vance Papers*, 1:261; McKinney, *Vance Papers*, 20:304, 20:333, 20:753, 20:845, 19:370, 20:831. The information on Drs. Swann and Love comes from the *Vance Papers*, 19:321, 24:287. For the Flanner-Wilkings duel, see Sprunt, *Chronicles*, 231-237. For Flanner's involvement with the *Mariner*, see NCSA, Military Collection, box 36, file 11. See also ORA, 4:3:1117. The information on Royal is from the *Whiting Papers*, Chapter II, vol. 347, dated 27 February 1864, also the *Daily Journal*, 12 July and 10 November 1864. The information on John Smith is from Powell, *North Carolina Biography*, 5:381-382 and William S. Powell, *When the Past Refused to Die: A History of Caswell County, N.C., 1777-1977*, 211-213. The information on the coal from Chatham County is from the *Vance Papers*, 19:367, 19:529-530, 19:619, 638-639 and 19:724.

19. *Vance Papers*, 25:459-461; *Whiting Papers*, II:336, entries dated 14 and 15 January 1864. *The Story of Fayetteville and the Upper Cape Fear,* John C. Oates (Charlotte: The Dowdy Press, 1950).

20. Wise, 96-97; *Whiting Papers*, II:335, letters dated 25, 27 April, 1, 24 May and 20 June 1863. *Daily Journal*, 2 July, 3 August and 22 October 1863; Colonial Office (Bahamas) 23:165; Sprunt, *Chronicles*, 453. *ORN*, I:9, 131-133, 141, 235, 474-475. According to Captain Case, Caleb Huse paid $2,200,000 in Confederate currency for the *Merrimac*, *ORN*, I:9, 133. See also Jim McNeil, *Masters of the Shoals* (Cambridge, Ma.: DaCapo Press, 2003) 66-68. *Vance Papers*, 25:390-391; *Wilmington Morning Star*, 23 February 1894. *Daily Journal*, 11 September 1863. Thomas Truxton Moebs, *Confederate States Navy*

Research Guide (Williamsburg, Va.: Moebs Publishing Co., 1991). Bleeker, 105-106. Bleeker quotes Huse as commenting that there were no means of repairing the Merrimac in Wilmington, but "it was easily accomplished as soon as she passed into private hands." When the steamer *Banshee* arrived at the end of May, Whiting "impressed" 15 iron plates, as well as other items; perhaps they were to be used on the *Merrimac*, see *Whiting Papers*, II:336, 20 may 1863. *ORN*, I:152, letter dated 25 July 1863; *Whiting Papers*, Ch. II, vol. 346, undated, late 1863. There were several pilots named Burris running the blockade. Porter, *Civil War*, 839.

21. *The New York Times*, 8 January 1893. Fonvielle, *The Wilmington Campaign*, 258; internet website, http://familytreemaker.genealogy.com/users. The Porter family had nine children, six boys and three girls. Only Seth and his brother Samuel survived the war. One of Porter's sisters, Laura, married into the Roosevelt family. She married Cornelius Van Schaack Roosevelt, a New York businessman who amassed a fortune in his lifetime. Upon his death in 1887, his estate was valued at somewhere between 1 and 2 million dollars. As Cornelius and Laura were childless, he bequeathed much of the money to his many nieces and nephews, but a lawsuit tied the estate up for some time and at one point Seth and Anna Eleanor (later to become the wife of Franklin D. Roosevelt) were involved. After Laura died in 1900, her nephew, President Theodore Roosevelt inherited between $100,000 and $150,000. See The *New York Times*, 28 February 1888, 3 July 1900, 14 December 1901 and 19 April 1902.

22. *Whiting Papers*, II:336, letter dated 11 March 1864. Wise, 156-157. *Whiting Papers*, II:336, dated 1 and 20 May 1863.

23. Sprunt, *Chronicles*, 488-489; Manarin, I:326.

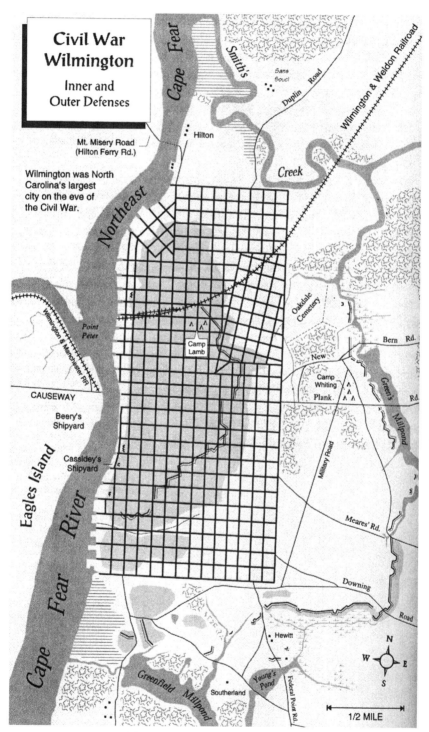

Civil War
Wilmington

Inner and
Outer Defenses

Mt. Misery Road
(Hilton Ferry Rd.)

Wilmington was North
Carolina's largest
city on the eve of
the Civil War.

Map courtesy of Mark A. Moore

14

The Department of the Cape Fear

ajor Thomas Sparrow, of the 10th N.C. (Artillery) Regiment, was Colonel Thorburn's replacement as city commandant. A lawyer before the war and a native of Washington, North Carolina, Sparrow was captured at Fort Hatteras in 1861, then spent time in confinement at Massachusetts' Fort Warren. Sparrow was then paroled and ordered to Wilmington. Prior to taking command of the city, he served as Judge-Advocate for several courts-martial in town. Several batteries of the Tenth Regiment remained in the Cape Fear area for most of the war, but it was the Tenth Battalion (Heavy Artillery) that constituted the main garrison troops of the city until late 1864 when they were sent to help defend Savannah, Georgia. Many of the men in the 10th Battalion fought bravely while in Georgia and South Carolina. Two members of the Battalion, Sergeant J.E. Harriss and Private H.M. Underwood, were commended for bravery by General Lafayette McLaws in February 1865, when they volunteered to burn a bridge that the Yankees were attempting to take. The following month, the unit would again prove their mettle at Bentonville, N.C., where they fought as infantrymen and suffered heavy losses. While stationed in Wilmington earlier in the war however, they seemed to be a lot more lax.[1]

When they were in the area, the battalion manned the defensive positions around town. The city, which was defended by batteries along the river, also had "A system of ponds, dams and earthworks extending in a crescent half around the northeastern side…then from Northeast River to Smith's Creek and across a sand ridge to the Cape Fear River a mile or more below the City[.]

There were dams with water gauges at each of these ponds, and it is said to have been a very skillful piece of engineering. In the city were two batteries of 10-inch [Columbiad] cannons...One battery was on a bluff at the upper side of the city, and the other on a bluff near the southern suburbs. These batteries and chain of dams along with several government sheds...were the principal points to protect the 10th Battalion...There were ten or twelve posts to be guarded which required a [force] of about forty men daily."

The duty officer was charged with visiting all posts during the day and his reports were forwarded to headquarters. The battalion had picket posts at the foot of Market Street. A guardhouse was located at the Market House with a Napoleon cannon inside. The men patrolled the streets and the railroad depot. Lieutenant Powell reported, "Many foreigners and strangers were in the city at all times coming on the blockade runners, so that a patrol guard policed the city day and night...The 'red light' district...was especially closely watched and many suspicious persons were arrested."

Soldiers often rode the trains and examined the passes of those aboard; movement along the river at night was suspect. After dark sentries at the Market Street ferry landing had standing orders to fire on any vessel or boat that attempted to pass that post. The Navy's guard ship, the *CSS Arctic*, once a lightship, now used to train future sailors, was stationed at Point Peter, just north of the city to monitor river traffic. On at least one occasion, the *Arctic* halted the Fayetteville steamer *A.P. Hurt* and a party of sailors boarded the boat. Equipment needed by the *Arctic* was seized and the vessel was allowed to go on its way.

When General Whiting was informed of the incident, he was furious and penned a note to Lynch. He said the Navy had no "right to stop any boat in this district except your own or those of the enemy...Matters like this do not lend cordiality of intercourse."[2]

The roads leading in and out of the city were fortified and manned; soldiers prevented unauthorized persons from leaving town. In May 1864, naval commander Lynch was notified that one of his Marines had been shot and killed by a sentry while trying to pass through the lines. Lynch was quite upset because it was the second time in three months one of his men had been killed in such a manner. He wrote to Whiting expressing his outrage and requested that more sentries be placed where they could be seen, so as to "overawe resistance." Lynch was aware that liquor played a part in the man's death, but railed against placing a sentry "in ambush as it were." Deadly force, however, was seen as a necessary evil to deter possible desertion.

Sentry duty was boring and offered ample opportunity for the men to get into trouble. In 1864, several soldiers stationed at Dam Number 2 were reported

Roads and ferry crossings around Wilmington were posted with sentries.

intoxicated. Sometimes, while checking passes, the men stole produce from the wagons they were searching. When a fire was needed to cook a meal, nearby fences were torn down. Even the old fence around the Poor House was not excepted. In June 1864, the superintendent reported that the pickets stationed there had removed parts of the fence surrounding the property, but the men on duty shifted the blame onto the drivers of the salt wagons that had stopped there to cook their noonday meal.[3]

There were other, more serious problems with the units stationed in town. Just what happened in March 1863, is not known, but whatever it was, the commanding officer of Company A of the 10th Battalion, Captain William B. Lewis, resigned "while under charges of conduct unbecoming an officer." The fallout continued when, on 6 April, a court martial dismissed Lieutenant George S. Boxley from the service and ordered him to report to a conscript camp at Raleigh. Former Lieutenant Boxley, an Alabaman, was then enrolled as a Private in the 48th N.C. Regiment.

That same month Private Alexander Hargrove, of Company A, was confined while awaiting trial to determine whether or not he was to be shot for "cowardice." Hargrove's life was spared when a new court was convened and he was returned to his company.[4]

The Tenth Battalion remained in town for nearly two years and served as both artillerymen and provost guards. Formed in May 1862, it was essentially a heavy artillery unit, composed of three companies until July 1863, when a fourth company was organized. August proved to be a bad month for Company A, as at least eight of its men deserted. In December 1863, the battalion was ordered to Fort Caswell on Oak Island. With the new year they were sent to nearby Fort Campbell, but the desertions continued and Lieutenant Charles Powell recorded that "while at this fort we had an oyster boat that kept us supplied with oysters and clams. One night the crew with the boat deserted and rowed out to the gunboats."

Six men from the 10th went over to the enemy in February 1864. The day after they made their escape, Union Lieutenant Commander William B. Cushing entered the river and led a raid on General Louis Hebert's headquarters in Smithville. Hebert was away in Wilmington, but his adjutant, Major John G.

Gen. Louis Hebert

Kelly, was snared. General Whiting was convinced the deserters guided Cushing.

At least one deserter was caught before he could get away. Private Ransom Gallamore was arrested and confined until his court martial. His punishment was decreed to be death by a firing squad composed of his own comrades-in-arms. His execution was to serve as a warning to others who may have harbored thoughts of desertion.

Michael Turrentine, a soldier stationed at Fort Caswell when the execution was carried out, wrote home: "The day appointed for the execution was Friday…At daybreak, a very heavy fog overspread the ground and obscured the sun…but at 10 o'clock [the sun] shined and the fog had… disappeared. The Reg't. formed in the usual order upon the parade ground and by a series of very awkward evolutions was formed into a hollow square with one side open and waited for the hour of the execution."

Eighteen members of the regiment had been chosen to act as Gallamore's executioners, with ten rifles loaded with cartridges and eight with blanks. Turrentine reported that the men were "pale and seemed loth [sic] to perform their duty." A stake was pounded into the ground facing the men and at eleven o'clock the condemned man, followed by a minister, was slowly walked around the square. The Reverend Andrews addressed the men, reminding them that their death was as close as that of the prisoner. The minister then shook hands with Gallamore and stepped away. After being blindfolded and forced to kneel with his back to the stake "he awaited his doom with commendable

Executions by firing squad were sometimes carried out when deserters were recaptured.

fortitude...A flourish of the sword and a roll of the drum announced that the moment had arrived...Ready-Aim-Fire and the prisoner with a bound fell forward upon his face... pierced through the breast by two balls, one passing through his heart. Thus died a man who was branded with the infamous epithet Deserter."[5]

Lieutenant Powell, writing after the war, recalled that the oyster boat the deserters had used had a "forty-two pound conical shell" as an anchor. "On their desertion, that put an end to the oyster business and the shell lay on the sand, used by the soldiers in athletic performances. Supposing all the powder had been washed out of the shell, I took it for a firedog in my new fireplace. About three hours thereafter, it exploded wrecking the chimney[,] damaging the building and slightly wounding my orderly[.]"

Besides a few jokes now and then, there were "outrages and depredations" alleged to have been committed by troops in the area. These were promptly reported to General Whiting, who had all charges investigated. If the damage was proven to have been done by members of certain unit, the men were identified and forced to pay. If the men did not come forward or could not be found, the entire unit was forced to pay.

In 1864, more serious charges and specifications were leveled against the Tenth Battalion's commander, Major Wilton Young. The charges were brought against him by Major Alexander MacRae, who commanded the 1st N.C. (Heavy Artillery) Battalion. Major MacRae was probably one of the oldest officers on active duty. He was 70 years old when the war began and had fought in the War of 1812.

MacRae preferred charges against Young for having cruelly punished two of MacRae's men. One of the men, said to be a malingerer, had been hung for several hours by his thumbs, while both men were also forced to carry two twenty-four pound cannonballs around for several days as part of their punishment.

Yet another soldier, Private Joseph Stancowitz, was singled out by Young because he "was quartering in a portion of the building occupied by Capt. Harriss & other officers as a kitchen. Pvt. S nightly had 2 women of ill fame to visit his quarters & remain all night & while quartered those women rec'd. visits from the soldiers of the garrison, thus virtually making his quarters a retail house of ill fame as this man ... made it a matter of speculation."[6]

When the guards broke into his room, they found the two women with Stancowitz and Private Charles Barton, Major MacRae's cook. All the charges against Major Young were dropped.

Those charges would have landed the men in jail. The prisons were full of men who had been drinking, fighting, were stowaways, Yankee and rebel deserters, murderers and thieves. Men who had overstayed their leaves were thrown in jail to await a court-martial which, because of a lack of suitable officers, was delayed for months. The problem became a major one when it was seen that there were no more jail cells available.

An indication of the conditions prisoners faced might be garnered from a letter written to the governor late in 1863. The writer described the lock-up at Weldon, where his brother had recently been incarcerated. The unfortunate soldier was "fed scanty rations, maggoty, stinking...crowded in a small, dirty room filled with vermin and filth - Great God! All this for refusing to carry [a] log." The writer referred to the place as the South's "Black Hole of Calcutta."

In town, some of the incarcerated men idled away the time by removing pieces of the plaster walls and ceilings and, while waiting for just the right moment, threw the pieces at hapless passers-by. One citizen noted that "yesterday any one passing along the side walk had to be watchful or else he would be struck by some missile thrown from the upper windows."

Wilmington became a prison depository for other commands. Charleston had begun to send prisoners to town so that they could be sent "beyond the lines," presumably aboard a blockade runner. General Whiting advised that city not to send any more prisoners to Wilmington. All available space was utilized. In the fall of 1864, when a barbershop moved out of the rooms under the City Hotel, Quartermaster Styron was ordered to fit it up "for a guard house." At the same time the city was filling up with all sorts of people. Whiting telegraphed Governor Vance in August that there was a problem with "[numbers of men claiming] foreign protection...[who] were banished from Georgia by Gov. Brown for refusing to bear arms in defence [sic] of the State." They were, Whiting concluded, "a great nuisance."

Mothers, fathers and wives all pleaded with the authorities to release their relatives from jail. The prisoners themselves often pled their own cases. Several wrote to Governor Vance asking him to take an interest in their plight. One soldier who languished in prison was William M. Stevenson. He had already spent seven months in jail with no end in sight. He tried his luck by writing to Vance, admitting, "under the influence of the intoxicating Drug, I deserted my company." Repenting and indicating a desire to return to his unit, he was released at the end of November, just in time to partake in the battles for Fort Fisher.

Another who remained in jail was George W. Johnson. Johnson had been arrested in the fall of 1863 for having stolen a locomotive from Richmond and, it was rumored, had run it to Goldsboro. In giving Vance the details of his supposed crime, he told of being arrested on the evidence of "two unknown men" who claimed to have heard him in a saloon, boasting of the deed. He denied the accusation and asked, "How is it supposed that I...could...take from any...Depots or Workshops an Engine, or any other article of such unwieldy proportions[?]" Assurring the governor of his innocence, he lamented that he had already been in prison for 91 days "all to satisfy the malignant hatred of two unknown enemies." He continued, "Here I have languished...suffering...and prevented from rendering assistance and support to a destitute and starving family. In consequence those destitute ones have now died and now sleep their last sleep beneath the cold sod of mother earth."

Indeed, for lack of anywhere to stay, Johnson's wife, who had come to Wilmington with her infant child to help her husband, had been living in an outhouse and it was there they were found dead. The coroner pronounced the cause of death "want of assistance." At the insistence of a judge, Johnson was finally released by an order from General Whiting.

Governor Vance was quite perturbed when he received a letter from yet another citizen who run afoul of the military. William Whitley, who claimed to be a railroad employee, had been shot, arrested and confined in Raleigh. "[I] was home to get shoes[,] have been a cripple for seven years and not required... to join any armed service...I was getting shoe work done [with a knock] at the door...one of the party presented a gun at my breast & snapped a cap but the load did not go off[;] he immediately fired the other barl [sic] the contents of which lodged in my left leg to the number of sixty-three shot."

Vance immediately called for a "full and careful investigation by the military. It was discovered that Whitley wasn't telling the governor the exact truth. There had been a scuffle at the house, in which he had been wounded and taken to the hospital. The authorities could not "ascertain which Road he claims to be on...About two weeks since his Negro wife came to the hospital to visit him[;] he came away with her & has not since been heard from, from all accounts he is a bad character."[7]

Some prisoners seemed fatalistic about their confinement while others appeared mortified. Several privates from the 1st N.C. Battalion admitted their crime: "[W]e have been in military prison for six months & for nothing but going home one time. We are very tired of being confined...We are brothers and never heard the Army regulations read. We were ignorant of what was our duty."

Several others readily admitted the error of their ways. Two members of the 22nd N.C. wrote Vance: "It has been our sad misfortune to have violated Military Discipline in overstaying our...furlough," thereby incurring, "a very unwelcome imprisonment in the Military jail of this City." They implored the governor to have them released, stating that their State needed them to repel the "Vandal foe that daily threaten her."

Due to paperwork errors, some men who were not deserters were accused of that crime. Twenty-two year old William M. Peck had enlisted in the 18th N.C. Regiment in June 1862 and was shot in the hand in the Battle of Cedar Run, Virginia. Sent to the hospital at Danville, he later came down with Erysipelas.[8] Evidenced by a swelling and redness of the infected area and sometimes referred to as the "eel thing," it was quite painful. Erysipelas is a streptococci infection which also causes constitutional problems. It was treated initially by isolating the patient as the disease was highly communicable. The surroundings had to be kept scrupulously clean while the infected area was treated with oils or lard. It was one of the most fatal diseases soldiers of both sides had to deal with.

Peck's doctors treated him as best they could, then gave him a furlough home. This was done for several reasons. First, he would receive better care from his friends and family and secondly, valuable hospital space was secured for another patient. When the soldier's illness did not require a doctor's care, but the man would be incapacitated for longer than thirty days, he was usually granted a furlough, "not to exceed sixty days." The Confederate medical officers took a wait-and-see attitude with many diseases. If the furloughed soldier needed more time, a certificate from the family doctor was required. In addition, a justice of the peace had to certify that the physician was of good standing in the community. If the patient recovered, he was expected to report back to duty. If he didn't, well, at least he would die at home.

Peck arrived in Wilmington and checked in at General Hospital No. 4 where he was examined and allowed to go home. He had to check in with the doctors every so often and was usually notified by an ad run in the local paper advising those "in private quarters" to return to the hospital. After some time at home, Peck was advised that he was listed as a deserter. After securing a certificate from the doctor who had treated him and passing that along to his commanding officer, his name was removed from the list.

In Wilmington, he may have visited Walker Meares or Lippett's drug store to obtain "Airam's Salve." That medication was said to be "peculiarly adapted to wounds exhibiting symptoms of Erysipelas." It could also be used for "cuts, bruises, burns, scalds...blisters, ulcers...and for all wounds of every description." After a year, with still no recovery, Peck applied to be transferred a local unit, the 1st N.C. Battalion. The response was "disapproved, owing to the applicant being diseased." Denied, he tried several times to reenlist, with no success. On 26 June 1864, Peck died from the disease.

There were conscientious objectors lodged in the prison. When the two Hockett brothers, who were members of the Society of Friends, were drafted, they were told they could perform non-combat duty, such as nursing the sick or working at the State Salt Works near Wilmington. They refused all such duty and were placed in confinement. They were later assigned duty with the 1st Company A, 36th N.C (the Wilmington Horse Artillery) and that company, later transferred to the 10th Regiment, was on duty in the Cape Fear area. When they again refused to do any duty, their commanders were in a quandary.

Walker Meares (NHCPL)

Letters flew back and forth and they were told that "They may report to Col. J.M. Worth, Salt Commissioner, or cook, or soldier, 'but must do one thing or the other.' " The Hocketts steadfastedly refused and were again put in jail. After three weeks in confinement and still adamant about their refusal to serve in the army, they were "set to hard work such as digging up stumps, cutting wood & all of the hard & disagreeable work of the Camp."

Eventually sent to the military prison in Wilmington, a court-martial sentenced them to six months at hard labor. Major Sparrow, in command of the garrison, filed a report which stated in part: "Private Hockett was sent to this Post on the 10th August. The next day the ball [a 12 pdr., attached to his left leg] and chain was placed upon him and he was confined in the guard house, on account of indisposition, he was not put to work during his sickness."

H.M. and F.D. Hockett, loyal Quakers, were at last set free by a proclamation of the President. Upon paying a five hundred dollar "fine" to the state and an additional one hundred dollars to the Confederate Government, they were released and discharged from the army.[9]

Sending men like the Hocketts to the Salt Works was not unusual. Salt Commissioner John Worth, whose family members were all Quakers and who himself had been raised in that religion, played an important part in their employment. Worth had lived in Randolph County, where many Quakers resided. He wrote in September 1862 to newly-elected Governor Zeb Vance: "I have about 200 men...one third of whom are quakers [sic], whom at my suggestion Gov. Clark directed me to take at the time of the draft[.]" These men were needed to "pump water, cut wood, drive wagons...attend the pans and furnaces, to make repairs, and bag salt."

Worth was often at odds with Major General Whiting because he thought the general saw not only the workers as a ripe field for the conscript "reapers," but cast his eyes on the work's steamer *J.R. Grist*, formerly run as a packet to Fayetteville. Whiting did covet the drivers with their many horses and mule teams; he needed such laborers to work on the defenses of the region. Many of those men were either woodcutters or teamsters who hauled the salt to Wilmington. The woodsmen would soon have to travel further and further to gather the enormous amounts of fuel required to feed the fires that burned night and day. These salt work fires were often used by the U.S. Navy blockaders as a point of reference.

Encompassing about 220 acres, the works produced anywhere from 200 to 300 bushels per day and supplied "that necessary article" to various counties throughout the state. In 1864, the salt commissioner reported the works had delivered 21,000 bushels to seventy-five counties at well below the market rate. Sold more cheaply, salt was meant to help support soldier's families as well as the poor and needy. More than just a seasoning, the product was utilized to preserve meat and

A marker near the site of the old salt works.

became all-important at hog-killing time.

When Governor Vance decreed an embargo on the shipment of certain articles out-of-state because many of those very items could not be found in the state, salt was included. Wilmington lawyer Thomas C. Miller wrote to him and objected on behalf of many owners of private works. He pointed out that salt which arrived via the blockade was not subject to such restriction and neither were other works within the state, those run by "foreign" [i.e. out-of-state] owners.

Miller stated that others "bring their labor and teams...but do not bring provisions for either, which is another great drain on the already impoverished growers of this section." Salt was consequently removed from the embargo list.

In a later letter, Miller advised Vance that many businessmen had "abandoned" the occupation due to the high cost of supplies. Mules now cost

Salt works like the one above were a vital necessity during the war.

between four and five hundred dollars, while wood was becoming increasingly scarce. If the salt workers were "impressed," not only would there be less salt, but it was the season for harvesting rice. That crop would suffer also, if more hands were taken by the army to work on the area's defenses.[10]

Another reason many were getting out of the business was because it was risky. The U.S. Navy made such enterprises a special target and raided many of them along the coast. "Another Raid," one account announced. "It would seem that the blockaders were quite active along shore on Sunday...We are...informed that they destroyed the Salt Works [at New Topsail Inlet]. The Salt Works belonging to D. McMillan, Esq., are mentioned positively, and we presume others may be included...From information obtained pretty directly by underground railroad from Beaufort, we learn that the Yankees there openly avow their determination to destroy all salt works on the different sounds."

General Whiting considered the salt works a traitor's nest, whose occupants would wreak havoc when invasion threatened and he tried several times to shut down the operation.

Disease almost did the deed. During the 1862 yellow fever epidemic, the works were effectively halted and the workers scattered. Upon starting up again in December, Whiting called for Worth to come to his office, where they held a conversation.

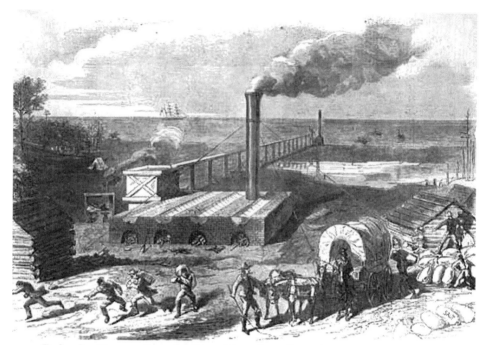

Federal raids on salt works along Masonboro Sound were a constant threat.

"Gen'l W.: I understand you have too many men at your works, and have also learned that you on that account are making the salt cost the State more than any other salt that is made hereabouts.

"[Worth]: if any one has told you that I have too many hands and that my salt costs more than that made by private parties they told you a d____ lie.

"They eyed each other for a few moments in silence, when the Gen'l. without another word told his Adj. Genl. to countermand an order he had made taking away 150 of [Worth's] men[.]"

One who contracted the fever and died was John Worth's seventeen-year-old son. The loss may have affected his work as he resigned his commission the following summer.

Realizing the importance of such a commodity as salt, Vance appointed yet another Worth to the job, this time the outgoing commissioner's nephew, David Gaston, whose father was state treasurer. The men at the works were eventually formed into militia companies, but were excused from drill. They were certainly not prepared when more than one hundred Federals raided the works in April 1864. The raiders "made prisoners of every one they could and set fire to the works." Fortunately, only a portion of the Masonboro works were destroyed and Commissioner Worth hoped to have the site back in full operation by mid-May. General Whiting had had enough and he ordered the removal of the works away from the Sounds. The removal was not immediate however, and was not completed until the following month.

The workers were not to go to the army however, as the works were then set up at Riverside, across the Cape Fear River in Brunswick County. David also found himself on the defensive; one salt purchaser wrote to Governor Vance that, "I had very good reason for believing that half of the salt that is made at one of the State's Salt Works is sold for cost and the other half for the highest price that could be obtained for it in Wilmington."

In taking over the works, David reported that he had some 270 workers, but "Of this number, about 40 are permanently diseased, and the greater part of their time unfit for service. At the time I took charge of the works there were 460 names on the roll – about 190 have died, been discharged, and taken by the enemy."

It is likely that many of the men employed by Worth voted for W.W. Holden in the election of August 1864. Worth was forced to concede that at least a part of his work force might be disloyal. He agreed to cooperate with General Whiting and allowed a detective to infiltrate among the employees, in an attempt to discover any treasonous activity. He still maintained that there was absolutely no communication between the salt works and the U.S. Navy vessels, other than through the "occasional desertion." In June 1864, Whiting ordered the cessation of salt making "between Dr. Anderson and the head of the Sound." To insure there would be no misunderstanding, he told his officers, "You will convey the accompanying order to Mr. Worth & similarly direct him to remove his force without delay."[11]

The risk of desertion by Confederate soldiers increased the closer they got to the Union fleet. With the Quartermaster, Commissary, Ordnance, Engineer Departments, the Conscript officers and the Nitre Bureau, soldiers stationed at the many gun batteries and forts in the area, and troops on furlough or passing through Wilmington, it remained a solid military town throughout the war. As the army presence increased, it was found necessary to appoint another assistant quartermaster. Major Cameron recommended Private Isaac B. Grainger.

Grainger's reputation must have preceded him for General Whiting did not hesitate to endorse his recommendation. The army had taken over several steamers to supply the forts along the river, and newly promoted Captain Grainger, along with his other duties, was placed in charge of them.

Whiting, in a letter to General P.G.T. Beauregard, complained about the state of available river shipping. It was, he commented, "lamentably deficient." He reported that he had "a few old [used] up river boats[,] mostly stern wheel, high pressure." Whiting thought nothing of impressing a steamer if he needed one.

In May 1863, when the *Harkaway*, a British vessel, limped into port, Whiting seized the ship for his use. The vessel had been dismasted, so he used it as a lighter and pushed for its purchase by the War Department. When the military and the owners could not agree on a price, Whiting refused to submit to arbitration and looked elsewhere.

In July, when the Consolidated Steamship Company's steamer, *Virginia*, came up the river, Whiting liked what he saw. The sleek, one hundred and sixty-foot steamer, originally named the *Flora*, was an iron-hulled twin-screw blockade runner with eleven successful runs to her credit. The ship, built in England in 1862, was seized by the general that summer and was finally purchased for $500,000 (in cotton) in the fall of 1863. Although Whiting may have originally wanted the vessel to assist in the defense of the harbor, the steamer soon became the army's primary means of transportation. When sold to the government she was renamed to better reflect her domain. Skippered by Captain Guthrie, the *Cape Fear* was run down the river three times a week for civilians, who needed a pass to board the boat and were not, in times of emergency, allowed aboard. The vessel was run for the military the other days of the week.[12] When on military duty, the *Cape Fear* was usually seen towing a lighter or flat full of assorted cargoes destined for the forts downriver.

The steamer *John Dawson*, piloted by Captain Oliver A. Jenkins, was also pressed into military service. Jenkins, an Alabaman, was a refugee from Pensacola who had made his way to Wilmington. As the skipper of the river steamers (he also piloted the *Flora*), he earned $100 per month. Although he was an excellent seaman, at least one complaint was lodged against him. Major James Stevenson, stationed at Fort Fisher, reported that one of his men detailed to bring mail to the *Flora* from a blockade runner, was not given enough time to "get on and off safely, & that [his] boat nearly went under."

Colonel Lamb investigated and responded to the charge by writing that, "Capt. Jenkins has always been exceedingly accommodating to me and I trust this matter was the result of undue haste to make his trip & not a disregard for the lives of the men."

When the *John Dawson's* mechanical system required repairs, she was turned over to Robert's Clarendon Iron Works. Sometimes there were more serious problems with the steamers: their crews. When it was found that the crew of the *Dawson* was drunk on duty, they were removed and replaced by free black workers. In July 1864, one of the *Cape Fear's* crewmen was discharged for the same reason and by the fall of that year, the vessel was still short of crewmen. Liquor was still the bane of the military.

In June 1863, a mutiny took place at Fort Johnston. The men of 2nd Company H, 40th N.C. Regiment, said to be normally "hard workers" and "generally well behaved," were found drunk and unruly. After the war an historian would add that the company was "composed principally of Irishmen, and no better or more loyal men, or better soldiers could be found in any company." That June, however, they were arrested by the Officer of the Day.

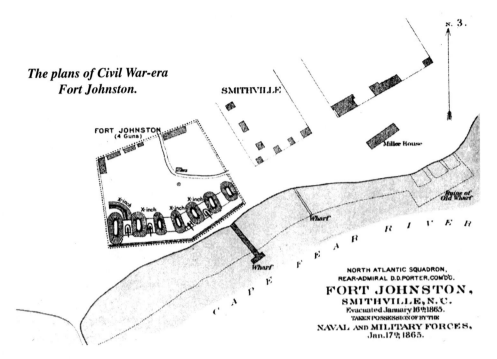

The plans of Civil War-era Fort Johnston.

General Whiting reported the rest of the sad story: "The ring leaders being confined attempted to force the guard assisted by and encouraged by those outside – The Officer of the Day ordered the guard to fire and the principal mutineer was instantly killed. The commanding officer with much difficulty disarmed the company without further loss of life."

Some men of the company were arrested and confined at the fort. Private James Stephens, apparently "the principal mutineer," was shot and killed by the guard. It might be interesting to note that several of the mutineers, whether by coincidence or design, were admitted to General Hospital No. 4 in the summer of 1862. Perhaps the seeds of discontent were already being sown by that early date. Upon further investigation by Lieutenant Fairly of Whiting's staff, it was discerned that liquor had been secretly smuggled to the men by an engineer aboard the steamer *Petteway*. That crewman was arrested and court-martialed. Virtually all the participants in the mutiny were sent to infantry regiments and several other members of that infamous unit transferred to other commands after the incident. For sometime afterwards, anyone found drinking at the fort was severely punished. When Sergeant John O'Connell was found drunk, he was "reduced to [the] ranks." A week later, Corporal John Sweaney was "killed by the guard while trying to arrest him." The evils of demon alcohol would be stamped out one way or another.[13]

Captain William James, Whiting's Chief Engineer and a Yankee by birth, had been an engineer in the U.S. Navy. He married a Southern girl and remained

South when war came. Stationed in town, he located his office on the second floor nearly over Walker Meares drug store (known as the "Iron Front" building) on Market Street. James not only dealt with the military, but with overseers and owners of slaves brought to labor in the area.[14] For every twenty-five slaves brought to town, one overseer, paid $100 per month, was allowed. Owners were paid twenty dollars every month, with "clothing, rations and medical attendance furnished." In time of danger, slaves were to be removed to an area of safety. This, of course, was not only for the protection of the workers, but also to ease the worry of the owners that they might lose their flesh and blood investments.

The workers were taken by steamer to labor at the forts downriver for a set period of two months, but the time actually varied. Slave owners were often found at James' office demanding the return of their human property. Those voices reached fever pitch around harvest time as the crops needed to be gotten in and the workers needed at home to help out. That was when irate letters wound up on the Governor's desk. One, written by former Governor David S. Reid, noted that: "[The slaves] have been brought to the Town of Wilmington, where some are employed at one business and some at another, some standing to horses and other little jobs not at all necessary for the public defence [sic] or even the health of Wilmington. Some of the owners have visited Wilmington and made inquiry as to when their slaves would be returned, but the authorities there have failed to give them the least satisfaction in regard to that matter."

Gov. David S. Reid

At times there was such a congregation of people on the street that customers had a difficult time getting into Walker Meares' store. Meares complained to the commanding general and a notice was run in the paper advising people to keep off the street and to allow access to the drug store. In mid-April, Governor Vance sent an aide to talk to Whiting about the problem of his keeping slaves well past their time. The aide received a promise that the he "would have the Negroes discharged immediately," but by the middle of the following month, Vance had to again order that the slaves "be returned without delay."

Captain James was assisted by Captain Francis Hawks. Hawks supervised not only the workers at the forts, but also those working on pilings, rope and chain obstructions in the river, and those building wharves and gun batteries along the beach.

Hawks, a native of New Bern, had worked for the Atlantic and North Carolina Railroad before the war. He was the son of the "famous divine and historian, Dr. Hawks," who "had fallen into disfavor with his [New York] congregation" and had resigned. After he returned from Charleston, where he had examined "torpedo boats." Hawks was detailed to help construct the army's torpedo boats at both the "Army Navy Yard" (Cassidey's shipyard) and Beery's shipyard. In the fall of 1864, he was sent downriver to build a wharf at "Sugarloaf," a line of Confederate works several miles north of Fort Fisher.

Captain James worked closely with Captain John C. Winder and his company of engineers who were engaged in building Fort Holmes on Smith's (Bald Head) Island. Another assistant sent to help James was Lieutenant John Kent Brown (with whom he would go into business after the war).

Engineers James and Brown were kept busy simply exchanging groups of workers. As one group was returned home, another was sent to take their place. If a slave died or escaped while in the employ of the Engineer Department, the owners, after filing a claim, were compensated for their loss. When one poor unfortunate in Confederate employ suffered a hernia and was not likely to be able to work anytime soon, his owner was awarded over eight hundred dollars. The necessary paperwork, if a slave's signature was required, had to be witnessed by three people.

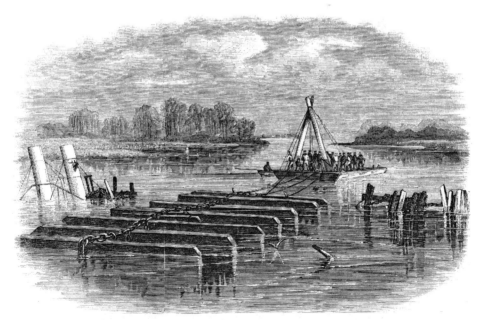

Confederate troops laying river obstructions on the Cape Fear.

In the spring of 1863, James wrote to Governor Vance telling him that he could not get enough provisions for his work force and requested the governor to have the owners send meat and bread, for which he would pay market prices. Although the work to strengthen the defenses of Wilmington continued right up to the fall of the city, there were never enough workers for the job. As late as November 1864, Whiting ordered calcium lights for the harbor and to help insure they got there safely, he asked that the 19 cases of lights be sent "in tried vessels with tried Captains who have frequently been here."

General Whiting often relied on the advice of his mentor, General P.G.T.

Capt. Benjmin Beery, who ran the Army-Navy Yard on Eagle Island.

Beauregard, now at Charleston, on how best to defend the port. Both locations had many similarities; Sullivan's Island was likened to Smith's Island. If the Yankees gained that spot, they might soon control the mouth of the river. One of the reasons Fort Holmes was constructed on the island was to prevent its occupation by Union forces. In addition to gun batteries on the riverbanks, patrol boats loaded with as many as 75 men, drifted slowly along the entrances to the river. Sentries were placed along the river with orders to halt and examine all boats found on the water.

General Whiting was both amused and irritated when a corporal on sentry duty hailed his rowboat as he and Lieutenant General Holmes made their way back to the city after their steamer had grounded on a bar: "To the hail of the sentinel I answered Comd'g. Gen'l. He was not satisfied, but ordered the boat in. I complied & he said he did not know me & required a pass. He was directed to call the Corp'l. of the guard...I had to write my own pass[.]" Admitting that the occurrence was annoying, he "was glad to see vigilance" along the river.[15]

If Engineer James' office was busy, so was the Provost Marshall's office. Originally located in a hotel (the Pilot House), it was later moved above Mr. Eiler's grocery store at the intersection of Water and Market Streets. Whiting had trouble getting a good officer for this post. Connecticut-born Captain W.S.G. Andrews, a paroled veteran of the Hatteras fight, was his first selection. Andrews saw to it that hotels obeyed the law that they send a list of their boarders to his office every day. He was also responsible for registering not only the salt workers, but all male citizens in town. Andrews, however, was not up to the job physically. Chronic diarrhea kept him often in the hospital and when it was discovered that he spent much of his time away from his company, a call went out for his arrest. Forced to resign, he moved to Goldsboro, where he entered into a business partnership. For much of 1862, the office of provost marshall was held by Captain George D. Parker. By October of that year, he was assigned to the 36th Artillery regiment at Fort Fisher, leaving the position vacant once more.

Captain Swift Galloway, "dangerously wounded at Malvern Hill," was Whiting's next choice, but as soon as he recommended that officer, he withdrew his application because Galloway was the subject of a complaint by a citizen of the town. Instead of becoming the town's main military policeman, Galloway was arrested.

Whiting then asked for Captain John Wooster to be appointed provost. Wooster had been wounded and permanently disabled during the Seven Days battle. He was to be mustered out of the army, but still desired to serve his country. "The position," reported Whiting, "is very important here, where there is so much ingress and egress." In August, Wooster moved into the office at Front and Market Streets, but was not there for long. His tastes, it was said, ran more to the literary and "his mild nature shrunk from contact with the multitudes." He later accepted the offer to become librarian for the Wilmington Library.

In November 1863, young Lieutenant Armand deRosset was chosen for the job. He too had been badly wounded and was still recovering. Yet another man, Doctor Duncan Buie, later reported that he was the town's Provost Marshall from February 1863 until the end of July 1864. It must have been a very trying job.

Although he did not work directly for General Whiting, James Madison Seixas often assisted him. He was the War Department's agent in Wilmington and as such represented Secretary Seddon. Seixas, who processed and paid claims against the Department, came to Wilmington from New Orleans where he had served with the famed Washington Artillery. Enlisting as a private in the 5th Company of that unit, he was wounded and cited for bravery at Shiloh. "Promoted to lieutenant for gallantry on the field," he was recommended for the position by Lieutenant Colonel Thomas L. Bayne, head of the "Bureau of Foreign Supplies."

As several departments of the government desired to send cotton abroad, the Secretary of War created the bureau to eliminate conflict and competition. Posted to Wilmington, Seixas was to coordinate cotton shipments on board government vessels.[16] He paid any bills charged to the War Department and since he represented that department, Whiting often relied on his business expertise, especially when dealing with blockade runners. It was he who set the wages of the Pilots, officers and seamen on the runners. When applications were made for coal, Whiting turned to Seixas for an answer. Seixas's answer to that particular problem was to prioritize the requests, with the military getting first crack at the limited supply, with the remainder divided between the runners, the railroads and other businesses requiring that commodity. It was later reported that Seixas had "failed to get 700 bales of cotton on the correct ship," and in March 1864, was relieved by Quartermaster General Alexander Lawton. Apparently, with cotton hard to come by, Lawton had gathered the cotton at Augusta and sent it on to Wilmington, where it was to be given to Power, Low and Company, in exchange for a "large lot of shoes," but Seixas placed it on one of Crenshaw's steamers and the cotton was run out instead. Although Lawton may have tried to have him removed, quite possibly General Whiting intervened

Benjamin Ficklin

on his behalf. Seixas stayed in Wilmington where he continued to assist the general.

Another of those elusive officers who flitted in and out of Wilmington was Major Benjamin Ficklin, the very same man who, in 1864, would purchase Jefferson's Monticello. Ostensibly a Confederate treasury agent, it was he who, in 1862, was sent to England to purchase engraving supplies and engravers. Traveling with C.S.N. Lieutenant Wilkerson, they also purchased the new steamer *Giraffe*, which had been recommended to Treasury Secretary Memminger by Ficklin. Leaving the vessel under the command of Wilkerson at Nassau, Ficklin took a steamer to New York to visit friends, passed through Washington, D.C. and

then returned to the South. Formerly an officer in the 45th Virginia Infantry, he is sometimes referred to as the "Mystery Man of the Confederacy."

Ficklin was born in 1827 and educated at the Virginia Military Institute. At some point in his career, he worked in a bank in Fredericksburg, served in the U.S. Army during the Mexican War and, in the 1850s, "worked with stagecoach and mail lines from Missouri to San Francisco." He was an advocate of the transcontinental railroad and helped begin the famed Pony Express in 1860. After the war, Ficklin returned to Texas and, once again in the mail business, hauled mail from Fort Smith, Arkansas, to San Antonio and El Paso. He died suddenly in 1871, choking on a fishbone. His legacy lives on in Texas: the town of Ben Ficklin (near Fort Concho in Tom Green County) was named, by his friends, in his honor.

Whiting's Ordnance officer was Major Sloan. Sloan was responsible to see that the forts were properly armed with both artillery and the necessary small arms and ammunition. His complaint was nearly the same as everyone else's: there was never enough transportation (wagons, drays, carts, steamers and river flats) for the work that had to be done. Whiting's Chief of Staff was his brother-in-law, James Hill. It was Hill who read and passed on correspondence to the general and it was he who accompanied him to Fort Fisher in January 1865. At that battle Whiting was seriously wounded. Both he and Hill were sent north to prison on Governor's Island (Fort Columbus) N.Y. Hill remained with Whiting in jail, refusing a parole until it appeared the general was recovering. Upon his release he made his way back to N.C. Whiting took a turn for the worse and died in March 1865.

Near the corner of Water and Princess Streets is where Captain C.S. McKinney could be found. He was the department's Commissary officer who took charge of such things as flour, bacon, peas, wheat, rye, rice, coffee and meal. Not only was he responsible for feeding the troops in town, but had the charge of sustaining the garrisons at the forts downriver. "Nassau" bacon (so called because having been left on the docks at Nassau, it had begun to rot) was delivered to him. McKinney would "survey" it and determine what was spoiled and what could be given to the troops. The condemned bacon was not discarded. It was in high demand as grease, oil and candles, or as an ingredient for soap. McKinney had a lot of problems with break-ins and thefts from his warehouse near the docks. Even with the sentries placed, coffee was found on occasion to be missing. If, as happened on a few other occasions, there was not enough food for the troops, McKinney was authorized to impress what was necessary from the town or surrounding countryside.[17]

Captain William M. Swann was the chief enrolling officer in Wilmington for much of the war. One day, while in his office, Captain Daniel L. Russell came in and began striking Swann with a hickory walking stick: "When bystanders managed to stop the fray, young Russell broke away and was about to shoot Swann when a third party deflected his arm and sent the bullet into the wall."

Captain Swann, it appeared, resented the "often voiced view" of Russell's father, Daniel, Sr. The older Russell was critical of Confederate conscription policies and, as a Unionist, was many times quite vocal and critical of Richmond. Swann replied in kind, and Daniel, Jr. took offense and raised the stick to defend his father's honor.

Or perhaps the feud had even earlier origins. In 1851, in the State of Mississippi, Daniel Russell, Sr. was running for the office of Auditor against a

The government commissary in Wilmington.

man named Swan. The election was heated and Russell was on the stump in the country. He solicited and regaled the "dear people" with the following: "Ladies and Gentlemen: I rise – but there's no use telling you that, you know that I am up…I am not only the politest man but the best electioneer – you ought to see me shaking hands…I will allow that Swan is the best Auditor in the State; that is, until I am elected…My competitor Swan, is a bird of golden plumage, who has been swimming for the last four years in the Auditor's pond, at $5,000 a year…Time's almost out. Well, I like to forgot to tell you my name. It's Daniel, short for Dan. Not a handsome name, for my parents were poor people. Dan crawfished out of the stand, bobbing his head…amid the cheers for 'Dan,' 'A d__m Russell,' and 'Young Davy Crockett.'"

Maybe that election was the catalyst for the ongoing dispute between the Russells and the Swanns. Young Dan, for assaulting Swann, was arrested, confined to quarters and after a court-martial, reduced to the ranks. Major General Whiting wrote him that he had taken time to reflect "upon the violent manner you displayed in my presence the other day. From a thorough investigation of all the circumstances I find it uncalled for, the provocation you received existing only in your imagination. It can be excused only from the fact that existed by the peculiar and difficult circumstances in which you were placed, you mistook an order for an insult."

The general went on to speak to the young hothead and offered him this advice from "an old soldier, go quickly to your company without…making any attempt to have your sentence changed." Russell declined to follow his advice and returned to his Brunswick County home. His father secured his appointment as a county commissioner and Governor Vance certified his exemption.

Yet another confrontation began between Whiting, Russell and Vance. The N.C. Supreme Court, in 1864, decreed that young Russell was indeed free of the military. Whiting persisted. The case was finally settled when Russell was restored to the rank of captain and returned to his company. Two months later he submitted his resignation.[18]

Captain Swann survived the war, only to be killed in a tragic accident. He had gone to the railroad depot of the WC&A to await a shipment of lumber. He sat down on the track and watched as the train backed up towards him. As it got near, he rose and began to move away, but the load of lumber broke loose, with the first piece landing on Swann's feet, trapping him in place. The remainder of the lumber fell on him, killing him.[19]

Daniel L. Russell, Jr. later in life.

Major John W. Cameron was the army's chief quartermaster for the district. In January 1863, Cameron, who was paymaster as well as quartermaster, married Amoret Bradley. This marriage created quite a stir among society in Wilmington because Amoret had been engaged to marry Edward Meares, who was killed at the battle of Sharpsburg in September 1862. It was expected that Amoret would don mourning clothes, possibly for the rest of her life, as some women in similar situations did. Instead she married Cameron four months later, which some considered "shocking and unbecoming haste."

Cameron's able assistant was Captain Christopher Styron. As quartermasters, they were responsible not only for quarters, but also for troop transportation, ordnance and supplies for those men. They were called upon to render aid to blockade runners when required and were responsible for transporting coal down from Fayetteville. Applications for clothing, blankets, shoes and cooking utensils were part of Styron's domain. He handled bills against the quartermaster department, including rents charged by landlords, and many times had to deal with owners who wanted to raise the rent of buildings occupied by the army.

Late in 1863, when Doctor William A. Berry attempted to raise the rent of Styron's own office and warehouses, he was told that the "Commanding General is not disposed to allow any unreasonable increase in rents." The owners persisted and in the fall of 1864, when it appeared that a huge rent increase was about to take place, Whiting authorized Styron to "impress" the houses required by the military, much to the dislike of those who claimed to be patriots. An advertisement in the *Journal* reported on a meeting held in town with "the objects...to organize a moral resistance to the exorbitant and oppressive demands of certain landlords in Wilmington[.]"

In the midst of a housing crunch, landlords began auctioning their rental properties, causing rents to skyrocket. In the fall of 1864, Dr. Armand deRosset, Jr. informed the military authorities that he too was raising the rents of his properties presently occupied by the army. One of those buildings was

Confederate headquarters in Wilmington.

Whiting's headquarters. The general responded by refusing to pay and notified the War Department as well as other landlords who tried to raise their rents. In a letter to Dr. deRosset, Whiting told him that the issue was before Secretary Seddon. He told them: "I am inclined to think that in the case of premises occupied heretofore at any price satisfactory at the time to owners it will not be considered as coming under the impressments law & therefore it will be left to the Dept. to decide whether an increased rent shall be paid[.]"

When claims were made for damages caused by soldiers, it was Styron who investigated and made the decision as to how much should be paid. He made contracts to supply the wood and received the department's supply of corn, fodder, hay, peanuts and oats. He supplied transportation requests, whether for horseback, wagon or railroad. Styron was allowed to impress or confiscate what he needed and actually took over the Poor House to use as a storeroom. When he asked for additional feed for the horses engaged in the laborious task of hauling carts through the deep sand, his request was turned down by Richmond.

Even General Whiting pleaded the animal's case. "Many cases arise here in the matter of forage, especially with the Light Batteries on duty on the coast, where the severe labor, heavy dragging in the sand and utter want of anything like grazing, is very hard upon the teams, and some increase from time to time is required."

The missive to Quartermaster General Lawton did no good, so Whiting was forced to use salt grass as an added supplement to the animal's diet. In the autumn of 1864, Whiting answered a request by saying that "all forage brought from town is equally divided between Caswell and Ft. Fisher. The marsh grass is used by all the animals also at Caswell and in the Eng'r. Dep't. without injury to them." [20]

Another of Styron's duties was to visit the hospitals in town, to collect for distribution the unclaimed personal effects of deceased soldiers. Tragically, in many cases there were no effects worth anything. Many men died in the hospital possessing no more than the clothes they wore, a pair of drawers and a simple nightshirt. These belongings, pronounced "worthless" by the quartermaster, were relegated to the rag pile.[21] One of Styron's assistants was Lieutenant Jones, who was the officer in charge of the Confederate stables, located at Dock and Eighth Streets. Jones required a signed request before an animal was issued to anyone, but throughout the war there were complaints that most of the horses in Confederate service were "played out" and should have been disposed of long ago.

If the animals were tired and hungry, so was the populace.

Endnotes

1. Manarin, I:512; Thomas Sparrow Papers, Special Collections Department, J.Y. Joyner Library, East Carolina University, Greenville, N.C. Sparrow later commanded the garrison at Washington, N.C. See NCSA, Quartermaster records, box 44.5, folder 6, letter dated 5 October 1864.
2. Wilmington *Star News,* 7 March 1976. The *Arctic* had been used by Dr. Elisha Kane in 1850-51 on his polar expedition to find the Englishman Sir John Franklin, who had been lost since 1845. See the *Herald*, 31 July 1865. On duty at Frying Pan shoals, she was known as Lightship No. 8; she was subsequently sunk in the channel as an obstruction, was later (June 1866) raised and again used as a lightship off the coast of Massachusetts. She was finally sold for "junk value" at public auction on 16 April 1879. See *Dictionary of American Naval Fighting Ships* (Washington, D.C: G.P.O., 1959)I:55-56; *Daily Journal,* 13 June 1866 and 30 January 1867. Whiting Papers, II:335, letter dated 25 May 1863, II: 336, letter dated 7 October 1863.
3. *Whiting Papers*, II:347, letters dated 23 May, 24 May, 27 June 1864.
4. Manarin, I:514, 517; *Whiting Papers*, II:335, entry dated 28 April 1863.
5. *Powell Papers*, 7. Powell also wrote that Sandy Ivy (or Ivey), one of the deserters, was a member of his company. After the war Ivey told Powell that he was forced to go along, but, as Powell noted, Ivey applied for a federal pension,

"which means that he had joined their ranks." Manarin, I:527. Michael Turrentine Papers, Perkins Library, Duke University, letter dated 7 February 1864. Turrentine noted that Gallamore left behind a wife and six children.

6. *Whiting Papers*, II:338, letter dated 12 May 1864. Private Stancowitz remained with his company until late 1864.

7. *Whiting Papers*, II:348, 102, dated 10 October 1864. *Vance Papers*, 21:270, letter dated 17 December 1863. *Daily Journal*, 21 March 1863. LCFHS, "Soldiers & Letters, 1864," letter dated 16 November 1864. Private Stevenson was captured and sent to Elmira prison where he remained until May 1865 when he returned to his home in Guilford County, *Whiting Papers*, II:338, letter dated 20 November 1864. *Whiting Papers*, II:336, letters dated 20 February, 7 March 1864. It was not until the latter part of 1864 that military courts were convened. *Whiting Papers*, II:336, letter dated 7 August 1864; II:338, letters dated 13 October, 26, 28 November 1864. See also 23 November 1863. *Daily Journal*, 21 January 1863. The information on William Johnson can be found in the *Vance Papers*, 21:965-966, 1019 and the *Daily Journal*, 14 November 1864. *Vance Papers*, 20:1037.

8. *Vance Papers*, 20:646-647, 24:285-286. Erysipelas could be contracted through a wound or surgery. It also caused a painful swelling in the mouth.

9. Manarin, I:153, 179. *Whiting Papers*, II:346, entries dated 10 August and 9 November 1863; *Daily Journal*, 11 August, 22 October 1863. The N.C. General Assembly exempted Quakers by virtue of an act passed 7 July 1863. Bradley, I:5, entries 54 and 106, dated 15 April and 1 May 1862. *Daily Journal* 11 August 1863. It is likely the Hocketts spent well over a year in various jails.

10. Isabel M. Williams and Leora H. McEachern, *Salt: That Necessary Article* (Wilmington, N.C.: privately published, 1973) 56, 58, 117. Johnston, 246-247; Cheryl Lynn Martin, *The Heritage of Randolph County, North Carolina* (Charlotte: Delmar Printing, 1993) I:88; *Vance Papers*, 19:553-555, 26:656-657, this letter was signed by many of the private owners in the area. See also *Vance Papers*, 26:843-847, 24:341-343, 20:916-918; ORA, I:33, 1303-1304. Rain also affected the work's output by diluting the cisterns.

11. *Daily Journal*, 19 August 1863. North Carolina sent workers to the mines at Saltville, Virginia. The salt gathered there often languished for want of transportation. D.G. Worth's report to the governor, dated 6 May 1864 indicated that he was using flatboats and was able to discharge "at least twenty two-horse teams," see Documents, Document No. 10, Adjourned Session 1864, 2-5. *Whiting Papers*, II:336, letter dated 6 June 1864.

12. *Whiting Papers*, II:336, letters dated 17 and 22 May 1864; *Daily Journal*, 2 August 1864. Isaac Grainger, a native of Ireland, died at the age of 37 in 1878, in Williamsport, Pennsylvania while en route to a meeting of bank presidents. He was buried in Oakdale Cemetery, see the *Morning Star*, 27 August 1878. At the time of his death he was president of the Bank of New Hanover, the

Hibernian Benevolent Society, the Wilmington Building Association and receiver of the Carolina Central Railway. See the *Whiting Papers*, II:336, letters dated 9 November 1863, 15 March, 6 May and 21 June 1864. *Daily Journal*, 21 November 1863, "The Government steamer 'Virginia,' Capt. Guthrie, will... leave Wilmington at 11 o'clock, on Tuesdays, Thursdays and Saturdays. Returning, will leave...Smithville (touching at Caswell and Bald Head) at 9 o'clock A.M., on Mondays, Wednesdays and Fridays." Captain Styron placed the ad as Grainger had not yet assumed his post. *Whiting Papers*, II:335, dated 10 June, 20 October 1863; Wise, 101, 299-300.

13. *Whiting Papers*, II:348, 48-49, dated 13 September 1864. Ibid., II:347, entries dated 14 July and 23 September 1864. Manarin, I:479-489; Clark, 2:753-754. RG 109, Medical Department, General Hospital No. 4, Register of Patients, 1862-1863. *Whiting Papers*, II:335, letter dated 9 June 1863.

14. Clark, IV:417-418.

15. *Whiting Papers*, II:336, 79, letter dated 9 June 1863. *Vance Papers*, 26:1099-1100. *Daily Journal*, 11 August 1863. Whiting Papers, II:338, letters dated 3 September and 25 November 1863. Whiting's letter about the calcium lights is dated 1 November 1864. Whiting was writing to Flag Officer Lynch about being stopped along the river because Lynch had recently been halted by the same man. Whiting promised that the man would be severely punished, see the *Whiting Papers*, II:338, 7 September 1864.

16. Rosen, *The Jewish Confederates*, 91. Seixas (pronounced "Sayshus") was born in Charleston in 1829, but at the age of 24 moved to New Orleans. A partner in the firm of Gladden and Seixas, he was a cotton broker who married Julia Deslonde, whose sisters were Mrs. John Slidell and Mrs. P.G.T. Beauregard. He died in 1889 and was "buried in the Army of the Tennessee tomb in Metarie Cemetery, truly an unsung hero of the Confederate war effort." The information on Seixas was graciously provided by Mr. C.L. ("Lon") Webster. See also Harold S. Wilson, *Confederate Industry: Manufacturers and Quartermasters in the Civil War* (Jackson: University Press of Mississippi, 2002) 10, 165, 171, 175; see also *Whiting Papers*, II:348, entry dated 19 October 1864. As the War Department's agent, Seixas was involved in a rent dispute.

17. The information on Ficklin came from Wise, *Lifeline of the Confederacy*, 99-100; John M. Carroll, *List of Field Officers, Regiments and Battalions in the Confederate States' Army* (Mattituck, N.Y.: John M. Carroll and Co., 1983) 42; John Wilkinson, *Narrative of a Blockade Runner*, 88-106. Ficklin is buried in Charlottesville, Va. Internet websites: www.tsha.utexas.edu/handbook and www.fortours.com/pages/hmtomgreen.asp. *Confederate Veteran*, 16:72, 39:262. ORA, I:9, 282. *Daily Journal*, 19 March 1864; Whiting Papers, II:336, letter dated 25 June 1864. *Daily Journal*, 28 February 1863. *Whiting Papers*, II:347, letters dated 12 April, 1 and 2 November 1864. Whiting also borrowed engineering officers from Charleston, especially when he encountered difficulty

in placing torpedoes (mines) in the surf at Fort Fisher. Major Sloan had replaced Major Frobel who had been with Whiting since late 1862. After the war Sloan was said to be "teaching school somewhere in the mountains of South Carolina, according to Sprunt, *Chronicles*, 484. *Whiting Papers*, II:335, letter dated 30 May 1863. Whiting also asked a runner's consignee for furniture and bedding, to be used "for hospital purposes." He implied of the price was not right, it would be taken anyway.

18. LCFHS, Vol. XX, No. 3, May 1977, 1-2. *Daily Journal*, 16 December 1851; *Whiting Papers*, II:347, 211; "Cases Argued and Determined in the Supreme Court of N.C. From June Term 1863 to December Term 1864," 388-392. Manarin I:281.
19. *Morning Star*, 8 July 1888.
20. *Southern Women*, 8:16:68. *Whiting Papers*, II:338, letters dated 16 August 1864, 1 September 1864 and II:348, dated 28 August 1864. *Daily Journal*, 27 February, 27 August 1863.
21. RG 109, Medical Department Records, Register of Deaths and Effects, General Hospital No. 4, 1864-65, chapter 6, vol. 284.

15

I Would Like To Know What He Is Afightin' For

kyrocketing inflation hurt many throughout the Confederacy. Quartermaster Styron paid two hundred dollars for six window sashes at the end of 1863. When Engineer James bought files from merchant Jonas Levy, he paid over eleven hundred dollars for fifteen dozen of the tools. That comes to over six dollars per file. In March 1864, he paid twenty dollars for two paint brushes.

Not only inflation, but the lack of transportation hampered every facet of the war. This was certainly true in North Carolina. Soon after being appointed the C.S.A. Quartermaster for his state, Major John Whitford received a letter from Richmond.

"The distress in Genl. Lee's army for corn is beyond all comparison," it said. "The feed is reduced to five pounds per day for each horse and even this will have to be curtailed if there is not some remedy…[S]tretch every nerve in your direction in sending corn to Richmond."[1]

It was not the price of corn, but the lack of transportation that was delaying the delivery to Lee's equines. Earlier in the year, Governor Vance allowed the use of the train, "of ten cars" pledged to state service, to be used to haul corn from Tarboro and Weldon to Richmond. Later, Major Whitford was told to "please bring trains of the Atlantic Road to [the] aid of the government in [the] shipment of corn at Charlotte – 40,000 bushels."

If Richmond needed corn, Wilmington needed flour. In December 1863, the town fathers attempted to buy flour to be distributed to the poor and needy, perhaps in an attempt to avoid the riots that had occurred in Salisbury and

Richmond earlier that year. They bought the flour in Salisbury, but when the army quartermaster in that section became aware of the purchase, it was immediately impressed. Major General Whiting was soon involved in the mess and recommended "all permissions to purchase provisions be revoked." The final word had to come from Richmond. A flurry of heated telegrams demanded to know why the flour was not forthcoming, even after the Secretary of War's permission had been secured. By fits and starts, the flour rolled into town on the railroad.

Gen. James Longstreet, CSA

At about six dollars a barrel in 1859, the price of flour by the fall of 1863 had climbed to well over one hundred dollars for the same amount. With the delivery of the Salisbury flour, prices, at least locally, declined somewhat to between eighty-five and ninety dollars. By January 1864, price inched back to one hundred dollars. By early September, citizens were informed that flour was "in demand, and very little if any [was on the] market," but when offered, it fetched almost two hundred dollars a barrel. By the end of that month no flour "of consequence coming in, and the stock on market has been all worked off." It was now at three hundred dollars and by year's end, the price rose to four hundred dollars. Just before Wilmington fell to the bluecoats, a barrel of flour sold at anywhere from seven to eight hundred dollars. Prices were pretty consistent throughout the state.

Even if flour and corn were available, shippers had to contend with limited rail facilities. When Longstreet's Corp moved through North Carolina in September 1863, Major Whitford notified his superior, "troops arriving & departing with dispatch. We are overrun with corn here. I fear I have been too fast with transportation as Capt. Venable...cannot receive it at Weldon. At Gaston everything is full. When we get through with troops [we] will put everything [to move corn]."

When Lt. Col. Sims, Whitford's superior, notified the major of the last of the troop movement, he added: "Corn movement commences." As late as December of that year, 1863, William Harvey, Superintendent of the A&NC,

telegraphed Whitford: "Forty thousand bags of corn exposed to the weather waiting transportation – Please hurry Atlantic transportation forward." Even when it arrived, the corn was not always in the best condition. General Whiting asked if the poor women of Wilmington could not be utilized to repair the torn bags that came in on the trains. No matter how fast the trains delivered the corn, it was not enough. In January 1864, huge supplies of corn were being detained at Charlotte and Wilmington. Telegrams to Whitford implored him to move it to Richmond more quickly. By the 14th, another message from Richmond reported: "Still no corn from Charlotte – 2 weeks – Lees' army is starving[,] only one train load here."

In Fayetteville in January 1864, one would still have to fork over anywhere from eighty-five to ninety-five dollars for a barrel of flour, but in that town at least cattle were still available for sale. In Wilmington, beef was being brought to market "sparingly." Also for sale in Fayetteville was corn whiskey at forty-five dollars a gallon. Liquor was not advertised in the Wilmington papers, but was most certainly available in saloons as well as in the alleyways. In the fall of 1863, Mr. T.C. Craft and fellow grocer Mr. Hardwick, offered to sell meal "by the peck" to "families in straightened circumstances at one dollar[.]" They warned that no more than one peck would be sold to the same person at one time.[2]

While the basic food needs of the poorer classes may have been met, another crisis loomed. By the winter of 1863-64, the price of that most necessary fuel, wood, had risen beyond the reach of the poor. The *Journal* editorialized about the problem: "Wood! Wood! Wood is now selling on the wharf at twenty-four dollars per cord for pine wood, and twenty-eight dollars… for oak[.] Draymen demand anything from one to two dollars per load for hauling it from the wharf to the residences of citizens…It takes four loads to a cart, so that a cord delivered will cost something between thirty and thirty-five dollars. Can the less than wealthy class of citizens stand this?"

Apparently the town commissioners read the article, for that very day they passed a series of ordinances, the first of which read: "Ordered: That the prices to be charged by Drays and Carts…shall be fifty (50) cents for every load carried any distance under two…blocks…and ten cents for each additional block…Any Drayman who shall charge more than [this] shall forfeit his license[.]"

The fathers also tried to ease the hardships of the poorer classes by authorizing the purchase of $50,000 worth of both provisions and wood, "to be sold to parties for charitable distribution, or to indigent persons in limited quantities."

The army's need for wood was also dire. To fill that need, they took over Edward Kidder's sawmill, "idle because of defective machinery." An officer was dispatched to the several sawmills in town in hopes that they required parts could be obtained.

The Wilmington Relief Association, another charitable organization that sprung up to fill a need, helped by purchasing foodstuffs at the lowest possible price and then selling it to the needy at a discounted price. There were many who had never known want who now cried out for assistance. In July 1863, Mrs. Elizabeth Sampson, whose husband was with Lee's army, wrote to Governor Vance about her plight.

"I take the liberty of writing you…to ask you if you can't make some better arrangement about the soldier's families[.] Their families is a suffering… When he first went I got aplenty to eat…as soon as he was sent to Virginia my rations was cut down…provisions is so high I am not able to get them[;] I am only getting fifteen dollars for to support me and four children…My children crys [sic] a many a time for something to eat[.]"

Elizabeth poured out her heart to Vance, pleading with him to provide the family with not only food but clothing and fuel. She told him she used to get two loads of wood every month and when it ceased, she questioned the Association and was told "they could not give it to me." Despair and defeatism mingled in her letter as she informed the governor: [I] would like to know what he is afightin' for[;] he has nothing to fight for[.] I don't think that he is afighting for anything only for his family to starve and go naked."

Her husband John, an Irish immigrant, had been among the first to answer the call when he enlisted in the 3rd North Carolina in June 1861. Wounded at Chancellorsville in 1863 and again at Payne's Farm in November of that year, he was later captured and sent to a POW camp. He survived the war, as did Elizabeth and her children.

Others were not so fortunate. The town fathers tried to alleviate want by requesting that a clothing factory be established in Wilmington. Several prominent citizens wrote to the governor outlining a plan to employ "the poor women of our city…[we] would respectfully suggest the following plan – if you have any more clothes to be made, for our State troops…please allow Mr. James McCormick a very worthy and experienced tailor…to take charge of the cloth, cut it up and divide it out among the most needy[.]"

The city's infrastructure was playing out. Due to the "uncertain supply" of lightwood, many an unexpected blackout was experienced. The rising price of gas forced many to do without. Many of the streetlights had burned out and had not been replaced. There were complaints of broken sidewalks and muddy potholes; even the once-beautiful trees which lined the streets were run down. The bark had been either eaten off or rubbed off by the horses and mules, which crowded the lanes.

One wit wrote: "[The mules] have not left a show of bark, and next year there will be hardly a show of leaf. To be sure the trees are now defended by substantial boxes, but as we fear it is rather late...We would suggest that the lamp post be also boxed up – perhaps next year it will bloom out with a crop of young lamps, a thing very much needed in these dark nights, when garroters do most abound."

The town clock was run down and would not be repaired until 1866. Many homes remained abandoned, their owners awaiting the city's fate from afar. Fire destroyed some structures and these remained as a portent of things to come.[3] Necessity was most certainly the mother of invention in Wilmington during those lean years. From the firearms devised by William Utley and Louis Froelich (rifles and a thirty-six shot revolver, respectively) to Mrs. Reston's ink (made from gallberries and sold by the half-pint to the soldiers at the depot) there was still a lot lacking.

In the summer and fall of 1864, Raleigh Quartermaster Henry Dowd sought peanut oil from manufacturers in Wilmington. His search proved fruitless and he was told: "there is not a barrel of peanut oil in this place for sale." The oil was being made, but the two companies in town had orders well into the new year. Thomas Colville tried his hand at making the product to be used for lubricating purposes, but when it was tried out at the Fayetteville Arsenal, it was found to be "not quite equal to the best sperm." At this point of the war, most substitutes were "not quite equal" to the genuine article.[4]

It was long believed that an attack on Wilmington was inevitable. It was the last major port open to the outside world and the main supply route for the Army of Northern Virginia. Yet the Federals hesitated until late 1864. Prompted in large part by two Confederate raiders (the *Tallahassee* and the *Chickamauga*) that homeported in Wilmington, the Yankees finally took notice of the town. Those raiders left in the fall of 1864 and created havoc among northern east coast shipping. When insurance rates started to climb, cries from northern ship owners reached the ears of the Lincoln administration. Major General Whiting was right when he said that the Yankees would not allow this activity to go on for long. One journalist correctly surmised: "There is abundant cause for thinking that Wilmington is the great thorn in the flesh of the Federals at this moment."[5]

At this crucial point, when the combined forces of the Union Navy and Army formulated its plan of attack on the Port City, Richmond replaced Major General Whiting with Lieutenant General Braxton Bragg. Whiting continued to work for the cause he believed so deeply in. He visited the forts and made recommendations and memos. He requested phosphorous, to be used on cannon sights. Painted on the sights, the gunners would be able to see the sights and aim their guns in the darkness. He pleaded for poles and submarine cable to connect

Fort Fisher with Smithville. When regular copper wire could not be obtained, he asked if "baling rope in sufficient quantity can be had. Might not the…baling wire be spliced in some way." Even if the wire was obtained and put in place, it was too late to prevent an attack by the Federals.

In late December 1864, citizens in town could hear the sounds of battle at the mouth of the river. Fort Fisher had beaten off a massive Union attack and the town began to breathe a sigh of relief, but it was short-lived.

Less than three weeks later, Admiral David D. Porter's fleet returned and again opened fire on the fort with more than six hundred guns. The three-day battle ended with a Union victory. Now it was just a matter of time before Wilmington itself was attacked. Union forces slowly worked their way northward and one report told of a "poor, demented woman" who paddled across

Gen. Braxton Bragg, CSA

the Cape Fear River and offered her small boat to the attackers, who used it to obtain more river crafts and "the town was thus invaded by a hostile army."[6]

On 22 February 1865, Mayor John Dawson surrendered the old town to Major General Alfred Terry appropriately enough, on the steps of City Hall. Installed as the military commander for the Cape Fear section was Brigadier General Joseph A. Hawley, a native of Connecticut and a founding member of the Republican Party in that state. The Confederacy was soon to be no more. If W&W Superintendent Fremont needed any further proof, it came in the form of a letter sent him in early March, just before he was taken prisoner at Magnolia: "Enclosed you will find the $2,600…you sent me. I have done my best to get it off, but can do nothing with it. It is only worth in Richmond, forty dollars and hard to sell at that."

The writer, H.B. Bryan, was an agent of the W&W at Tarboro and was trying to purchase lard. He was forced to buy it with his own money and informed Fremont: "You owe me…twenty two hundred and nineteen dollars, which you will please send me immediately, as I need it at this time." He continued the letter with a litany of high prices: "lard and bacon were selling at $8 a pound while pork was $5, corn $100 per barrel." Nervous about his money, he again requested immediate payment and closed with, "My expenses to Richmond I also had to pay out of my own funds, of course the road will pay for that." It would be quite a while before Bryan would get any money from the W&W.[7]

Endnotes

1. *NA*, Citizen's Papers, J.P. Levy file, reel no. 584. *NCSA*, John D. Whitford Papers, box 89-4, letter dated 10 August 1863.

2. *Daily Journal*, 7 December 1859, 16 December 1863, 6 January, 7, 28 September 1864 and 15 February 1865; *Fayetteville Observer*, 22 February 1864. for the flour controversy, see the *Daily Journal*, 16, 20, 22, 23 December 1863; see also the *Whiting Papers*, II:346, entry dated 12 December 1863, II:336, letter dated 12 December 1863. The flour began arriving just before Christmas. The problems with corn are found in the *Whitford Papers*, 89-4, letters dated 14, 16 September, 18 December 1863, 7, 14 January 1864. *Daily Journal*, 2 October 1863.

3. *Daily Journal*, 24 and 30 September 1863. *Vance Papers*, 18:830-832. *Daily Journal*, 31 October 1863 and 3 November 1864. Wilmington *Weekly Journal*, 12 May 1864; see also 12 August 1862, 28 October 1863 and 3 February 1864 for the rising prices of gas. James Mitchell, one-time gas fitter, tried to sell his tools, but there was not another gas-fitter in town. See the *Daily Journal*, 1 July 1863. Any homes that were abandoned had their gas fixtures removed. Vance Papers, 25:223. The town built boxes around the trees, but it was to no avail, *Daily Journal*, 15 June 1864, *Weekly Journal*, 16 June 1864; *Herald*, 22 March 1866.

4. [Weekly] *Raleigh Standard*, 31 July 1861, 7 August 1861; *NCSA*, "Mrs. Charles P. Bolles Reminiscences" box 44-5; *NCSA*, Civil War Collection, "Quartermaster Records," letters from E. Murray, dated 25 October, 9 November 1864.

5. *Lawley Covers the Confederacy*, "Confederate Centennial Studies," edited by William Stanley Hoole (Tuscaloosa: Confederate Publishing Company, 1964) 80. Lawley's article (15 November 1864) appeared in the London *Times*.

6. *Whiting Papers*, II:338, letter dated 31 December 1864. *Confederate Veteran*, IX:445, (1901).

7. *NCSA*, Fremont Collection, letter dated 8 March, 1865.

Refugees and released POWs make their way to the Wilmington waterfront after the city fell to Union troops in February 1865. (NHCPL)

16

The Aftermath

O n 22 February 1865 it was fitting that the white flag of surrender hung on the roof of grocer H.B. Eiler's store near the Wilmington waterfront. That building had housed the Confederate provost marshall's office. With the fall of Wilmington, Lee's defeat was just a few months away, now that the "door that fed the rebellion was closed."

Union troops flooded the streets of the town for some months to come. Trade was stagnated for a few months with the exception of northern merchants, notably the firm of Cutter and French. George Z. French and his son George R. had been merchants in Wilmington before the war, while William B. Cutter came to town with the Federals. Their company was probably the first, and certainly the largest, of several that quickly filled the merchandising vacuum left by the collapse of the blockade running industry. The removal of that business, which had sustained (though many would say contaminated) Wilmington, and the war's end in April, left many workers idle.

When released Federal officers flooded through Wilmington in a prisoner exchange in late February, Cutter and French generously provided nearly 900 of them with much-needed clothing and money, "trusting to time and the honor of the officers for their payment[.]" The firm's trust might have been misplaced; five months later they still awaited payment.

Paroled Union prisoners from Andersonville and Florence nearly overwhelmed the occupying authorities in town. Many died shortly after reaching safety. With the dead from the recent attack on Fort Fisher to bury, wood for coffins soon disappeared. It would appear that the premises of the

Former Union prisoners of war in Wilmington.

former undertaker, Mathew Lawton, were taken over by the authorities who quickly cleaned out his stock of "wood, ornaments, screws, plates, glues, paints, varnishes, brushes … and coffins."

Hospitals were quickly staffed and soon filled up with sick and wounded soldiers. Doctors were in short supply, so several of the town's physicians, including Doctors James King, Edwin Anderson, Duncan Buie and William Berry, were employed as contract surgeons for the U.S. Army. Former prisoners who were able to travel were fed, put on steamers and sent to northern ports.

Along with the sick on board the steamer *General Lyon*, formerly used to transport the 3rd and 7th New Hampshire regiments to Fort Fisher and later used to carry Confederate prisoners to their incarceration, were many discharged men of the 56th Illinois Volunteers. These men, veterans of the battles of Corinth, Champion's Hill, Vicksburg and Sherman's March to the Sea, had been mustered out and were on their way home.

Among the members of that unit was Private William C. Tate, who had fought and been wounded at Corinth. Sent from Sherman's army to Wilmington, he boarded the steamer along with the Gowdy brothers, Henry, William and John and more of their extended family, Cyrus and Henry. Everyone on board had to be feeling relief, for they were out of the war and heading home. They were still, however, surrounded by the war's aftermath. The *General Lyon* was packed with "troops and refugees to the number of some four or five hundred," in addition to the two hundred or so from the 56th Illinois.

The steamer left the wharf at Wilmington on 29 March and headed for Fortress Monroe, only to be delayed for a night off Smithville. After passing the bar, it was found that the sea was calm, but soon became "boisterous" and as the wind increased to hurricane force, many of the passengers, now seasick, went below decks. Some sixty miles off Cape Hatteras, several barrels of kerosene, stored in the boiler room, rolled over and smashed into the hot boiler. Kerosene filled the boiler room and erupted into flames.

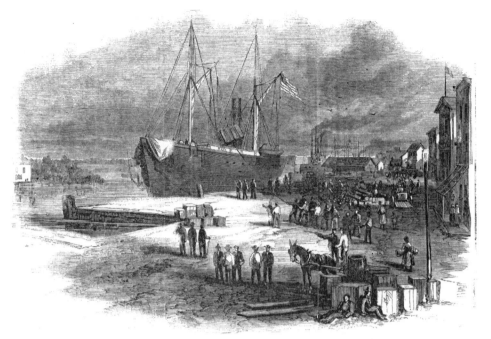

Union transports unloading along the foot of Water Street.

The fire was quickly discovered, the alarm sounded and the crew began to fight the fire valiantly. Some of the soldiers helped to man the pumps and hoses, but the fire, now fueled by a nearby barrel of oil "steadily gained headway [and]...soon spread over the centre portion of the deck...The hatches had been closed in consequence of the decks being so constantly under water, but those below, alarmed by the smoke which was spreading through the cabins, rushed on deck, only to be driven back by the flames."

Others below began to climb up the ladders to reach the main deck, but by now panic was widespread. Those still below pulled others back down as they scrambled for the ladders. The ladders fell into the hold; attempts to set them upright failed. Soon the "frightful shrieks of the women and children... were drowned by the roaring of the storm." They now realized that the ship was lost.

One of the first to rush to a lifeboat was the steamer's Captain. It was apparent that "the captain had lost all control of himself, and was evidently crazed with fear." Screaming "the ship is gone, lower away the boats," he was "among the most eager to seek safety in the first boat lowered." He got the boat into the water but the small craft was pulled toward the stern and struck by the steamer's paddlewheel. The steamer was still underway, and "the Captain was thrown out." The boat and skipper were smashed to pieces.

Many who had survived the rigors of prison were plunged into the cold sea. As it was quite stormy, a rescue vessel, the *General Sedgewick*, also loaded with passengers, found it nearly impossible to come to the aid of the stricken ship. They did manage to pluck more than two dozen men from the sea, saving them from a watery grave. Of the approximately 600 persons on board, only 24 were rescued. In Wilmington, word was received of the disaster and although many of the civilian refugees lost were from the interior of the state, many were known to those now occupying the town.

Captain E. Lewis Moore, of the 7th Connecticut, penned in his diary: "We hear with profound grief the loss of the *General Lyon* – the ships company and many of the passengers were known to us (I was on board just before she sailed)."

Listed among the dead were Private Tate and all of the Gowdy clan.[1]

Rev. Alfred A. Watson (above), and the Union commander of the city, Gen. Joseph Hawley (below). Hawley occupied the Bellamy mansion as his headquarters.

That same month the Episcopal Minister of St. James Church, Alfred Watson, ran afoul of the Union authorities. While still in the Confederacy, the church offered prayers for Confederate leaders, but even with the new administration Watson felt he was not authorized to change the liturgy to include prayers for President Lincoln. General Hawley felt Watson and his congregation were exhibiting disloyalty so the church was taken and converted into a Union hospital. Watson knew full well what was going to happen. During the war he had received a letter which chronicled a scene which took place in February 1862, after Alexandria, Virginia had been occupied by the Federals.

"The following narrative has been furnished me by the Rev. Dr. Stewart, who you will recollect was dragged from his Church [St. Paul's] in Alexandria, during the performance of divine service, for refusing to pray for the President of the United States.

"'The services had progressed...and I was conducting the services... when a confidential agent of Sec'y. Seward arose in the front of the chapel and demanded that I should pray for the President of the U.S.[.]'"

A shout came from the pews. The agent, named Morton, rose and demanded that Stewart read the prayer for the President. Being ignored by the pastor, Morton again repeated his demand: "Immediately, Captain Farnsworth, of the Eighth Illinois cavalry...arose and demanded that he should read the prayer. Still refusing, Captain Farnsworth ordered his sergeant to arrest [Stewart.]"

Elon Farnsworth approached the pulpit and grabbed the minister's prayer book and tossed it aside. Harsh words flew from Farnsworth's lip as he called him "a rebel and a traitor" and arrested him "in the name and by the authority of the President of the United States." Stewart shot back, "and I summon you to appear before the bar of the Lord of Lords and King of Kings, to answer upon the charge of interrupting his Ambassador, by armed violence[.]"

The pastor lost the argument and was unceremoniously taken from his congregation. The Reverend Stewart was later released from arrest and sent south. Later in the war, Farnsworth, by now a general, would answer to the "King of Kings" on 3 July 1863 when he was ordered by General Hugh ("Kil-Cavalry") Kilpatrick to charge a strong Confederate line during the Battle of Gettysburg.

With Wilmington's Reverend Watson's refusal to alter the prayers, General Hawley ordered the pews of the church to be taken out and the congregation turned away. Furniture and other hospital necessities were taken from the Seaman's Home (formerly Confederate General Hospital No. 4), and put in the church. Writing to President Lincoln, Watson implored him to return the church to its members, but Lincoln was killed before he could respond on the issue. The church was returned to its flock in December 1865.[2]

Headquartered in one of the finest ante-bellum homes in Wilmington, the John D. Bellamy mansion, General Hawley was in charge of the several surrounding counties. Bellamy, arguably one of the richest pre-war residents of the town, was a physician, rice planter and director of the W&W railroad. The home had been built in the months just prior to the outbreak of hostilities, with the Bellamys moving in three months before Fort Sumter was fired on. An ardent secessionist, Bellamy nonetheless sent his family to safety when yellow fever struck the town in 1862. With the end of the war, he attempted to regain possession of his home, but was refused by General Hawley, who responded, "having for four years been making his bed, he must lie on it for a while." In September, after Doctor Bellamy secured his pardon from Washington, the family was allowed to return home.

Dr. John D. Bellamy
(NHCPL)

In May 1865, General Hawley hosted the Chief Justice of the Supreme Court, Salmon P. Chase, at the mansion. Justice Chase addressed a crowd of nearly 4,000, mainly recently emancipated slaves, from the front balcony. The mansion soon became an adjunct of the recently established Freedman's Bureau, as Hawley and his staff gave out passes and otherwise assisted the black population.

Another famed guest was William Tecumseh Sherman. General Sherman telegraphed ahead to make no special arrangements, but to have a steamer readied for him to travel on to Charleston. Once in Wilmington, he was invited by Hawley to take lunch in the mansion and then continued on his way south. Delayed for a time at the mouth of the river,

The Bellamy Mansion as it appeared in the 1870s. (Bellamy Mansion Museum)

Sherman entertained a bevy of officers who had gone along for the ride. Captain Moore recalled that Sherman delighted in telling a story about the many requests for autographs that he received. Likewise, many admirers asked for a lock of his red hair. Sherman delegated the task to his orderly who, having a mane the same color as the general, was also instructed to enclose a lock of his hair.[3]

April was a bleak month. On the 15th, Wilmington citizens read of Major General Whiting's funeral in New York. In Washington, President Abraham Lincoln died from an assassin's bullet. When that news was reported, a committee of the town's leading citizens met to condemn the murder. All businesses were closed and flags lowered to half-mast. Several days later, the U.S. military proclaimed a day of mourning. At the foot of Castle Street, a "handsome arch of evergreen; from the top of which were suspended the words 'We Mourn.'" was erected. Beneath the arch a gun, draped in black, was fired every half hour from sunrise to sunset.

Former tailor Horace H. Munson edited the town's remaining paper, the Unionist *Herald of the Union*. The paper remained in publication until late May when it was sold to Thomas M. Cook. Renamed the *Herald*, it soon became the semi-official organ of the occupying Federals.

Justice Salmon P. Chase

Cook had been the *New York Herald's* war correspondent and came to town "with the naval squadron that bombarded Fort Fisher." During his wartime career, Cook was seemingly everywhere there was news. In May 1863, he was with General O.O. Howard's XI Corps when "Stonewall" Jackson launched his famous flank attack at Chancellorsville. From his vantage point he described the confusion and panic of that day. "It was my lot to be in the centre of the field when the panic burst upon us," he wrote. He was at Vicksburg with Sherman, disregarding his order not to allow any reporters to travel with the army. After the Battle of Resaca, he was General Dan Sickle's aid when that officer was sent to investigate the possibility of Governor Andrew Johnson being Lincoln's running mate in the 1864 election. On 2 July he was with Meade's army at Gettysburg and in August, was with Admiral David G. Farragut when the successful attack on Mobile Bay was made.

Told by Gustavus Fox that his report of the Mobile battle was "the best account...of the fight," he was soon aboard the *USS Montgomery*, the vessel set aside for the press at the December battle for Fort Fisher. Upon his return, after having probed the remaining Wilmington defenses in February 1865, Lieutenant Commander Cushing revealed to Thomas Cook that he had heard General Braxton Bragg exhorting his men at Fort Anderson. In reality, it was Colonel John D. Taylor, of the 36th N.C. Regiment who spoke to his men at the fort. After the forts were taken, Cook continued on with the Federals to Wilmington and soon purchased the local tabloid from Munson.

The decidedly Union paper and its editor were not well liked by several in town. Among them was James Fulton, editor of the opposition paper, the *Journal*. In what was to be one of his last editorials, Fulton lashed out at Cook: "A vast majority of our citizens will no doubt be greatly surprised to learn that we have, really, an oracle in our midst, and that oracle is the editor of the...*Herald*...[He] is neither a native nor a citizen of North Carolina...as he has only lived here since the Federal occupation[.]"

At the close of the war, on 29 April, Cook scored a coup when he interviewed Robert E. Lee. It was the only interview Lee would ever give. Lee's message was one of conciliation and acceptance of defeat.

Writing in Wilmington in 1865, it didn't help matters when Cook came out strongly in favor of W.W. Holden for governor. Having been appointed by President Andrew Johnson, Holden was already serving in that capacity. The *Journal* backed Jonathon Worth. Cook warned the populace that if Worth were elected, it would hamper the state's readmission prospects.

As often as Cook had faced danger, it was in Wilmington that he came close to being shot. Surprisingly, it was not over politics. In June 1865, he reported that a local physician, Doctor William Love, had visited a patient who had died suddenly, the cause unknown. Cook reprimanded Dr. Love for "needlessly alarming the community" when it was discovered that the deceased did not die of yellow fever, as the doctor had first diagnosed. The day after the article ran, Cook was visited by Theodore James, a one-armed veteran of many battles. James delivered a note from Doctor Love demanding a retraction. In his note, Love stated that the article was full of "incorrect statements and unjust censures." If there were no apology, Love hoped Cook would "afford him the satisfaction usual among gentlemen."

As James waited for a response, Cook remarked that he would not answer the note. The following day, several handwritten notices were posted around town. They read in part: "TO THE PUBLIC. Whereas an article appeared in the Wilmington *Herald*...full of incorrect statements, and reflecting upon my...character, and the editor of said paper, T.M. Cook, has failed to make any amends for this injury...and had refused to give me the satisfaction due a gentleman, I hereby denounce him as a libeler, a slanderer and a base coward."

The entire proceedings were published in next issue of the *Herald* and Love found himself up against the power of the press. Entitled the "Code

Duello," the article condemned dueling as "a relic from the dark ages." Cook pointed out that Love could have simply come to his office and explained his position. Unable to resist a parting shot, Cook picked up his pen, wielding it as a sword. "In conclusion, as we [were] branded...with being a coward...we [do not] now propose to arm ourselves...Those better skilled with pistols or knives can use them when they find antagonists of like education."

Upon selling his newspaper and leaving Wilmington, Cook continued his journalistic career, working at one time for the *New York Sun*. He established a newspaper in Detroit and would, by 1892, be something of a "muckraker." When he questioned the chief of the Jersey City, N.J. Police Department about corruption, he was jailed overnight.[4]

In order to reopen their stores, those merchants who had backed the rebellion were required to appear before the provost marshall to take the Loyalty Oath. This requirement was meant to insure that "none but persons of undoubted loyalty and good character [would] be permitted to trade." The Treasury Department sent an agent to town to issue permits and make sure the required bonds were filed by those same people.[5] Other merchants, hoping to reestablish their businesses, took the first available steamer north to purchase goods for the fall season.

One former prominent merchant who relocated permanently to New York was Oran S. Baldwin. Baldwin, a leading clothing merchant, had been in Wilmington for several years but was found in New York as early as the beginning of February 1865. Remaining in that city, he advertised in the *Herald* that he was ready to supply his former clients with all sorts of clothing. A long-range battle between Baldwin and local merchant James McCormick soon developed. McCormick advised his friends that the N.Y. firm had "no confidence in southern merchants or people [and] does not deserve their patronage."[6]

While there may have been a rush to take the required oath to start a business, many of the town's citizens did not come forth to raise their hands. The *Herald* lamented that as late as September only 40 citizens had qualified to vote. One week later the paper reported that throughout the county, only 500 voters were eligible. Restrictions against those who had refused the oath were severe: they could not hold public office or vote; they could neither vote in stockholder elections nor could they sell any produce at market. They could not import or export any goods and could not open or run a business in town.[7]

Saloonkeepers were the one class of businessmen who were quick to secure the required permissions. Bars, saloons and groggeries sprang up everywhere. Houses of prostitution, needing no such permission, also appeared all around town. In July, the provost guard raided the saloons on Water Street, where, it was reported, "hundreds daily assembled and gambled publicly."

Intoxication and drunkenness soon degenerated into fights and shootings and became a major problem for both the military and civilian authorities.

One instance recorded the "remarkable agility of a drunken tar," who, it was said, was "trying to walk on both sides of the street at the same time, or else imagined himself to be in a heavy storm at sea, with his ship rolling and pitching at a terrible rate."

A near riot occurred in November. "About half-past eleven…last night, a party of the colored crew of the revenue cutter lying in the stream…in passing a crowd of police and citizens near the Market, commenced firing on them… The rapid pistol reports brought several policemen to the spot, when the sailors ran to the foot of Market Street and seized a boat from the ferryman…[They] were fired upon by one of the police…They, however, made their escape to the Cutter[.]"[8]

Fights were not always between black soldiers and white citizens. In July of that first year of occupation, the *Herald* reported: "Like all other cities in the South that are garrisoned by negroes, Wilmington has a riot when white soldiers are brought into the city."

Members of the 2nd Massachusetts were passing through town and embarking on a steamer for Fort Fisher, when one of the men "made a purchase…[from a vendor] and under the apprehension that he had paid for it walked off and the guard arrested him." His comrades moved in on the guard and tried to wrest him from the grips of the provost, but more and more guards responded to the altercation. Firearms were loaded and "shouts of aim, fire, shoot, and everything else were heard[.]" No shots were fired though, and with the appearance of the provost marshall himself, peace was restored. Realizing the real cause of the fight, the Provost ordered all saloons shut down for the remainder of the day.

An actual mutiny took place that summer among the members of the 37th USCT. The regiment, recruited from eastern North Carolina among the recently freed "contrabands" was initially designated the 3rd N.C. Colored Infantry. Attached to the Army of the James, the unit served at Norfolk and Portsmouth until April 1864. Reassigned to the 18th Corps, they took part in several actions in Virginia including the battles about Petersburg. They were reassigned to the Army's 25th Corps, then preparing for the attack on Fort Fisher. They participated in both battles at the fort and were with General Terry as he moved to capture Wilmington. After pursuing Generals Braxton Bragg and Joe Johnston, they returned to Wilmington. Stationed there as garrison troops, they spent their days unloading ordnance stores from vessels, as well as performing fatigue and camp guard duty.

John Eagles was a proud man that 15th day of September 1865. Having enlisted in Wilmington on 1 March of that year, he had just been promoted to

First Sergeant of Company D, of the 37th Regiment. The Union army recruited many from the town that spring. Nearly one-hundred seventy free men joined the 37th USCT in early March and John Eagles was one of them.[9] Little more than a week later, he found himself in deep trouble. On 23 September 1865, while encamped at Camp Hilton at Castle Hayne, north of the city, a civilian boatman reported two soldiers for having stolen some wood from him. The 37th's commanding officer, Major Phillip Wienman, ordered the regiment to fall in while their tents were searched. The wood was found in Private James Fisher's tent and Fisher was arrested and hauled off to headquarters where he was "tied up" as punishment.

Several members of Fisher's company picked up their firearms and went looking for their comrade. Finding that he had already been released, they returned with him to the company area. One of the troopers celebrated by firing off his musket. The Officer of the Day, Lieutenant James Mellon, quickly ran to the noise, but couldn't find the offender. Major Weinman also came to the spot and ordered the company to fall in. When he asked who fired the gun, he received no response. The Major then ordered the men to "present arms." Then he turned and walked away.

The men became restless and asked First Sergeant Eagles how long they would have to stand there. When told they would have to remain in that position for several days if necessary, until someone confessed, the thirteen men in line broke ranks, saying they would "not fall in and stand for days for him or any other man."

Hearing of the disobedience, Major Weinman "had the drum beat for the regiment to fall in." Calling out the guard, he proceeded back to Company D's area. For some reason, at this point Weinman had Sergeant Eagles arrested and sent to the guard house. Ordering the miscreants to fall in, the major later described what happened next: "Instead of obeying my orders they loaded their guns, and one man replied, 'if we have to die, we might as well die now.' After this I ordered [another company] to load their pieces…and marched them to the spot for the purpose of arresting the mutineers."

As the major and the few men he had gathered returned, the mutineers saw them coming and "fired a volley at [Weinman] and Lieut. Mellon, killing the latter[.]" Another man, Henry Mitchell, of Company A, also fell mortally wounded. As Weinman turned and ran, another volley was fired at him. Gathering members of yet another company, he later recalled: "I tried to bring them into line, to fire into Company D [the mutineers]. The men refused to obey orders. I then tried the same with Co. K with no better effect."

The men were finally arrested and confined in the military prison to await their court-martial. Six men were originally arrested, but two, Thomas Goss and Anthony Eagles, had the charges dropped. Four men (and "others unnamed") were put on trial, charged with the crime of mutiny and the murder of Lieutenant Mellon. One other mutineer, Ben McLoud (or McLeod) of Company E, didn't wait around. He deserted two days after the shooting. Of those involved, Fisher, Manual Davis and the hapless Mitchell had been enlisted at Wilmington.

The trial was held in January 1866 and after hearing the evidence: "The accused were then called into Court, the proceedings...were read and approved. The accused having no testimony to offer any defence [sic] to submit, the Court was closed...and Manual Davis, Samuel Alderman, George Smallwood and Isaac Moore...are Guilty[.]" For their crimes, the men were to be "shot to death with musketry."

A court again convened later that year at Fort Fisher to review the sentence. Not present at those proceedings was Major Weinman. He had been sent to Fort Macon in March, where he died of disease. Although some of the wording was changed, the sentence remained the same.[10]

Other soldiers of the 37th also committed mayhem, this time at Federal Point. Stationed at Fort Fisher, several men of the regiment attempted to rob a home in January 1866. After hearing a knock on the door late at night, Miss Mary Pickett called for her father. As he opened the door, a shot rang out and Thomas Pickett fell dead. Several blacks made their way into the house, firing as they did so, rousing other members of the family. Some of the victims attempted to escape through the back door or the windows, but were driven back by other soldiers outside. There were at least four or five men involved and after ransacking the home and beating the women, they ran off. Witnesses identified the men as soldiers, most likely from Fort Fisher.

A short time later, the *Journal* reported: "It gives us great pleasure to be able to state, that through the untiring exertions of the military authorities, combined with the citizens, four of the supposed murderers...have already been arrested, and, we think, identified."

The paper commented on the arousal of the citizens in the area, many of whom called for "summary vengeance." Three of the four were Union soldiers, so they would not be tried in a civilian court. The army would try these men. The *Journal* set the tone when it stated that "A little stretching of hemp would have a salutary effect" on the rampant crime in the region.

Early the next month, the offenders were brought to trial. The court listened to the evidence presented by various witnesses, including not only those at the house, but nearly a half-dozen others who testified they were with the accused the night of the murder. When Lieutenant J.L. Rhoades, still the Judge Advocate of the trial, took the stand as a defense witness, the outcome was foreseen. Summing up the evidence and making a final statement before the court, Major William A. Cutlar, counsel for the defense, said: "It now becomes my duty to appear in defence [sic] of four humble men who were formerly slaves, and who at the first dawn of the day of Liberty nobly entered the service of our country, and have since risked life and limb for the preservation of that country."

After refuting statements of the accusers, he concluded with an appeal to the military judges: "They have shown a lofty spirit of Patriotism by enlisting... They have nobly and heroically defended the Star Spangled Banner at a time when it would have been almost certain death if they had fallen into the hands of our Country's enemies as the Fort Pillow massacre too fatally proves...They have always been ready and willing to go into the thickest of the strife...This has been well proven, in "front of Petersburg, upon New Market Heights, in the assault upon Fort Harrison, in the charge at Fair Oaks...and in the part they took in the reduction of Fort Fisher and the capture of Wilmington."

In mid-March, the four were acquitted and the case closed with no one brought to justice for the murder. Several years after the war, the incident still rankled many Wilmingtonians. One townsman, recalling those tumultuous days, wrote: "Witness the case of Mr. Pickett, murdered in his bed at midnight, by three black Union soldiers who...fortunately for themselves, were of a coal black color, and truly 'oil.' In spite of the most positive evidence brought against these men, the military court acquitted them, the Judge Advocate appealing to the passions of the court, if they would convict the loyal...soldier upon the testimony of white unrepenting rebels."

It would appear that the prosecution witnesses that accused the four men – Corporal George Josey, Musician Washington Flood and Privates Jerry Pruden and Edward Newsome – were indeed mistaken. Lieutenant Rhoades testified that Private Priden had remained at his headquarters the night of the murder.[11] The men were released and returned to duty.

Sympathizers of the former Confederate States argued: "It is absurd to suppose that any idea of another appeal to arms, at least in this generation, is cherished by Southern people...Their blackened fields and empty houses would warn them far more impressively than a company of United States soldiers can do, that further wars are not to be thought of."[12]

Several former Confederates also saw the nature of things to come and allied themselves with the victors. One who quickly took the Oath of Allegiance and expected to pick up where he had left off was Wilmington attorney John A. Baker. Baker was the former colonel of the Third North Carolina Cavalry who had a checkered military record. Although he had been wounded at Kinston in December 1862, he was intensely disliked by both officer and men. In May 1863, the men of the unit circulated a petition. Addressed to Baker and signed by virtually all the officers, it stated: "believing you to be unaware of the universal dissatisfaction now existing in this regiment...and believing...that you are a man of too much pride and self-respect to remain in such a position [you will] resign the position you now hold[.]"

He was charged with being a horse thief, for firing at one of his men and for arresting several officers without good reason. Included with the petition were charges that in December 1862, Baker: "did while on duty...by false pretense decoy from her home into the woods, a Miss Amanda Curtis a respectable young lady...& did take advantage of her unprotected situation & of the privacy of the place to which he had decoyed her, did insult her, by asking her to consent to unlawful sexual intercourse with him; & for the purpose of gratifying his lustful desires before her, did take hold of her & handle her person & was restrained and repelled only by her threatening to raise an alarm & call for assistance."

Baker immediately responded to the challenge by ordering the arrest of all the officers involved in the cabal. One of those officers, Captain Abram Newkirk, was forced to resign. Later, the charges that had been filed against Baker were somehow "lost" and Baker continued in command. On 21 June 1864, he was captured and confined in a northern prison. As a prisoner, he was placed in the rebel line of fire at Charleston. After the war, as a member of the "Immortal 600" he should have been a Southern hero, but having done "something that angered his fellow soldiers" he was made unwelcome in Wilmington.

One lady reported: "Who do you think came yesterday from New York[?] Mr. John A. Baker – a deserter, a traitor, a miserable wretch – he has taken the oath, been released and talks loudly at the Street corners." After a short stay in North Carolina, he "fled to the West Indies" and never came back.

George Myers, a town merchant, was glad to see Federal troops take Wilmington. The widow of Colonel Gaston Meares (of the 3rd N.C.) wrote: "The Myers family are the only demonstrative white people in town. They raised a flag over their front door, the only one at a private home and [they] are exuberant and exultant beyond conception." Mrs. Meares wrote that the Myers also hosted a dinner for Union General Hawley and his wife.

William Poisson, now employed by the W&W railroad, applied for the position of postmaster at Wilmington. Although he stated that he had voted for the Union candidates at a secession convention, he was unable to subscribe to the Oath of Allegiance due to this service with the Commissary Department. He pled that he had been forced, by the Conscription Act, to go into the army and fight against the "Stars and Stripes." I took a position as clerk and government agent in the commissary department. This position I held until I could secure a position on the Wilmington and Weldon Rail Road."

Declaring further that he had always been opposed to the war, he added that he had taken "President Lincoln's amnesty oath" and if required, could also provide proof of his Union sentiments throughout the war. Poisson got the postmaster's job.

In 1860, Henry Bishop, who ran the Farmer's Hotel, sometimes fed as many as 300 people a day. When he reopened the hotel in October 1865, there weren't nearly as many customers. The old Globe Saloon was soon reopened, again under the ownership of Colonel L.J. Sherman, the very person who had fled Wilmington in 1862. He kept a few pets in his establishment as attractions. A pair of raccoons wandered about the place while a bear was kept chained at one end of the bar. The raccoons eventually walked out while the poor bear was always being challenged to a wrestling match by drunks. The bear never lost a fight. To attract ever more business, many of the bars in town began to raffle off watches as prizes.

The mayor's docket soon overflowed with cases caused by too much imbibing or fighting over a woman. One action was usually associated with the other. One of the most notorious madams of this era was Ann Jane Kennedy. Known as "Gentle Annie," from the words of a popular song of the times, she was in and out of jail during and after the war. Belying her name, Annie was often charged with assaulting the policemen who raided her house.[13]

The military authorities determined the best course was to shut down all saloons, and did so in the summer of 1865. Not only was there to be no drinking or fast riding in the streets, but also no indiscriminate discharge of firearms. Oakdale Cemetery was a favorite locale for this noisy demonstration. In short, the very same problems that vexed the Confederates were now facing the Federal authorities. The liquor ban failed, much as it did in earlier days. The provost marshall, given the authority to license the trade, issued permits only to those who swore to maintain order in their premises.

In the summer of 1865, it was determined that Wilmington was ready to be returned to civilian control. In preparation for the event, James Macomber, chief of the fire department, sent his report to the commissioners. It showed that the companies were in need of everything from engines to hose to tools. The question was raised, "What has become of the Hook and Ladder Company...? Some one has remarked that its death might be dated from the withdrawal of the conscript officer."

On a day in July in which the "sun came down with as little mercy as a limb of birch from a school marm's hand," James Mitchell, the fire department's chief engineer, ordered the several fire companies to turn out for a parade and equipment inspection. Of the five companies in town, only the black companies appeared on the designated day. The men, who composed three of the companies, were resplendent in their bright red uniforms. Their antiquated engines were quickly seen to be in need of repair. They were deficient, too small and not able to send a stream of water a great distance. Leaky hoses, with only 400 feet of hose for all five companies, compounded the problem.

The two white fire companies didn't bother to turn out at all. An investigation revealed that one of their engines was inoperative, but it would appear that they did not want to parade with the black firemen. It was suggested that during the war those companies "had a full and overflowing quota of members, who were exempt" but it now looked as if "the vocation is to be abandoned." In response, members of the Howard and Hook and Ladder companies wrote that they never "paraded" with the black companies and never would. The members pointed out that most of the white firemen during the war were not conscriptable and those that were (some 30 out of a total of 91 men), were indeed granted exemptions. They had to serve not only as firemen, but as police and home guards. With the war ended, they said they were still ready to turn out to fight a fire. In July, with the resumption of civilian control, a new police force was sworn in. Although they numbered about 50 men, it was still difficult to keep the peace. Squads of garrison troops of the 6th USCT patrolled the streets, as did the police, but many of the policemen went about unarmed. They were not allowed to carry firearms because Major General H.W. Slocum's General Order No. 10, which decreed that no one, except military personnel, were allowed to bear arms. This led to the impossibility of enforcing the civil law.

Even when Slocum's order was lifted, many policemen simply couldn't afford the twenty or twenty-five dollars a revolver cost. In many cases, when they encountered armed soldiers, they were forced to either look the other way or call for military assistance. There were several instances of fights between the police and soldiers, sometimes with fatalities. Unwilling to give up what they saw as a hard-earned right, many of the USCT continued to act as the law.

Shortly after the new men took to the streets, a squad of soldiers arrested Paul McGreal, who was once more the Chief of Police. Hauling him off to jail amidst the cheers and jeers of the soldiers, McGreal submitted quietly and was soon released by the Officer of the Day.

In August 1865, a disturbance at Front and Market Streets turned deadly when a drunken trooper berated a police officer. Seeing that the man was drunk, the officer turned away and walked on, but the soldier followed him, drew his bayonet and stabbed him in the back. When the guard turned out, they arrested the wounded officer, but later released him. That same night, while walking his beat, a patrolman was shot and killed. As if that was not enough, later a policeman shot a soldier who was attempting to escape arrest. As the local paper reported, "Yesterday seems to have developed a mania for shooting and killing."

Most of the shooting was done by soldiers who were intoxicated, although some of the recently freed slaves also threatened the lives of the officers. Faced with these threats, the entire police force quit, en masse.[14] The army was then called upon to provide a guard in town and shortly after this, the mayor and Commissioners advertised for one hundred men to fill the void.

These men too, had problems. Many of them were found sleeping or drunk on duty or absent from their posts. They were fined and then returned to duty.

Confrontations continued throughout the year. In October there was a shoot-out between the two forces with two policemen wounded. Collateral damage included a cow, whose tail was shot off.

Nearly one year after the fall of Wilmington, yet another altercation took place between "a party of white soldiers" and the city police. The soldiers, armed and under the influence of alcohol, ignored orders to "conduct themselves in a more becoming manner" and began to curse at the officers. One cop attempted to arrest the ringleader, but was beaten and, being outnumbered three to one, the police retired, allowing the men to roam at will. Alcohol was the main culprit behind many of the problems.

In October a chaplain of the USCT harangued nearly 100 people on Dock Street. He railed against what he saw as injustices still being perpetrated against blacks. The Reverend Cheeseborough spoke against President Johnson, saying "he was not fit to hold the position he occupied." He referred to General O.O. Howard, chief of the Freedman's Bureau, in a "sarcastic manner" and in general abused the government, especially its judicial system, and the white officers of his own regiment. It was said that he was "highly applauded by the negroes present."[15]

It was widely rumored that the newly freed slaves would rise up and slay their former masters on Christmas of that year. Citizens formed militia-style companies and requested firearms, including the new Spencer repeating rifles, from the military authorities.

This request was denied when Major General Thomas H. Ruger replied that he had "no authority to order the issue of arms or ammunition to any militia." He added that the "matter of a possible outbreak on the part of the freedmen...has been brought to my attention; but I have been unable to ascertain that there is any credence of such insurrection on their part."

The military and police were on high alert when December 25th rolled around, but nothing happened except when two men were arrested and taken to jail, a mob rushed into the place and rescued the men. Quickly obtaining reinforcements, the police and soldiers rounded up nearly one hundred of the miscreants and lodged them all in jail.

For most of the townspeople, Christmas was celebrated as in olden days, except in many homes, the *Herald* noted, "there were many vacant chairs, but all seemed to feel grateful that so much remained to be grateful for." One week later, several hundred "colored citizens" came together and marched in a "procession...for the purpose of celebrating the 'Emancipation Proclamation.'" The event, which "passed off as quietly as expected," formed at the African Church on Front Street, marched through the town displaying various banners, ending at the old slave market. Speeches were delivered and the parade was "well conducted and the managers, and all engaged certainly deserve great credit[.]"[16]

In November, a shooting occurred which shocked the city. A well-liked member of a prominent Wilmington family shot and killed a man at a local saloon. John C. McIllhenny, once Lieutenant of Company E, of the 10th N.C., had been discharged from the army after suffering injuries in 1862. He and a friend went into the Wilmington Bar for a drink when McIllhenny was drawn into an argument with another patron. Words led to an altercation and as the two men grappled, McIllhenny drew a revolver and shot his antagonist. He was arrested and charged with murder. A change of venue took the trial to Cumberland County, where his infirmity was brought out as part of his defense. He was acquitted.[17]

When the army relegated power over the town, they specifically retained control over the liquor trade. In June, General Joseph Abbot ordered the cessation of sales of the "demon rum" and all other intoxicants. The following month he allowed the bars to reopen, but with restrictions; they were not to sell to enlisted men, nor to sell bottles of booze; they were not to allow a drunk to remain in their premises. The measures failed, so the next month the bars were again ordered closed. Vendors continued to ply their trades in the back alleys and risked not only confiscation of their wares, but also jail time.

One who was caught dispensing liquor was a black named Sheridan Newkirk, who was seen selling liquor while wearing green goggles. It is not known if Newkirk was jailed because he violated the liquor law, or the ethics of good fashion. Newkirk escaped the punishment meted out to a Federal teamster charged with the same crime; that man was tied up by his arms in public view on Princess Street.

The military also retained control over the sanitary affairs of the town. They had the town cleaned and swept by teams of unemployed men. Merchants were ordered to clean their premises and deposit the sweepings in a box outside the store where the town cart would take it away. Later that summer, a new machine made its debut on the streets. "[T]his homely but useful little contrivance commenced operations on Market Street yesterday." It was a water-sprinkling device which was employed to keep the dust down. By June, it was reported that the streets were again filthy. "In the rear of the buildings on Market…no one can pass without holding their breaths."

Another major problem was the lack of a certified coroner; no one wanted to give a bond for a position that they might lose when the army left Wilmington. It would not be until late in the year that someone stepped forward to take the job. At least one victim of small pox lay "uncoffined and unburied" for a little too long.

Another who had come in on the wings of a Federal victory was Flavel W. Foster. Foster, a recently discharged soldier of the 106th Pennsylvania Volunteers, arrived in March as the representative of the U.S. Sanitary Commission. He was sent to Wilmington aboard a steamer funded by the Commission to help in the relief efforts of both released prisoners and civilians. He filled a storehouse on Market Street with food and medicines. The supplies were needed immediately, as the town had quickly filled up with sick and wounded soldiers, over 8,000 former POWs, along with over 1,000 from Sherman's army at Fayetteville, overwhelming the town's facilities. Over fifteen hospitals were established. To aid in the cleanup of the town, Foster issued lime, which was utilized as a sanitizing agent. Men loitering around the corners were "impressed" into manning brooms and a regular schedule for the town drays to collect refuse was instituted.[18]

On more than one occasion, crowds of loiterers were simply gathered up, put on a steamer and sent to Savannah or Charleston. Late in September, when black stevedores went on strike for higher wages, white laborers rapidly replaced them. By that time, there were regular schedules to New York and other major northern cities. In the latter part of August, the steamer *Euterpe* plied between Wilmington and New York City for the Atlantic Coast Mail Steamship Company. This ship was built of white oak, chestnut and cedar, stretched 176 feet and drew 12 feet of water. She was soon joined by the *Twilight*, a new steamer some 150 feet long and having less than an eleven foot draft. Schooner rigged, she had three decks and was expected to "give satisfaction on her proposed route...possessing speed, strength of hull, and a variety of elegance of finish in her passenger department."

By mid-September, there were three lines of steamers operating to Wilmington. In November, the *Twilight* headed back to town from New York and hit a storm as she neared the Cape Fear. Grounding on a bar, she "went to pieces" and her entire cargo was lost.

One of those who lost their all was the "Soldier's Friend," Mary Ann Buie. She later advised her friends that she sought information on her trunks, which contained "all her clothing, together with a lot of specie and invoices." Her baggage had been "broken open and the trunks thrown overboard but she hoped someone might have saved something." The *Journal* questioned the loss of such a fine ship, "which went ashore in fine weather, within two miles of the bar, and with a pilot on board." The editors were quite upset because they suffered the loss of a "lot of paper" for which they had no insurance and stated the loss "comes particularly hard just now." Less than a month later, the *Journal* would suffer a more serious loss, that of longtime editor James Fulton, who passed away in December of that year.

In late 1865, the London correspondent of the *Times* voiced his opinion when he wrote: "If the Government intends to 'restore' the South, it cannot begin

Mary Ann Buie, in a soldier's sketch of the time. (NHCPL)

too soon to give back its liberties, to let it manage its own affairs...and to remove the military... [The South has] suffered more than any words could describe, and now to drive the iron further into their necks is a fatal policy... A gun boat in the river in front of this city and a detested body of negro troops patrolling its streets will never make the North Carolinians loyal." Soldiers continued to guard the railroad depots and to inspect trains. They continued patrols of the town and also guarded the various government storehouses.[19]

In the summer of '65, with the reins of government handed back to the municipal authorities, the provost marshall, as if to emphasize the exchange of power, moved out of City Hall and went into an office on Market Street. Mayor Dawson had a multitude of problems to contend with, not the least of which was the lack of commerce. Since the war's end, business had virtually come to a standstill. The market report for the time indicated the sales were "Cotton- dull; Naval Stores- brisk; turpentine- lively; spirits- scarce; rosin- dull."[20] There were still no banks open and currency was nearly nonexistent. Financial matters were handled by two brokers. There were only three post offices open throughout the State. The lighthouses were still inoperative.

One of the brokers in town was John Wilkinson. He handled such matters as cashing checks drawn on out-of-state banks and loaned money to businessmen. He suffered a setback when it was discovered that his nephew had broken into his safe and absconded with the funds. The nephew was last seen hightailing along the tracks of the Wilmington and Weldon railroad.[21]

In antebellum days, trade was pretty well done by June. Summer and fall seasons were normally "dull." After the war, commercial ties with the north, mainly New York, were slowly being reestablished, but at four or five steamers a week, it would be a little while before Wilmington resembled anything of its prewar days. F.W. Foster and other northerners in town looked for opportunities. Foster started a company that supplied laborers to the Cape Fear area.

Early in 1866, a steamer brought over 50 German emigrants to town. After trying in vain to hire local workers for his steam mill, Thomas C. McIllhenny hired "the whole of them, the men at $15, the women at $10 per month[.]" Unfortunately for McIllhenny, his mill was destroyed by an arsonist from among the group shortly after he hired them. It was reported that the men, former U.S. soldiers who could find no work in the north, were very dissatisfied working at the mill.

Adding to the economic woes was the low stage of the Cape Fear. The river was at its lowest point for some years, cutting off trade with Fayetteville and the interior. This disruption in waterborne trade would last until late in October. The Wilmington and Manchester Railroad wasn't bringing in much produce. There was a break in their line because the bridge across the Pee Dee River was down. Along the line of the W&W, there was a temporary structure across the North East Cape Fear, put up by the Federals as they pursued retreating Confederates. The bridge piers and pilings interfered with river traffic since the pilings were not spaced far enough apart to allow flats loaded with lumber and naval stores to pass through. The flats had to be cut in half, passed under the bridge and then put back together again. The process was laborious and time-consuming. The railroad had been taken over by the military and was not returned to civilian control until August, although as early as mid-July private freights were being shipped to town.

Thrown back on older means of transportation, people could go by train to Warsaw and take a stage (almost fifty miles) to Fayetteville. The stage ran three times a week. The old road between Fayetteville and Wilmington was once again busy with the clattering of wagons. The town clock, long since "upon a war footing" and no longer working, was of no use for persons trying to regulate their business. The U.S. gunboat *Tacony*, in an attempt to relieve this want, displayed a pennant from its main peak at exactly twelve o'clock. Those within sight of the ship, which was anchored off the town, were thus able to "regulate their time." The ship also contributed to the commerce of the town by computing the tide table, which was then published in the papers. The nine o'clock curfew bell was brought into use again, signaling to the artisans in town that it was quitting time.

On 13 July 1865, an English schooner arrived in port. It was the first foreign vessel to call at Wilmington since the blockade had been raised. In September the British steamer *Harold* left town with the first cargo of sawed lumber since May 1861. When the brig *Persia* left for Liverpool in October, it was the first vessel to sail directly to England since North Carolina's secession.

The naval stores business, neglected since the occupation, was also at its lowest ebb. To obtain turpentine and rosin, the pine trees needed to be "boxed," but by early January and February they remained untapped.[22] In August, it was reported that there was almost no foreign market for shingles and they were becoming hard to sell, but by the end of 1865 business appeared to pick up. Both Bailey's Star and the City Hotels had reopened. "First Class Performers" were wanted for a minstrel band at Baileys, although other hotels, the Farmer's House, the Rock Springs and the Franklin were still up for rent. Harry Webb was again serving liquor and "Oysters, fish and all kinds of game in season."

The theater had been open for some time and when a tightrope walker ascended the rope which was stretched from the stage to the gallery high above, the audience cheered. Reaching his goal, he turned to walk down, but slipped, falling into the gallery and "becoming mortified at his partial failure, he remounted the rope and attempted to descend to the stage backwards, but after proceeding a few feet from the gallery he again lost his balance, and then commenced a painful and thrilling struggle for life." Realizing that he was about to fall, he tried to swing onto the stage and nearly made it. His feet hit the stage, but falling backwards, he struck his head on the floor below. He was killed instantly.

Normalcy, of a sort, was returning to Wilmington.

The city hosted several distinguished visitors that year. Major General Ruger visited Fort Fisher, while Major Generals George Crook and George Gordon Meade also came to town. While Meade was at Bailey's Hotel, a band of the 2nd Massachusetts Heavy Artillery serenaded him. He later took a steamer downriver, probably to view Fort Fisher. Crook, who stayed at the MacRae house, assumed command of the department and made his headquarters at that home.[23]

The Southern Express Company was again in business, this time allied with the Adams and Harndens Express Companies. One who was pleased with little or no business was the mayor. At the Mayor's Court, held daily when necessary, it was said that the "docket was as bare of cases as a poor man's coffin of polish." The mayor's docket was sometimes the scene of poking fun at those caught by the police. At one such session, the mayor dismissed a case because the defendant argued that he had not stolen anything, but was merely trying to steal.

That year, 1865, there were many who decided to marry. Of the fifty-six marriage licenses issued, 41 were for negroes. By the fall, there were eight schools in session and it was noted that many of the town's merchants had returned from the north with all the latest goods. Shipping continued to increase, with naval stores and lumber brought to town from Elizabethtown and Lumberton by wagons. Exported were more bales of cotton, rosin, shingles, even sugar, coffee, beeswax and old iron were sent out as cargoes. Government tugs were hard at work, raising the wrecks of vessels accidentally or deliberately sunk in the channel. Commenting on the state of affairs after war's end, a local paper was pleased to write: "two years ago it was a crime to be a Unionist, now it is a virtue to have been one."

The paper might well have been speaking of Joseph Neff, the man who had so vexed General Whiting. He remained in Wilmington and after the occupation became quite wealthy and would even be elected mayor.

While many were content to resume the old ways, some felt that old scores had to be settled. In the fall of 1865, there was a court martial which showed just how deep the passions of the recent conflict had run. Two Bladen County men, Neill McGill and John L. McMillan, were brought to Wilmington to face military charges of murder. The murder, it was said, had been committed earlier that year, on 10 April, by the men, who were members of the Home Guard. Witnesses reported that Matthew Sykes, who had been, for a short time, a Confederate soldier in the 40th N.C. Regiment, was dragged from a friend's home near Elizabethtown at gunpoint by three men. The third man, William Wilkinson, had confessed to Sykes' relatives what had happened and was never charged. The victim's wife and relatives began searching for Sykes and found him strung up to a tree. More witnesses testified that McGill had sworn revenge because Sykes had "piloted the Yankees" to his (McGill's) home whereupon the Federals ransacked the place and made off with McGill's valuables. Sykes remained with the U.S. Army for a few weeks and returned home only a week before he was taken away. He was told "to bid his friends goodbye, he would never see them again." Wilkinson told Catherine Sykes that the three stopped to take some "liquid courage" as Sykes began to sob. McGill pulled him off the horse and began to beat him. Both McMillan and Wilkinson felt that Sykes didn't deserve to die, but McGill was determined that he should. Having passed out from the beating, Sykes was awakened only to be immediately hung.

The trial, which was convened by Major General Ruger, began in early October. Alfred M. Waddell and Adam Empie ably represented the accused. Splitting their defense strategy, Empie argued that the military tribunal had no place trying two civilians, who were charged with the murder of a third civilian, who happened to be a "Union man." Since the civilian courts were open, he asserted that the military had no jurisdiction in this case. Indeed, he continued, if the military held exclusive control, then any case that had been heard in any Confederate court since 1862 could be reexamined. Waddell's tact was to shred the evidence against the two. He insisted that all the evidence was circumstantial. No one really knew how or when Sykes had died. All the evidence seemed to come from one source – Sykes' relatives. Waddell attacked the credibility of those witnesses. Nearly every other witness admitted that both women – Sykes' mother Unity and his wife Catherine – had bad reputations. One man said that the mother was known throughout the community as a liar. Another offered the opinion that although Sykes' sister-in-law's reputation had been bad, it was getting better. The defense also suggested that, as the accused had stated, they had simply turned Sykes over to a patrol of Confederate cavalry that had been looking for him and it was that unit that had strung poor Sykes up.

Empie's tack failed. The army continued to try the case. On the last day of October, Judge Advocate Major Roberts, reiterated the charges: "that the men had willfully and with malice aforethought did kill and murder Matthew P. Sykes...who had acted as a guide for a portion of the United States forces."

He stated that the court did indeed have the right and duty to try the case as North Carolina had "been in armed rebellion against the authority of the United States...and her courts of justice [had] succumbed to the attacks of treason, and thus become incapable of administering the civil laws of the state." Roberts countered Waddell's arguments by showing that not only were Sykes' kin offering telling evidence, but so were several others who had no axe to grind. An attempt was made to bring the matter to the attention of the State Convention, then meeting in Raleigh, and a resolution was introduced requesting President Johnson to allow a civilian court to hear the case. It too failed and the court retired to deliberate.

As elections were being held in November, the court seems to have held off its verdict until later. It was a bad time for anyone being tried by a military court. In Washington, D.C., a highly-publicized trial had just ended with the hanging of the accused, Captain Henry Wirz, former commander of the Andersonville, Georgia prison.

Shortly after, the military court in Wilmington handed down its sentence – death by hanging. In January 1866, the military commission, which included General Ruger, who had handed down the verdict, recommended Executive clemency and forwarded a petition, which, it was noted, had been signed by many ladies, to Congress. "After careful study" of the case, the Judge Advocate General declined to request clemency. It appeared that the luck of the two had run out and the hangman would soon be placing a noose around their necks.

It was not to be. In February 1866, while still awaiting sentencing, the pair escaped from jail. Wilmington's *Daily Dispatch* reported: "They made their escape...between three and four o'clock, through the agency of the sentinel who was guarding the...building in which they were confined. A hole was made through the wall...The bayonet was the instrument chiefly used in making the aperture...The soldier who 'used the bayonet' so well, accompanied the escaped prisoners in their flight, and it is supposed received some compensation for his services." One author stated that it was Waddell himself who bribed the sentry on duty one evening and the pair quickly made their escape.[24]

Even with the war's end, bad luck and tragedy continued to strike some families. In October 1865 the widow of Colonel Gaston Meares ran an ad informing the populace that since the State had "repudiated...their fairly and honestly contracted debt, I and my children have been made losers to the extent of NINETY-FOUR THOUSAND ($94,000) DOLLARS[.]" Defaulting on the bonds of the WC&R railroad forced Mrs. Meares to go to work to support her family.

The family of Armand D. Young also experienced bad times. Young owned a 350-acre rice plantation, "Lyrias," some three miles north of town, on the Cape Fear River. In February 1865, released Union POWs streaming across the river at Castle Hayne were in a pitiful condition and required immediate attention. Federal authorities confiscated any foodstuffs from nearby farms to feed the starving soldiers and Young's plantation was hard hit when it was stripped of "bacon, beef, rice and fuel." The farm was pretty well wiped out with the seizure of "4,000 bushels of rice, 300 pounds of bacon, eighteen head of beef cattle, three dozen hogs and two hundred bushels of corn." When tallied up, the loss was greater than $13,000. Young sought relief from the Federal court and his case was one of many brought to the attention of the U.S. Attorney General. An act of Congress in 1871 allowed repayment to citizens who presented valid claims against the government. Young hired local attorney Edward Cantwell to press his case to the Commissioner of Claims. When it was denied, Cantwell wrote directly to the Attorney General stating that Young had been unfairly dealt with and that "Mr. Young's defness [sic]; the probability that he had been misunderstood, and more than all the apparent injustice done his loyalty to the U.S. under very trying circumstances & special temptation[.]"

Cantwell offered to secure testimony from Charles Bradley, a Unionist who had been run out of town in 1861, "who would prove the loyalty of Mr. Young[.]" Young pointed out that he had sent his son to the mountains to avoid conscription and although he had a brother and three brothers-in-law in the Confederate service, he "did not rejoice at the victories of either side...and was strictly neutral, yet sympathized with the Union cause." He even had the support of former Union General Joseph Abbott, who assured the commissioners that Young was pointed out to him as one who had been "secretly opposed to the rebellion, and was put down on [Abbott's] list of loyal men." The correspondence went on throughout the fall of 1874, without resolution. The outcome of the case didn't matter to Young, who had passed away in 1871. It was likely his wife who pressed the claim, but it was perhaps Young's statement that he had been "strictly neutral" that doomed his claim. The commissioners rejected the claim saying that: "Utter quiescence and strict neutrality" was not sufficient to establish a claim.

Cantwell would later apply for the position of Assistant District Attorney for the Eastern District, the Cape Fear region. It is probable that his quick leap from Confederate officer to Republican judge caused a split with his brother, former Confederate Colonel John Lucas Cantwell. John remained a firm believer in the "Lost Cause" and although both lived in Wilmington, the two rarely ever spoke to each other.

Jonas Levy also looked to the Federal Government for reimbursement for losses suffered during the war. When he appeared before the Claims Commission in 1871, he said he had been an "ardent and enthusiastically patriotic Unionist, one whose sympathies for the Union [n]ever failed; his patriotic devotion to the flag and the Government of his country glowed all the brighter during the dark days and nights in which the storm of battle and of blood lowered over the land."

The commissioners listened sympathetically, then showed Levy several letters he had written to U.S. officials supporting his claim. They asked him if the signatures were his. He replied in the affirmative. Unbeknownst to him, several letters written by him to Confederate authorities had been mixed in with the others. When he realized he had been tricked, the commissioners reported that he then :" [C]ommenced to equivocate and multiply his perjured falsehoods. He soon improvised a line of defense, and swore these letters were concocted by ... enemies, who had plotted his destruction and secured the aid of his confidential clerk, now dead[.]"

The trap had been sprung and Levy was caught. The letters written during the war had been provided to the commission by the U.S. War Department. Indeed, by 1864, the C.S. Quartermaster Department owed Levy some $20,000. The U.S. Commissioners blasted him by calling him a "shameless traitor, perjurer, and swindler" who "added the villany of... blackening the reputation of the dead as well as the living." To be sure, his claim was thrown out and it appeared from the tone of their response that Levy was fortunate he was not arrested.[25]

Not just Confederate sympathizers had their claims rejected. Sanitary Commissioner Flavel Foster had begun to establish himself in Wilmington but suffered a setback when the U.S. Army confiscated his wagons and mules – eighteen of them. Foster claimed to be out over $3,500 and asked the government for reimbursement. The commissioners turned him down because "[H]e had been too long in the Federal Army & too much of a businessman not to have known the value of vouchers."

In March 1866, an incident occurred that brought Wilmington into the news once again. Several blacks were convicted of larceny and sentenced to be publicly whipped. This was the normal prewar punishment for that crime, but when the Freedman's Bureau, headed in Wilmington by Major Wickersham, was informed of the sentence, he reacted quickly. Sending armed guards to the courtroom, he demanded the sentence be "suspended until he could have an opportunity to investigate the case." It was too late; the whip had already been administered. The courts were warned by Major Wickersham not to deliver such punishments in the future.[26]

By the end of 1865, Wilmington was slowly on its way to recovery from the effects of the war. On of the most distinguished visitors was General Ulysses S. Grant. He arrived early in December from Raleigh, received a salute from a gunboat and went to the City Hotel. He did not remain long and left the next morning on the Wilmington and Manchester Railroad.

It was said that "he left as he had come, not as a conqueror...but as a free citizen of a free country." When he left, a crowd of the curious gathered at the hotel to see the architect of their downfall. He was described as "a very unpretending middle aged gentleman, rather a small man...with a cigar in his hand, which he smoked most of the time."

That very December day, the Old Capital Prison in Washington was closed. The very next day, Wilmington's old jail "ceased to be a military prison." The war and its peripherals were winding down, but Wilmington would suffer the effects of the war for some time to come. Throughout the South the physical damages would eventually be repaired or rebuilt.

The following notice appeared in the Wilmington *Herald*, 7 August 1865: "DIED. Near Masonboro Sound, on Sunday morning, the 30th of July, John F. Herring. After an absence of eleven months, ten of which were spent in prison at Point Lookout, he was enabled to return to his wife and little ones, and although he only lived to enjoy them one short day, he expressed great thankfulness, that his prayer was answered, and he was permitted to meet them again on earth...He gave his dying blessing to his children, and met his last summons with perfect resignation[.]"

The unseen effects of hunger and deprivation would linger for more than a generation or two. Some writers have suggested that the South never really recovered from the Civil War until at least the Second World War. In Wilmington's case, this might well be true.

Endnotes

1. Fonvielle, *The Wilmington Campaign*, 427. [Wilmington] *Herald of the Union*, 7 April 1865. Commission Claims, no. 184, 141. The fire and sinking of the Sultana, which occurred later that month on the Mississippi River, killed about 1,700 men, many of whom were, like those on the *General Lyon*, were too weak to survive. Many of those on the *General Lyon* were from the 56th Illinois, about 35 women and 25 children also died. See The *New York Times*, 3 and 14 April 1865; the *London Times*, 27 April 1865. Perhaps some of those who owed sutler French money had perished in the disaster. Cutter and French loaned out over $4,000. *Civil War Notes*, recorded by Captain E. Lewis Moore, A.A.G.,

transcribed January 1995 by David M. Moore, manuscript copy, Fort Fisher State Historic Site. See also "Passenger List of the Steamer General Lyon," internet website (6 December 2004) http://home.att.net/~genlyon.htm.

2. *Daily Journal*, 9 June 1863; *ORA*, II:217-218; Fonvielle, *The Wilmington Campaign*, 455-456; Claims Commission, 135, claim of George R. French, president of the Seamen's Friend Society; LCFHS, Seaman's [sic] Minutes, 22, dated 28 March 1874. The Board requested president French to "push Congress for injury done the home" but the claim was rejected.

3. "The Civil War Years at the Bellamy Mansion," newsletter article by Jonathon Nofke, March 1995. Captain E. Lewis Moore, Civil War Notes.

4. J. Cutlar Andrews, *The North Reports the Civil War* (Pittsburg: University of Pittsburg, 1955) 70-71, 363, 554, 572; Louis M. Starr, *Bohemian Brigade: Civil War Newsmen in Action* (Madison: University of Wisconsin, 1987) 210. *Herald of the Union*, 4 August 1865. Horace Munson had been in partnership with P.J. Sinclair, editor of the *Daily North Carolinian*. Cook was also called as a witness in the Henry Ward Beecher trial. See the *Herald*, 5 September 1865; *New York Times*, 17 March 1875 and 24 December 1892. See also Evans, *Ballots and Fence Rails*, 46-48; Fonvielle, *The Wilmington Campaign*, 343. Fulton's editorial is dated 6 December 1865; he died 15 December 1865; *Wilmington Herald*, 29 June 1865.

5. *Herald*, 7 and 11 March 1865. Later justices of the peace could also administer the oath. It was said that the time allocated for such duties was quite short and interfered with the workday.

6. *Herald of the Union*, 13 and 22 March 1865; *Wilmington Herald*, 26 September 1865.

7. *Herald*, 8 and 12 September 1865. The *New York Times*, 25 March 1865; known as "Baldwin the Clothier" in New York, he was the agent for Carhart, Whitford and Company. Baldwin died in September 1886, see The *New York Times*, 9 September 1865.

8. *Daily Journal*, 28 December 1865.

9. Internet website, http://www.rootsweb.com/~ncusct/37usct1.html. Not all those enlisting that spring were from Wilmington. It was, at that time, a large refugee center.

10. National Archives, RG153, entry 15A, Court Martial Case Files, 1809-1938, microfilm no. 1105. *Daily Journal*, 22 and 23 December 1865. The case took some strange turns. Isaac Moore attempted to escape, but was recaptured. While awaiting trial, he was promoted to corporal. James Fisher was not charged, but deserted on 5 February 1866; Anthony Eagles followed suit the next day.

11. National Archives, RG153, entry 15A, Court Martial Case Files, 1809-1938, microfilm no. 3615. *Herald*, 14 and 15 July 1865; *Daily Journal*, 15 January, 20, 22 February, 5 March 1866. Transcripts, (1870) 8. North Carolina provided

the Union with over 3,000 soldiers. See Court Martial Case Files, microfilm no.
3615, statement of Major William A. Cutlar, 16. Lieutenant Rhoades would
have a dispute in 1866 with the new Chief of Police, "Ex-rebel Gen. Ransom"
over soldiers that had been arrested by Ransom's men. The two exchanged
heated words and ransom challenged Rhoades to a duel, see The *New York
Times*, 2 April 1866.

12. The [London] *Times*, 6 December 1865.

13. Sifakis, 28-29; LCFHS, Newkirk family File, "Charge of Conduct against
J.A. Baker, Col." *Southern Women*, deRosset papers, letter of Catherine
deRosset Meares, dated 28 March 1865. *Herald of the Union*, 26 April 1865.
The Papers of Governor W.W. Holden, letter dated 14 July 1865. Poisson
selected the *Herald* to publish the Post Office list of letters, over the objections
of the two other papers in town. The *Herald*, 23 February, 1866. L.J. Sherman
was said to be the "Chief Detective" for the U.S. Government, see the *Herald*,
21 August 1865, also 23 June, 1 July, 20 December 1865 and 17 January 1866.

14. *Herald*, 18, 22 and 25 July 1865. In November of that year, it was the black
fire companies that refused to turn out for fires, see the *Herald*, 13 November
1865. A black soldier was shot in the back as he walked along the streets,
Herald, 7 June 1865. See also 3, 4 and 5 August 1865. The entire police force
actually resigned on two occasions. It was not a highly-sought job. Applications
for 100 new men were advertised in the *Herald*, 6 August 1865, the pay was $50
per month. *Herald*, 4 January 1866. An editorial calling for the arming of
police is in the *Herald*. Shortly afterwards, the police had things firmly in
control, even to the point of making a raid on "Camp Jackson," known as a
"dirty, filthy quarter" where crime and disease ran rampant. *Herald*, 7 June, 20
July and 4 August 1865.

15. *Daily Journal*, 8 February 1865; *Herald*, 3 October 1 November 1865. The
Reverend Cheeseborough brought up a recent shooting of a white, one B.F.
White, and regretted that "he was not the one who shot him." See the
[Wilmington] *Daily Dispatch*, 1 November 1865. Cheesborough was "allowed
one of two alternatives": to leave town or go to jail. He was brought up on
charges by the Freedman's Bureau, but was soon with his regiment at New Bern,
Herald, 2 November 1865.

16. Dan T. Carter, "The Anatomy of Fear," The Journal of Southern History,
42:347. White troops had been replaced by the USCT in early June, see the
Herald, 5 June 1865. Events in Wilmington were certainly stirred up by the
headlines in the newspapers at this time. There was an insurrection in Jamaica
and it was widely reported that the "bodies of white men were horrible
mutilated" by mobs of blacks. The Jamaican rebellion was quashed, with the
hanging of over two hundred blacks, *Herald*, 11 November 1865. In
Wilmington, nearly a full regiment of militia was recruited, *Daily Journal*, 16

December 1865, *Herald*, 19 December 1865. As early as June, lawyer A.M. Waddell was writing to the Provisional Governor, W.W. Holden, that "the soldiers insult and curse the most respectable ladies in Wilmington…Unless there is a change for the better it will inevitably result in massacre." See Records of the States of the United States, (North Carolina), 1865-1868, reel 12, letter dated 18 June 1865. See also the *Herald*, 27 December 1865, *Daily Journal*, 2 January 1866.

17. *Daily Journal*, 27 March 1862; *Herald* 16, 17 November 1865; Sprunt, *Chronicles*, 340. McIllhenny died in September 1865. More than ten years after the war, a newspaper happily reported, "Paddy's Hollow has been on its good behavior lately," the paper suggested changing the name to Sleepy Hollow. See the *Morning Star*, 23 October 1878. Nicknames for some of the sections of the town were "Texas," "California," and "Oregon," all suggestive of a frontier-like existence.

18. *Daily Dispatch*, 17 November and 13 October 1865. The street sprinkler was in use by mid-October. *Herald*, 13 September 1865. The information on Foster is in *Morning Star*, 6 December 1902. The *New York Times*, 17, 25 August 1865; *Herald*, 17 and 24 November 1865; *Daily Journal*, 17 November 1865.

19. The [London] *Times*, 6 December 1865.

20. General Order No. 2 transferred government of the city to the mayor and commissioners on 24 July; see the *Herald*, 24 July 1865. The military issued liquor permits to 24 firms, see the *Herald*, 24, 26 and 28 July 1865.

21. Wilkinson's nephew took off with over $15,000, see the *Herald*, 18 and 23 October 1865.

22. Watson, 57. *Daily Journal*, 13 March and 21 October 1865; *Herald* 16 January 1866, 5 October, 13 July, 20 September and 10 October 1865. The *Persia* carried 657 packages of tobacco and 124 bales of cotton. The bridge over the Pee Dee was repaired in early 1866, but was still unbridged over the Brunswick River. *Daily Dispatch*, 4 February 1866. *Daily Journal*, 23 November 1865. Prewar rafts were 30 to 35 feet wide and sometimes 100 feet long. New rafts were 24 feet wide and were "divided down the middle before passing the bridge. Herald, 10 July 1865. *Morning Star*, 14 July 1907. The *New York Times*, 9 April 1866; the turpentine season ended by September.

23. *Herald*, 4, 13 and 26 September 1865. *Daily Dispatch*, 25, 30 November 1865. General Ruger came late in September also. See the *Herald*, 25 September 1865. Another visitor was General O.O. Howard, in command of the Freedman's Bureau.

24. *Daily Dispatch*, 31 October 1865. The Sykes case ran throughout October, see the *Daily Journal*, 3, 13, 14, 19 October 1865; see also the *Herald*, 10, 11 October 1865. *The Civil War: The Nation Reunited*, Richard W. Murphy (Alexandria: Time-Life Books, 1993) 37-39. *Daily Dispatch*, 13 October 1865.

The *New York Times*, 11 January 1866; Evans, *Ballots and Fence Rails*, 27-32; *Daily Dispatch*, 24 February 1866. Evans also wrote that Governor Jonathon Worth wrote to President Johnson seeking a pardon for the men. This may have been granted as a Neill McGill and J.L. (John Leonidas) McMillan are listed in the 1870 Federal Census as Bladen County farmers. See the 1870 Federal Census of Bladen County, N.C., copied by Mildred Lay Bryant (Elizabethtown, N.C.: Bladen County Historical Society, n.d.) 176, 160.

25. Mrs. Meares became a piano and voice instructor. "Letters to the Attorney General of the United States," Disallowed Claims, no. 186, Claim of Armand D. Young; no. 135, Claim of Jonas P. Levy. Levy would return to New York where he lived out his life; he died in September 1883.

26. The *New York Times*, 2 April 1866.

Index

About the Author

Robert J. Cooke, in front of the original Fort Anderson garrison flag, at Brunswick Town / Fort Anderson State Historic Site in Winnabow, N.C.

Robert J. Cooke

Robert J. Cooke is a New Yorker by birth and an avid historian by nature. He graduated with a BA in history from St. Francis College in Brooklyn, N.Y. After retiring from the telecommunications industry in 1994, Bob relocated to Wilmington, N.C., where he and his wife Joan and "a couple of dogs" now reside. Robert J. Cooke has also contributed articles and stories to several journals and magazines. *Wild, Wicked, Wartime Wilmington* is his first book, the result of more than a decade of research.

LaVergne, TN USA
05 January 2010
168950LV00004B/59/P